TRUST *hope* PRAY

Encouragement for the Task of Waiting

LUKE AND TRISHA PRIEBE

Foreword by Dr. David Doran

SONFIRE MEDIA

A PUBLISHING COMPANY

SONFIRE MEDIA, LLC 2010

Trust, Hope, Pray

Published by Sonfire Media, LLC
411 N. Main Street
Galax, VA 24333 USA

Unless otherwise noted, all Scripture is taken from the NEW AMERICAN STANDARD BIBLE®, Copyright © 1960,1962,1963,1968,1971,1972,1973,1975, 1977,1995 by The Lockman Foundation. Used by permission.

Scripture quotations marked ESV are from The Holy Bible, English Standard Version® (ESV®), copyright © 2001 by Crossway, a publishing ministry of Good News Publishers. Used by permission. All rights reserved.

Scripture marked NIV are taken from the HOLY BIBLE, NEW INTERNATIONAL VERSION®. Copyright © 1973, 1978, 1984 Biblica. Used by permission of Zondervan. All rights reserved.

NOTE: Bolded text in Scripture is the authors' emphasis.

Cover design by Christa Bryson
Interior book design by Larry W. Van Hoose

ISBN No. 978-0-9825773-5-6

What others are saying about *Trust, Hope, Pray*

Trust, Hope, Pray is a diary of faith from a Christian couple whose heartfelt trial of waiting for the adoption of their child teaches the importance of resting in God's good providence.

Exposing their thoughts and hearts, Luke and Trisha Priebe show what it is to wait and depend on God day after day. Their confessed confidence in God demonstrates that waiting time is not wasted time. Indeed, waiting increases the sense of divine dependency and intensifies the expectancy of divine intervention.

Luke and Trisha are convinced that God is incapable of disappointing those who wait on Him. Every entry has simple but pointed thoughts that encourage the reader to find contentment in the Lord and not in the circumstances of life. Although not every Christian shares the Priebes' particular trial, every reader who is waiting on God will find direction and encouragement to trust, hope, and pray.

> — **Michael P. V. Barrett,** President of Geneva Reformed Seminary Author of *Beginning at Moses: A Guide to Finding Christ in the Old Testament; Complete in Him: A Guide to Understanding and Enjoying the Gospel; God's Unfailing Purpose: The Message of Daniel; The Beauty of Holiness: A Guide to Biblical Worship; Love Divine and Unfailing: The Gospel According to Hosea; and The Hebrew Handbook.* He is presently working as co-editor with Dr. Joel Beeke on a King James Version study Bible.

* * *

Jesus tells us that sorrow comes with the birthing process, but great joy comes when the baby arrives (John 16:21). And though there are differences, the adoption process has a similar pattern of sadness and then joy. In fact, the pain of waiting can be even more difficult than physical birth pangs. In this 365-day devotional, the Priebes have provided the church with a wonderful gift to serve waiting couples with gospel grace and hope. I trust that God will use this book in ways beyond what we can ask or imagine as the church pursues adoption for the glory of God.

> — **Justin Taylor,** Managing Editor, *ESV Study Bible*; blogger, "Between Two Worlds"

Dedication

With love to our son.

For this child, we pray.

Trisha White Priebe

Acknowledgment

With hearts full of gratitude, we acknowledge the following contributions:

Without the goodness of God, we would be nothing.

Without the fervent, cheerful encouragement of our family, this book—and the events recorded in it—would tell a different story.

Without the wisdom of our pastor and the prayers of our church, our burden would be much heavier and this book would be much shorter.

Without the careful, thoughtful insight of our friend and editor, Vie Herlocker, the weaknesses in this book would be too many to count.

Without the faith and confidence of the Sonfire family, this book would be a rough draft in a closet somewhere.

To those who have prayed for us, we thank you.

— TRISHA AND LUKE

Foreword

We live in a culture that despises waiting!

Just this morning, as I waited in a long line to pass through an airport security check, I was surrounded by the moans and groans of travelers who could easily think of hundreds of more beneficial things to do than wait in line, especially this kind of line. I even moaned a little myself—especially when the lady behind me kept bumping into me!

It really is quite amazing to watch how "progress" seems to set us up to be dissatisfied and impatient. Here I was in Florida standing in a line for a plane that would carry me to Michigan before noon, but I was bothered by having to wait. I was about to make a journey in hours that would have taken days not that long ago (and weeks not too much before that). Modern technology has accelerated our pace through life, but it will never catch up to our expectations that we should get what we want when we want it (if not before!).

The problem really is deeper than technological progress. It touches the core of human existence—we want things, but we often don't have the power to make them happen. We are creatures, not the Creator. We are bound by time and space. We have limited resources and limited capacities. We are dependent on God.

Worse yet, the Bible is clear that we are sinful creatures, so we often want things that are not good, and sometimes we even want good things too much—not just as a desire, but as something we demand that God gives us. We don't have what we want and we don't like it.

In reality, the very reasons we don't like waiting are exactly why waiting is good for us! Having to wait reminds us that we are not in charge—God is—and it forces us to see that we need Him. When God puts us in a holding pattern, it is for our good.

Luke and Trisha Priebe have done us a great service by meditating on the challenge that waiting poses for us. By taking us to the Scriptures, they guide us to God's wisdom and direct us to God's help. What they really do is point us to God Himself, and we need Him more than whatever else we are waiting to receive.

We are prone to push and prod until we get what we want or accomplish what we desire. Pushing and prodding, though, too often lead us away from God. They are the tools of self-reliance and personal accomplishment. In many areas those are good things, but when it comes to spiritual realities, they can be deadly. My guilt before God because of sin cannot be removed by pushing and prodding. Spending eternity with Jesus Christ cannot be achieved by my effort. Trusting in ourselves is vanity.

The message of the Bible is that there is one God who alone is the true and living God, and that He acts on behalf of those who wait for Him (Isaiah 64:4). The good news announced in the Bible is that this Creator God has acted on behalf of sinners by sending His Son, Jesus Christ, to live righteously, die sacrificially for sins, to rise victoriously from the grave, and that He now offers to all the forgiveness of sins and eternal life through faith in what He accomplished. This message is good news precisely because it tells us that Jesus did all that needs to be done for our salvation. He did what we couldn't do and offers us these gifts on the basis of grace, not works, "For by grace you have been saved through faith; and that not of yourselves, it is the gift of

God; not as a result of works, so that no one may boast" (Ephesians 2:8-9). Grace and works are completely contrary to each other—you earn wages, not gifts. You receive gifts, and the gift of eternal life through Jesus Christ is received by faith (Romans 6:23).

Waiting on God means trusting Him; it means banking on the reality that He will keep His promises. It means you stop trying to help Him out and simply rest confidently in His Word. The most important waiting you can ever do is to wait for God's Son to come from heaven and rescue you from the wrath to come (1 Thessalonians 1:10). Until you have come to rest on God's promises in the gospel, you aren't ready to wait on God from day-to-day. Once you've trusted in good news about Jesus Christ, learning to wait on God daily is the path of discipleship you're called to walk.

You hold in your hands a great guidebook for that walk! The Priebes open the Word and their hearts to help you trust God more fully, to follow Him more faithfully, and to cultivate a heart that can say with the prophet, "But as for me, I will watch expectantly for the LORD; I will wait for the God of my salvation. My God will hear me" (Micah 7:7).

Dr. David M. Doran

President, Detroit Baptist Theological Seminary
Senior Pastor, Inter-City Baptist Church, Allen Park, MI

Introduction

We are professional waiters. No, not as in those who wear white aprons and solicit food and drink orders. Rather, we've spent a tremendous amount of our lives waiting. We've waited for a personal cancer diagnosis. We've waited to see if a loved one would recover from a devastating accident. We've waited as family members died of difficult diseases. And most recently, we've waited for over two years to learn when we will finally be able to adopt our child from overseas.

Our understanding of waiting has been transformed through these events. Previously we thought of waiting as an exercise in stopping. As children, we took many walks with our families. And as children often do, we would sometimes run ahead of the group until a parent would call out, "Wait!" Perhaps we had come to a busy crosswalk or met face-to-face with a neighborhood dog. At that point, we would put on the brakes until our parents were close enough. And then, after getting the signal, we'd run ahead once again.

This is *not* the picture of waiting on God.

The image of waiting on God depicts a life moving forward—not standing still. Paul David Tripp, in his book *Broken-Down House*, wrote, "Waiting is not only about what you will receive at the end of the wait. Waiting is about what you will become as you wait."

The image of a tree relying on the sun and the rain, yet growing, inch by inch, even during the night, serves as better imagery than the afternoon walk. In the darkness, when the tree is lacking what it wants, it doesn't fold its leaves and branches while it waits—rather it bends its limbs toward the sky in anticipation of daylight. And often, in the morning, growth is evidenced.

The following 365 entries are meant to encourage you in the task of waiting. Everything in these pages comes from our own journals and notes—gems given to us by those who cared enough to give hope during our time without sun or rain.

Each theme verse includes the words: *trust, hope, pray,* or *wait* because those are the themes of the journey. May God give you grace as you wait.

TRUST*hope*PRAY

DAY 1

Genesis 49:18

*For Your salvation I **wait**, O LORD.*

Waiting on God is the source of unfailing spiritual strength for the believer, but it is not a habit that comes easily.

Of waiting, Mrs. Charles E. Cowman wrote, "It may seem an easy thing to *wait*, but it is one of the postures which a Christian soldier learns not without years of teaching. Marching and quick-marching are much easier to God's warriors than standing still."

What, then, enables God's children to *stand still* and wait—to wait for an adoption, to wait for a diagnosis, to wait during the long days that separate request from response?

Simply put, we wait because of an unwavering belief in God's sovereignty.

No matter the circumstance, the sovereign will of God has ordered our steps—yesterday's, today's, and tomorrow's. And while that knowledge doesn't clear the pathway of thorns or pitfalls, or promise a trail of uncompromising ease, it enables us to walk with confidence on the path God has chosen for our lives, knowing our good guide is in full control (Psalm 37:23–24).

God graciously enables us to endure by strengthening us to trust, hope, and pray.

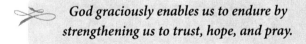
God graciously enables us to endure by strengthening us to trust, hope, and pray.

Waiting enables us to say with the psalmist in Psalm 123:1–2, "To you I lift up my eyes, O you who are enthroned in the heavens! Behold, as the eyes of servants look to the hand of their master, as the eyes of a maidservant to the hand of her mistress, so our eyes look to the LORD our God, till he has mercy upon us" (ESV).

DAY 2

Exodus 33:18

*Then Moses said, "I **pray** You, show me Your glory!"*

Waiting is a reality of life.

Like Moses in Exodus 33, we pray for God to show us His glory—in whatever life experiences we are called to face—and then we wait for Him to exalt Himself with whatever outcome He has ordained.

But waiting is more than a casual passing of the time or a youthful surveillance of the clock in anticipation of the next desirable thing. Waiting, in the most biblical sense, is active.

Waiting, though it requires us to stand still and fix our gaze upon God, also requires us to hope, to meditate, to believe, to pray, to endure, to rest … to *do* the things that God has commanded us to *do*, all the while expecting His glory to be evidenced in His response to our requests.

We waited over seven years for God to bless us with a child. While friends all around us seemed to marry and grow their families at the speed of light, we experienced miscarriages, health challenges, setbacks, and disappointments. We watched children we once took care of get married and enter parenthood. We watched newborns grow to school-aged children.

We waited for God to give us the desire of our hearts.

> **Waiting,
> in the most
> biblical sense,
> is active.**

Our once frantic or frustrated prayer became simply and wholly, *Lord, we want what glorifies You! Show us Your glory.*

DAY 3

Numbers 14:17

*But now, I **pray**, let the power of the Lord be great, just as You have declared.*

God's power is remarkable.

No cluster of cells in any human body has ever been too hard for Him to heal. No illness, enemy, or catastrophe has ever posed a threat to the supremacy of God. Death, itself, submits to His command (Galatians 1:1).

Yet this same powerful God, who created light with the words of His mouth (Genesis 1:3), has in His nature the desire to know us and hear our concerns, however large or small. He carefully governs our lives with the same authority that spoke the seas into existence.

So we must learn to trust this power with the entirety of our hearts— more than we rely upon the encouragement of our friends. We must thank the doctors, appreciate the caseworkers, and welcome the guidance of wise counselors.

But we must *trust God's power.*

> *There are no furrows of worry on the brow of the eternal God.*

We should agree with Dr. Alan Cairns who said, "The LORD has everything—time and all its events and all its people and all its possibilities—He has everything under control. There are no furrows of worry on the brow of the eternal God. There are no creases of perplexity, no wrinkles of care upon the face of our Father. He has everything in His control."

And so we trust Him.

DAY 4

1 Samuel 1:10

*She, greatly distressed, **prayed** to the LORD and wept bitterly.*

When Hannah prayed for a son, it was not the effortless prayer mumbled before a meal or the half-hearted request spluttered in the midst of a prayer group. It was the urgent, desperate prayer of a woman in distress.

Though silent to the ears of Eli the priest, Hannah's petition before the Lord was earsplitting. She was certain in her request as she "poured out [her] soul" (1 Samuel 1:15).

So it is when we pray for the deepest desires of our heart: it should not be the simple, carefree exchange of friends on a park bench; it should be the wholehearted, desperate plea of a beggar in search of sustenance. We should not be afraid to plead with our God.

The King of Kings has granted us an audience. Why would we be anything less than forthright?

One awesome reality of God's goodness in our lives is displayed in the endowment of prayer. Prayer does not exist as a communication tool for God—it is an instrument for us, as God's children, to speak with our Heavenly Father. Prayer, one of the greatest disciplines of the Christian life, was never intended to be viewed as a duty, but as a gift.

Prayer affords us the opportunity to enter the throne room of grace and pour our petitions onto the lap of our Heavenly Father.

Why would we choose to do anything else?

> *The King of Kings has granted us an audience.*

DAY 5

1 Samuel 1:12

*Now it came about, as she continued **praying** before the LORD, that Eli was watching her mouth.*

It is no coincidence in the plan of God that Hannah's name means "grace."

Along with women like Sarah, Rebekah, Rachel, and Elizabeth, she knew what it was to need God's grace to deal with the social stigma attached to childlessness.

Taunting. Insulting. Chastising.

So it was with Hannah and so it is with us. God allows difficulties, at least in part, to bring His children to the point of total dependence on Him.

Our God delights to answer prayer.

Sometimes when the situation looks hopeless, God intercedes on behalf of those who are praying earnestly to Him (Luke 1:16–17).

God didn't just *eventually give Hannah a child.* He gave her a son who would be instrumental in bringing revival, who would be both judge and prophet—responsible for anointing Israel's kings, one of whom would become the man after God's own heart.

Samuel was not only God's grace bestowed on Hannah. Samuel represented God's grace bestowed on the nation of Israel at a critical point in her history.

Our God delights to answer prayer.

DAY 6

1 Samuel 1:26

She said, "Oh, my lord! As your soul lives, my lord,
*I am the woman who stood here beside you, **praying** to*
the LORD."

Prayer is a privilege.

We have the ability to be involved in God's sovereign work in our lives through the activity of prayer. No other time is this opportunity felt so strongly or appreciated so fully as during the difficulties and complexities of life.

Our hearts are more pliable to prayer when God alone knows what we are feeling and facing. Our hearts are more peaceful when we seek the giver more fervently than we seek the gift. If we maintain an internal posture of prayer, then our lives are more blessed during difficulty than during any time of prosperity or success when prayer is an oversight or afterthought.

As our soul lives, we stand beside our friends and family . . . and we pray to the LORD.

The third verse of William Walford's hymn reads:

Sweet hour of prayer! Sweet hour of prayer!

Thy wings shall my petition bear

To Him whose truth and faithfulness

Engage the waiting soul to bless.

And since He bids me seek His face,

Believe His Word and trust His grace,

I'll cast on Him my every care,

And wait for thee, sweet hour of prayer!

DAY 7

1 Samuel 1:27

*For this boy I **prayed**, and the LORD has given me my petition which I asked of Him.*

"Prayer is God's ordained way to see His will accomplished."

Our pastor, Dr. David Doran, reminded us of this truth as we began the adoption process. We believed his words. Scripture is abundantly clear that prayer is an important component of the Christian life.

We must never underestimate the effectiveness of prayer.

But our awareness of the power of prayer was expanded when we knelt by our couch late one night and asked God to provide so that we could adopt. Like Hannah in 1 Samuel, we made a petition to God for a child.

The next day—right on schedule and in God's faultless timing—a check arrived in the mail for an overage we had paid in taxes, and to the penny, it met the need of our adoption application.

God wants us to pray.

If the direct command to do so (1 Thessalonians 5:17) isn't sufficient to the point, the Bible bears a conveyor belt of illustrations that show prayer to be essential. Abraham prayed for Sodom. Moses interceded for Israel. Elijah entreated for prophets. Nehemiah requested for Jerusalem. Paul implored for Philippi. And each prayer was key in accomplishing God's will.

We must never underestimate the effectiveness of prayer.

DAY 8

1 Samuel 2:1

*Then Hannah **prayed** and said, "My heart exults in the LORD; my horn is exalted in the LORD, my mouth speaks boldly against my enemies, because I rejoice in Your salvation."*

God, alone, knows our end from our beginning.

Hannah, Sarah, Rebekah, Rachel, and Elizabeth had no idea what God had in store for their lives. Even their earnest prayers fell short of what God had planned.

In time, these women gave birth to a prophet who would anoint the first two kings of Israel, the promised seed of Abraham, the father of a nation, the sustainer of God's people during the famine of Egypt, and the forerunner of the Messiah whom Christ would deem the greatest prophet born of women.

Had these women written the last chapter, it would likely have read much differently.

Waiting would be easy if we knew what the end entailed.

We said it one million times while waiting for the phone call—if we just knew when and if we would receive good news, the wait wouldn't be nearly as hard. Even disappointing news could be accepted, dealt with, and disregarded.

But waiting on God, without any concept of what the future holds, cultivates in us the type of trust our God desires. How genuine would the trust be if we knew the outcome?

God has proven Himself *trustworthy*.

We must prove ourselves *trusting*.

DAY 9

1 Samuel 8:6

*But the thing was displeasing in the sight of Samuel when they said, "Give us a king to judge us," and Samuel **prayed** to the LORD.*

God is not good because He gives us what we want—He is good because He gives us what is best.

Years before we decided to begin the adoption process, we were approached by a co-worker we barely knew who asked if we would be willing to adopt a brother and sister in need of a home. When we learned that the pair had been abandoned by all family, we did not hesitate to consider the decision.

We prayed about it, sought counsel, and by the end of a weekend were ready to uproot our lives to make room for these precious two. Within forty-eight hours of making the decision to adopt these children, however, an unknown non-relative came forward and took custody.

In addition to discovering our love and longing for children, we learned that God isn't the granter of what is *good*. He is the giver of what is *best*. We thought it would be good to move those children into our home and our lives. God knew it was best to wait.

No doubt Samuel approached the Lord in 1 Samuel 8 with some apprehension, disappointment, or even embarrassment at the people's insistence for a king. Clearly, he knew it was good for the people to retain God as their leader (I Samuel 8:7). But God, in His providence, knew it was best to allow the people to experience the leadership of Saul.

Anything that God allows into our lives to transform us into the image of His Son is best.

God is a good God.

DAY 10

1 Samuel 12:23

*Moreover, as for me, far be it from me that I should sin against the LORD by ceasing to **pray** for you; but I will instruct you in the good and right way.*

Peace is the presence of God.

As God's children, we find perfect peace through perfect resignation to Him and His decisions for our lives.

There is no other way to find peace—not through the self-help section of the bookstore, not through the support group (though kind and accepting the members may be), and not through the firm resolution that "everything will be okay"—a sort of laissez-faire attitude about life.

True peace in any situation is found in God. And *only* in God.

Perfect peace is maintained through ceaseless communication with the Father.

As the days grew closer to weeks, the weeks grew closer to months, and the months grew closer to years, we found comfort from these words in Arthur Bennet's Puritan Prayer, *The All-Good*:

This is my magnet, my attraction.
Thou art all my good in times of peace,
my only support in days of trouble,
my one sufficiency when life shall end.
Help me to see how good Thy will is in all,
and even when it crosses mine
teach me to be pleased with it.

DAY 11

2 Samuel 7:27

*For You, O LORD of hosts, the God of Israel, have made a revelation to Your servant, saying, "I will build you a house"; therefore Your servant has found courage to **pray** this **prayer** to You.*

God keeps His promises—no small achievement since the Bible, according to scholars, holds nearly 7,500 of them. What are some of these guarantees?

The Lord will give strength to His people (Psalm 29:11).

There is no want to them that fear Him (Psalm 34:9).

God is a very present help in trouble (Psalm 46:1).

So like the servant in 2 Samuel, we must find courage to bring our petitions to God, based upon what He has promised to us. Our prayers are strongest which begin, "Lord, You have said in Your Word . . ."

The encouraging reality is this: If we pray in God's name for God's will to be done, we will never be disappointed. No matter how long the day may be or how dark the night, our God has promised us an end to our discouragement.

We should, therefore, mean every word that we say in the presence of our Creator God, believing "he exists and that he rewards those who seek him" (Hebrews 11:6 ESV).

> *If we pray in God's name for God's will to be done, we will never be disappointed.*

DAY 12

2 Samuel 21:14

They buried the bones of Saul and Jonathan his son in the country of Benjamin in Zela, in the grave of Kish his father; thus they did all that the king commanded, and after that God was moved by prayer for the land.

God is moved by prayer.

If we would study the pages of the past—take just the Old Testament of the Bible and open it for consideration—we would find that prayer undoubtedly changes things.

Moses cried out to God, for instance, and the Sea was divided and the Israelites spared.

David, who was accused of great crimes against God, prayed for forgiveness and was recorded in Scripture as being a man after God's own heart.

> *God is moved by prayer.*

Jehoshaphat prayed and God silenced his many enemies.

Isaiah and Hezekiah petitioned for God's intervention, and 185,000 murderous Assyrians were killed by the angel of the Lord.

Daniel prayed and the lions, desperate for a meal, left him alone.

Elijah prayed and asked for rain, and after three years of not a single drop (also at his request), the skies opened and poured buckets on the dry earth.

We underestimate the power of prayer any time we choose worry over petition.

DAY 13

2 Samuel 24:25

*David built there an altar to the LORD and offered burnt offerings and peace offerings. Thus, the LORD was moved by **prayer** for the land, and the plague was held back from Israel.*

Prayer does not change God.

We know this because God is unable to be changed. But God does use prayer to accomplish His will. And we are commanded to pray.

Perhaps one of the greatest mysteries of heaven-and-human interaction is that God longs to hear from and respond to His people, sinful though we are.

That David's offering to the Lord—presented on an altar of rocks, dirt, or broken pottery—could so move the heart of God that He would withhold a plague from Israel, should persuade us that God loves His children and longs to hear from them.

We must believe there is power in prayer.

We began going to pray in the tiny room we had prepared for our child. Beside the small bed—with a backdrop of freshly painted brown walls and photos of animals—we began asking the Lord to be moved on our behalf. We didn't build an altar and we didn't request the rescue of an entire nation. We simply asked God to work in our family.

And we believed He could do it.

DAY 14

1 Kings 8:26

*Now therefore, O God of Israel, let Your word, I **pray**, be confirmed which You have spoken to Your servant, my father David.*

Though life is hard, God is good.

And, good thing for us, God's goodness has everything to do with God and nothing to do with us.

Early in our process of learning to wait on God, we were forced to make a choice. Would we place our exclusive confidence in our Heavenly Father, believing that what He said is true and trustworthy, or would we doubt His goodness and try to take matters into our own hands?

We could manipulate the system, demand prompt communication, and wring our hands when questions went unanswered. Or we could trust God and know that He was overseeing the details out of our control.

At several points throughout our adoption experience, we had friends ask why we weren't sharing regular updates. Our blog went untouched. Our e-mails went unsent.

The truth was simple: we had no updates to share. Months passed without any word about our child. We had unnumbered opportunities to wallow in worry.

In the book of 1 Samuel, Hannah prayed to God in desperation, and in so doing, exhorted us to do the same.

The reality is this. We can doubt God's goodness and try to take matters into our own hands, but the operative word is *try*.

God doesn't need our permission to accomplish His will.

DAY 15

1 Kings 8:28

*Yet have regard to the **prayer** of Your servant and to his supplication, O LORD my God, to listen to the cry and to the **prayer** which Your servant **prays** before You today.*

God is good, not only when He gives us what we do not deserve, but when He does not give us what we think we need.

How often have we prayed and asked for something, only to learn later that we wouldn't have wanted what we thought we needed had we known what God already knew?

When we laid eyes on our child—via a tiny snapshot taken in an orphanage halfway around the world—we were immediately grateful that God had disallowed us to begin our family a day earlier than He designed. Our child's huge brown eyes, sweet smile, and mop of dark hair melded into an image that fortified us for months and made us eternally grateful for God's perfect plan.

So when we bring our supplication to the Lord and ask Him to hear our cry and the prayer we make before Him, we must recognize that God is more aware of our desires than we are, and He is working on our behalf to do better for us than we ask or think (Ephesians 3:20-21).

> *God is good, not only when He gives us what we do not deserve, but when He does not give us what we think we need.*

DAY 16

1 Kings 8:30

*Listen to the supplication of Your servant and of Your
people Israel, when they **pray** toward this place; hear in
heaven Your dwelling place; hear and forgive.*

God never tires of hearing from us.

In Psalm 55:22, we are instructed, "Cast your burden on the Lord, and
he will sustain you" (ESV). And incredibly—unbelievably, perhaps—
we aren't given any limits, account parameters, or *maximum prayers
allowed in one day.*

In the history of the human race, no man has ever taken too much to
God.

And yet, when the trials come and the tribulations push us to our
limits, our initial response is often total loss about what to do.

We need more than a casual commitment to prayer. If we expect God
to listen to us, isn't it fair that He should expect us to talk to Him?

During Solomon's prayer of dedication for the temple, recorded in
1 Kings 8, Solomon said that heaven
itself could not contain God. Why?
God is everywhere—investing Himself
in us as His creation—aware of our
needs and meeting them before we
can do anything about them.

> *If we expect God to listen
> to us, isn't it fair that He
> should expect us to talk
> to Him?*

Amazing, isn't it, that He hears and forgives?

DAY 17

1 Kings 8:42

*(For they will hear of Your great name and Your mighty
hand, and of Your outstretched arm); when he comes and
prays toward this house.*

We all need the Lord all the time.

When we first began to travel the road of trial and disappointment—
as frequent voyagers and not just passersby—we did so quietly.

Yes, we had experienced a lot of difficulties both before and during
the adoption wait. But we didn't believe they were to be compared
to some of our brothers and sisters in Christ who were suffering so
much more.

Dear friends of ours had recently lost their mother. How could we talk
to them about waiting on God for finances? Both of our grandfathers
were dying. How could we talk to our family members about our
desire for expedient adoption paperwork? When, at one point, we
spent several long days and nights in the hospital waiting for a difficult
diagnosis of our own, we essentially kept it private. Surely there were
others facing worse situations.

In one day, Job from the Bible lost ten children. Our details paled
in comparison. What right did we have to tell others what we were
experiencing?

But then we were reminded, rather poignantly, that there are no levels
of needing God—no rungs in the ladder of faith or trust. We *have*
Him or we don't. We *need* Him or we don't.

We may be trusting God for our child while our neighbor trusts God
for her car payment. Both of us can mutually encourage each other to
wait on God in the most fitting way. Our trials are tailor-made for us.

God has invited us *all* to cast our cares on Him (1 Peter 5:7).

DAY 18

1 Kings 8:45

*Then hear in heaven their **prayer** and their supplication, and maintain their cause.*

God delights when His children trust Him.

Prior to beginning the adoption process—when we were waiting to see if cancer would play a significant role in our lives—we wrote these words in our journal:

> The God who saved us, who led us to get married, who brought us to
> our church, will continue to meet our needs as He has always done.
> We choose today to cast off our worries. God is more infinitely aware
> of our needs than we are. We will do our job to trust and leave the job
> of meeting needs to Him.

We learned, over time, that trusting God is a decision to be made every day. The choice to place all confidence in the Creator is not made once then written in the back of a Bible or printed on a certificate to be hung in the office. Trust in God is a continual undertaking. We must trust persistently.

Face a fear? *Trust God.* Face another fear? *Trust God again.*

Trust, trust, trust.

"You keep him in perfect peace whose mind is stayed on you, because he trusts in you" (Isaiah 26:3 ESV).

DAY 19

1 Kings 8:49

*Then hear their **prayer** and their supplication in heaven Your dwelling place, and maintain their cause.*

God maintains our cause around the clock.

Because God is both omniscient and omnipresent, we can never stray outside His thoughts. He does not need to be reminded, prompted, nudged, or nagged. He wants to hear from us in prayer, but not so that He can be "brought up to speed" or told again what needs to be done on our behalf.

He hasn't forgotten. He is more aware than we are.

If we could see from God's view and through His eyes, we would not fear tomorrow. We would know with certainty that the sovereign God of Heaven rules perfectly every day and in every decision, even when we are in the depths.

If we had God's knowledge and God's power and God's love, we would choose for us what He has chosen for us every single time.

But since we cannot experience that perspective, we must trust the one who can.

So that tonight, when we lay our heads on our pillows, we can know He is still working on behalf of His own. And we can rest securely.

> *If we could see from God's view and through His eyes, we would not fear tomorrow.*

1 Kings 8:54

*When Solomon had finished **praying** this entire **prayer** and supplication to the LORD, he arose from before the altar of the LORD, from kneeling on his knees with his hands spread toward heaven.*

God shows no partiality (Romans 2:11).

He does not listen closer to the prayers of the pastor or the king than He does to His other children. God is not impressed by purple robes or jewel-studded crowns. God holds the king's heart in His hands (Proverbs 21:1).

God is pleased by prayer.

And whether the prince or the poor approach God's throne of grace, both must eventually kneel and be quiet in the presence of God.

Which means we cannot go to God expecting Him to be impressed with us.

Which means, no matter who we are (or who we are not), or what we have done (or what we have not done), we can go to God believing He'll listen on the basis of who He is and what He has done.

Our confidence in times of trial or ease is not grounded in our ability to cling to God, but rather in God's inability to lose hold of us—no matter who we are (Romans 8:37–39).

With this confidence, let us assume a posture of spirit that kneels before the Lord with hands spread toward heaven.

God is pleased by prayer.

DAY 21

1 Kings 9:3

*The LORD said to him, "I have heard your **prayer** and your supplication, which you have made before Me; I have consecrated this house which you have built by putting My name there forever, and My eyes and My heart will be there perpetually.*

We must pray to God as beggars plead for a piece of bread.

Supplication has as its Greek root the concept of lacking or deprivation. A prayer of supplication, then, is a not a prayer mentioned along with gratitude for supper or in combination with confession over a fleeting, inappropriate thought.

Supplication is single-focused, intensified, razor-sharp prayer that is fixated on the Supplier. A beggar doesn't come with a list—he asks for the item he needs most.

We must beg God for help and then wait for Him to respond.

Shortly after hitting a speed bump—of which we quickly had a collection during our adoption—we went to God as beggars. Shortly afterward, we were encouraged by this song written by Katharina A. von Schlegel:

Be still, my soul: thy God doth undertake

To guide the future, as He has the past.

Thy hope, thy confidence let nothing shake;

All now mysterious shall be bright at last.

Be still, my soul: the waves and winds still know

His voice who ruled them while He dwelt below.

DAY 22

2 Kings 4:33

*So he entered and shut the door behind them both and **prayed** to the LORD.*

Going to God should never be an afterthought.

In today's hyper-connected, electronic age, we can actually fire off a text message, e-mail, phone call, or status update before ever leaving the doctor's office. It's possible for people who live thousands of miles away to know something simultaneously with someone sitting next to us.

This potential for fast and furious communication can be good when asking others to pray, and bad when we, ourselves, should pray.

The morning we found out that we were facing a potential cancer diagnosis and subsequent surgery, we contacted our entire immediate family before we ever pulled our car into our driveway. Thanks to speed dial, we didn't even need to know phone numbers!

But going to God for His help and comfort should be our knee-jerk reaction to all of life's events—before ever dialing a number or logging on to a computer.

When Elisha was called to heal the Shunammite's son in 2 Kings, he demonstrated what God desires for us. He entered the house, saw the need, shut the door, and prayed to God.

There is no indication that Elisha asked anything of anyone else before going to God.

And neither should we.

DAY 23

2 Kings 18:5

*He **trusted** in the LORD, the God of Israel; so that after*
him there was none like him among all the kings of Judah,
nor among those who were before him.

The ground for our confidence in God—is God Himself.

We trust God because God is trustworthy. We trust God because it doesn't make sense to trust anyone else.

The country from which we planned to adopt our son fell heavy with civil unrest just months before we planned to travel and meet him. Imagine our frustration when we watched the images of large-scale political demonstrations, heard the warning of imminent terrorist attacks, and read of the potential disasters that awaited us in our child's home country—if and when we would ever be permitted to go. We entertained the worst kind of thoughts until our minds came to rest on Psalm 91:1-2: "He who dwells in the shelter of the Most High will abide in the shadow of the Almighty. I will say to the LORD, 'My refuge and my fortress, my God, in whom I trust'" (ESV).

More powerful than the most belligerent dictator, more knowledgeable than the wisest captain, more protective than the strongest shield, and better than the kindest medic . . . is our God.

We *must* trust Him because He is trustworthy.

We trust God because God is trustworthy. We trust God
because it doesn't make sense to trust anyone else.

DAY 24

2 Kings 19:15

*Hezekiah **prayed** before the LORD and said, "O LORD,
the God of Israel, who are enthroned above the cherubim,
You are the God, You alone, of all the kingdoms of the
earth. You have made heaven and earth."*

To maintain the right spirit before God, we must maintain the right perspective of God.

We must believe that God, in His providence, is in control of it all.

For some of God's children, the fact that God's invisible hand directs all of the events of their lives is a source of frustration. If God is in control, then He is responsible for the difficulties, disappointments, and discouragements. And that, for some people, is too difficult to accept.

But thinking of God as incapable of permitting our difficulty is just as flawed as believing He wants us to be frustrated.

Both perspectives lack an understanding of the word *frustration.*

That God, in His providence, is in control of all things means we should not be *frustrated.* The literal definition of frustrated is to be thwarted in our goals or plans. If our objective is to trust God and maintain a right perspective, we can't be frustrated.

God's will and ways will never be thwarted.

To maintain the right perspective—and ultimately avoid frustration— we must ensure our goals align with His.

DAY 25

2 Kings 19:19

*Now, O LORD our God, I **pray**, deliver us from his hand that all the kingdoms of the earth may know that You alone, O LORD, are God.*

More than happiness or healing, we must want God to be glorified.

Earlier in 2 Kings (verses 11–13), Hezekiah prayed that God would answer his request to show Himself strong and to defend Himself. Hezekiah's primary concern was not that Israel be protected. Hezekiah wanted God to be glorified.

God must be glorified.

God's character is at stake in His glory. All the world exists for this supreme purpose (Colossians 1:16–17).

Who else would we want God to glorify but Himself?

God must be glorified.

So it is in our prayers, we must pray—not for an outcome that makes us happier or healthier—but for a result that best displays the magnificence and splendor of God.

Later in 2 Kings 19, God responded to Hezekiah, and in part said, "For I will defend this city to save it, for my own sake and for the sake of my servant David" (2 Kings 19:34 ESV).

The power of God in Hezekiah's prayer—and all of our prayers—must be for God's power to be made undeniably clear.

2 Chronicles 6:19

*Yet have regard to the **prayer** of Your servant and to his supplication, O LORD my God, to listen to the cry and to the **prayer** which Your servant **prays** before You.*

It is a theological reality that God sovereignly determines the path His children will take.

It is also a reality that the decreed will of God for our lives at times necessitates waiting and, at times, includes suffering. Very few people are exempt from dark days or deep waters. Very few people receive instant responses to their deepest desires.

Some on this earth will experience a season of winter in marriage or a verbal stoning in ministry. Others will face the heartache of wayward children or the insecurity of financial ruin.

None of us will take the same path in life, but all of us will experience disappointment.

Herein is our security: Yahweh, our Sovereign God, is in control of all things. And He always enables His children to complete their earthly assignments. Called to endure something difficult? You aren't expected to do it alone. Called to wait? God gives the grace to endure.

While powerlessness to control the future poses great frustration for some people, for others, it brings tremendous security. Little can be done to alter the course that God has designed. Meaning, a Pilot more skilled than we are is controlling the vessel that is our lives, and we have His permission to rest and trust.

"God is our refuge and strength, a very present help in trouble. Therefore we will not fear though the earth gives way, though the mountains be moved into the heart of the sea, though its waters roar and foam, though the mountains tremble at its swelling" (Psalm 46:1–3 ESV).

DAY 27

2 Chronicles 6:21

Listen to the supplications of Your servant and of Your
*people Israel when they **pray** toward this place; hear from*
Your dwelling place, from heaven; hear and forgive.

None of us are without the need for prayer.

When Solomon knelt and prayed in 2 Chronicles 6, he was demonstrating king-sized humility. It was not the typical behavior for kings to acknowledge the sovereignty of anyone else. Later in the Old Testament, Daniel would be thrown in the lion's den for acknowledging that someone other than Cyrus the Great was sovereign.

Not so with Solomon.

None of us are above
the need for prayer.

Solomon recognized his need for dependence on God. Living a life independent of God's strength is futile at best.

So it is with us. We will not find God to be trustworthy until we trust Him. We will not find God to be responsive to us until we ask Him. We will not find God to be sufficient until we recognize that we are not above the need for prayer.

Joshua, the military strategist, recognized from where his strength came. Gideon the warrior knew that he was helpless without God. King David and King Solomon knew not to put their trust in position or wealth. Joseph—after growing from nothing to everything and shrinking back to nothing—knew that his livelihood depended on God.

None of us are above the need for prayer.

DAY 28

2 Chronicles 6:39

Then hear from heaven, from Your dwelling place, their **prayer** *and supplications, and maintain their cause and forgive Your people who have sinned against You.*

Nothing can happen to us apart from the permission of God.

Every incident from our conception to our death is decreed or permitted by Him. To not want this for our lives is to grossly underestimate who God is and what He wants for us.

Angry, resentful questions about the painful circumstances of life become unnecessary when we begin to grasp that God does everything for us in love. And though we will never fully comprehend this love— as someone tossed in the ocean with a yardstick could never begin to measure the width or the depth—we can trust His goodness based on what He has already done.

The Bible is clear.

God loves you. He longs to hear from you, forgive you, and sustain you.

On several occasions, in random places, for different reasons, we heard this song written by S. Trevor Francis in 1875. It became to us a comfort and a well-known landmark along our journey:

O the deep, deep love of Jesus,
Vast, unmeasured, boundless, free!
Rolling as a mighty ocean
In its fullness over me!
Underneath me, all around me,
Is the current of Thy love
Leading onward, leading homeward
To Thy glorious rest above.

DAY 29

2 Chronicles 6:40

*Now, O my God, I **pray**, let Your eyes be open and Your ears attentive to the **prayer** offered in this place.*

Prayer glorifies God.

Our lives are often filled with events and attempts to exalt God, yet sometimes we get busy doing what we think God wants us to do to the neglect of what He has actually called us to do most often: pray.

It is the single biblical command we are told to do ceaselessly. Yet, sometimes we struggle to do it at all because we're actively trying to do everything else.

During times of waiting, prayer can feel like the opposite of activity—when, in fact, it is the most needful task we can accomplish.

When we begin to realize that prayer is not just about us—it isn't simply us bringing requests to God—it is finding God to be good and true and faithful, we will pray more often and with more resolve.

To be sure, we will glorify God when we pray.

The wonderful truth about prayer is that we need not make an appointment. We need only make it a priority.

C. H. Spurgeon rightly said of 2 Chronicles 6:40: "This is so pointed that we may not imagine that any one single hour of the day or minute of the hour are we removed from the eyes or heart of God."

> *The wonderful truth about prayer is that we need not make an appointment. We need only make it a priority.*

DAY 30

2 Chronicles 7:1

Praying, *fire came down from heaven and consumed the burnt offering and the sacrifices, and the glory of the LORD filled the house.*

God's purification process, alone, is responsible for making us holy.

In 2 Chronicles 7, fire fell from Heaven onto the offering at the Tabernacle to signify God's purifying presence in the Temple. Fire has long been understood to be a chief purifying agent.

The biblical imagery of fire and trials is clear. Both biblically and currently, fire is used to represent the purification process of trials in our lives (Malachi 3:3).

In the way that fire rids precious metals of inconsistencies and impurities, so trials have the capacity to rid our lives of the same—shaping us for better usefulness (Job 23:10).

And isn't that the goal? We ought to want usefulness by God as much as we want life.

One of the songs we actively meditated on during our trials—humming, singing, or discussing almost daily—was *How Firm a Foundation*. One of the verses reads as follows:

When through fiery trials thy pathway shall lie,

My grace, all-sufficient, shall be thy supply.

The flames shall not hurt thee; I only design

Thy dross to consume and thy gold to refine.

DAY 31

2 Chronicles 7:14

And My people who are called by My name humble
*themselves and **pray** and seek My face and turn from their*
wicked ways, then I will hear from heaven, will forgive
their sin and will heal their land.

The shortest route to answered prayer is wanting what God wants.

Since the Garden, mankind has struggled to believe that God wants the best for their lives. Eve was not content to leave alone the tree of the knowledge of good and evil—and she bought the lie of Satan that God was not aware of what was best (Genesis 3:4).

Since the Garden, man has struggled with the same deadly deception.

Here is the wonderful plan we had for our lives: We were going to get married, finish graduate degrees, and start a family two years later. We would raise our children in a brick bungalow with a white fence and a happy dog.

Here was God's plan for our lives: Seven years later, after experiencing two miscarriages and facing countless disappointments, we would just be starting a difficult adoption process. (Note: We did have a happy dog.)

And here is what we learned: We must be vigilant to want what God wants for us more heartily than what we want for ourselves. In 2 Chronicles 6, Solomon asked God to make provision for the people of Israel after they had sinned. God's response, in 2 Chronicles 7:14, indicated He wanted more for the Israelites: humility, prayer, searching, and change.

We must, by humble prayer, desire what God wants for our lives.

2 Chronicles 7:15

Now My eyes will be open and My ears attentive to the
prayer *offered in this place.*

God is listening.

As the Great Engineer of our lives, the Almighty has not left us to
figure things out by ourselves. In addition to telling us that the very
hairs of our head are numbered (Matthew 10:30), God has granted us
an open door policy for coming to Him with our cares and concerns.
This is truly an incredible demonstration of care in light of the many
ways we have disappointed Him.

God longs to meet His children at the throne of grace.

And unlike King Ahasuerus from the Book of Esther, God has made
it clear that we need not fear approaching His throne. We will not risk
our lives or livelihood by bringing petitions or requesting help.

In fact, our lives and livelihood are in danger when we do not seek
His intervention.

His eyes are open and His ears attentive. There is no greater assurance,
no sweeter promise in all the Bible than this: "I will never leave you
nor forsake you" (Hebrews 13:5 ESV).

We are blessed.

> *... God has granted us an open door
> policy for coming to Him with our cares
> and concerns.*

DAY 33

2 Chronicles 14:11

*Then Asa called to the LORD his God and said, "LORD, there is no one besides You to help in the battle between the powerful and those who have no strength; so help us, O LORD our God, for we **trust** in You, and in Your name have come against this multitude. O LORD, You are our God; let not man prevail against You."*

Belief in God's sovereignty during times of waiting, combined with an unwavering conviction that God is good, will lead us to trust and not fear any potential conclusion to our concerns.

On the days when it is hardest to open the Bible—because of the wars being waged inside our hearts between truth and error—it is then we need the Bible most.

On days when we are doubtful, we must read the Word until we believe with our whole hearts that God saved us to be more than a Savior to us for all eternity. He saved us to be our Savior now—today—in addition to the splendor that awaits us after death.

And Scripture alone will lead us to this conclusion.

Believing with certainty that God is our Savior in this life will enable us to say with the hymn writer, Frances Havergal:

Every joy or trial falleth from above,

Traced upon our dial by the Sun of Love;

We may trust Him fully all for us to do—

They who trust Him wholly find Him wholly true.

2 Chronicles 33:13

*When he **prayed** to Him, He was moved by his entreaty and heard his supplication, and brought him again to Jerusalem to his kingdom, Then Manasseh knew that the LORD was God.*

Trials are often pathways to greater trust.

Manasseh was, at one time, a wicked king who did evil things in the sight of God (2 Chronicles 33:2). On his list of misdemeanors, he practiced witchcraft, worshiped idols, desecrated the temple, and killed his own children.

> *If life were easy, many would never take note that God is the greatest joy and hope for the believer.*

Manasseh was not someone we would easily forgive.

In Manasseh's moment of weakness, though—when his freedom hung in the balance—he cried out to the Lord. And because the Lord was gracious to answer this man who had spent his life in contempt of all things holy, Manasseh came to the knowledge that God was real.

The trial formed the trust.

If life were easy, many would never take note that God is the greatest joy and hope for the believer. Trials present believers with opportunities to publicly trust God—to authenticate on the dark days what is said when everything is sunny.

God does not allow trials into our lives as a means of making us miserable. There is always something good at work.

DAY 35

Job 4:6

"Is not your fear of God your confidence, And the integrity of your ways your **hope?**"

While living his worst nightmare, Job trusted God.

There is no doubt that Job suffered immensely, but while he suffered, he trusted God, proving both can be done concurrently. In the verses immediately following his string of losses—including his livestock, servants, wealth, and children—we learn how Job responded. "Then Job arose and tore his robe and shaved his head and fell on the ground and worshiped. And he said, 'Naked I came from my mother's womb, and naked shall I return. The LORD gave, and the LORD has taken away; blessed be the name of the LORD'" (Job 1:20–21 ESV).

The reality is that Job may never have understood why God allowed the events of that difficult day. Job certainly never paged through a Bible to the story where God and Satan discussed the test.

That the Bible includes the backstory of Job's testing is for our benefit—not Job's.

Job trusted God on the day of testing because Job trusted God before the day of testing.

God had already proven Himself trustworthy long before the test.

The truth remains: Job may have been confused about the circumstances, but he was never confused about his God.

DAY 36

Job 6:11

*What is my strength, that I should **wait**? And what is my end, that I should endure?*

There is no shortcut to waiting on God.

No *insta-prayer*, no *ten steps to endurance*. He will not change His mind because we are more penitent or push things forward faster because we are more earnest.

A god who would cause our pain to cease because we begged or blubbered would not be the God who lovingly ordained the events in our lives because of His goodness. He would be a god who responded to us as an exhausted parent might respond to a pleading child.

But our God loves us too much to give us what He knows we should not have.

God's agenda will transpire on time. We are invited to request, yet we are instructed to wait. He has ordained our experiences as an expression of His goodness.

So we wait for the phone call. We carefully count out the days between now and important events. We eagerly turn the pages on the calendar.

And we endure patiently.

We find our strength in the reality that all waiting on Earth directs us to the one thing we are ultimately waiting for—Heaven (Philippians 3:20–21).

DAY 37

Job 8:14

*Whose confidence is fragile, and whose **trust** a spider's web.*

Trust enables us to obey God and wholeheartedly believe Him when our minds would otherwise be conflicted with despondency or doubt.

It is the gracious gift to every believer that we are equipped to trust in this way. If we didn't have God as our hope, our confidence would be brittle and our trust easily broken. We would put hope in men and seek salvation in possessions. The days would be

Forgetting God produces the most fragile confidence imaginable.

long and the nights even longer. Like the spider's web, our convictions would serve their short-lived purposes and be gone.

Forgetting God produces the most fragile confidence imaginable.

That our Heavenly Father has chosen to work all things together for our good and His glory should *allow, enable, fortify, and strengthen* us to trust and obey.

That God can be nothing other than good should so empower us that we can do nothing other than trust.

No matter what.

DAY 38

Job 11:18

*Then you would **trust**, because there is **hope**; and you
would look around and rest securely.*

Regardless of our circumstances, we can rest in this: *God is bigger
than I am and He knows better what I need.*

Walking by sight is always easier than walking by faith. Sight affords
us the opportunity to better see where we are going—determine
whether the next step is one we want to take.

Walking by faith is a completely separate matter.

Walking by faith necessitates confidence in God regardless of
circumstance, feeling, reason, or desire. With one hand firmly planted
on the shoulder of our guide, we cross the busy intersections of life
blindfolded. And we hear the honking and the yelling—we feel the
wind of passing traffic as we walk. Our lives are in His hands.

But we know that God has designed it best that our security be found
in Him—not in our ability to see where we are going.

In the opening pages of *St. Augustine's Confessions*, he wrote: "You
awake us to delight in praising You; for You have made us for Yourself,
and our hearts are restless until they find their rest in You."

 *Walking by faith necessitates confidence in God
regardless of circumstance, feeling, reason, or desire.*

DAY 39

Job 13:15

Though He slay me, I will **hope** *in Him. Nevertheless I will argue my ways before Him.*

Waiting on God is the clearest demonstration of hope.

We hope; therefore, we wait. When we cease to hope, we cease to wait.

The moment a child believes his father is not coming home from work is the moment he ceases to watch for him out the window. Likewise, the moment we believe God is incapable or unwilling to meet our needs, we stop watching for Him to work, and we lose hope.

Many of us lose hope long before we come in danger of being slain.

We must trust God so wholly that even when it seems to us that God is knowingly and actively choosing the painful paths for our lives, we still trust Him because we believe He is good. We must never tire of the promise that all things will work together for our good (Romans 8:28).

This truth is reciprocal.

Waiting on God develops hope. Hoping in God strengthens our ability to wait.

Our hope should be brightest when our days are darkest. The valley of the shadow of death is but a momentary necessity to reach the Kingdom of God.

DAY 40

Job 14:7

*For there is **hope** for a tree, when it is cut down, that it will sprout again, and its shoots will not fail.*

Hope is the difference maker for the Christian.

What separates a believer from a non-believer is not intelligence, talent, commitment, or kindness. Some non-believers actually embody virtue to the shame of those who have Christ living within.

What separates the believer from the non-believer, then, is where the hope is placed.

For the nonbeliever, hope is placed in externals—circumstances, career, finances, and family. For the believer, hope is placed in God, resulting in a peace that surpasses disappointment, sadness, grief, or failure (Philippians 4:7). The believer has hope, based on what Christ did, that he will live forever with Him (John 14:19).

A trust in God for eternal salvation must manifest itself on Earth as hope in God for everything else. What the non-believer sees as disastrous, the believer must see as sovereign.

> *What separates the believer from the non-believer, then, is where the hope is placed.*

What the non-believer views with pessimism, the believer must view with Christ-centered expectation—the definition of Christian hope.

If not for hope in God, what difference is there?

DAY 41

Job 17:15

*Where now is my **hope**? And who regards my **hope**?*

Every part of pain has a purpose.

From our perspective, it is no mystery why God allowed Joseph to be thrown into prison. There is little question why God sent the strongest part of Gideon's army home. From our vantage point, God had plans to bless Job all along—he was going to receive twice what he had from the beginning! And Gideon's battle was won before he fought.

But sometimes, when we stand on the outskirts of our own disappointment and pain, we have a difficult time believing that Joseph's God, Gideon's God, and Job's God is the author of our story as well. The untrusting part of us is inclined to believe we are suffering for no good reason.

But, like a sequel written thousands of years after the original story, our lives exist to bring glory to the same God as those men who lived in the Old Testament.

We have the advantage of reading God's purposes for a group of men who never owned the Bible. We can cling to promises they never held in their hands. We have more information in our time—through written history and all the promises of God—to know that God acts with perfect wisdom and with a faultless plan.

We must believe that God has never made a mistake and never will.

DAY 42

Job 22:27

*You will **pray** to Him, and He will hear you; and you will pay your vows.*

Getting mad at God hinders us from worshiping Him as we ought.

Misguided counselors would encourage us to "be honest with God"—even shake our fists at Him if it would help us cope with our grief. "God understands your anger!" they might say. And though He does know us better than we know ourselves—flawlessly deciphers the intention of our thoughts and emotions—He never permits us to be guided by feelings to the point of sin.

He always requires us to be faithful to truth.

Being angry with someone insinuates he or she made a mistake. And we know that God is unable to make a mistake (Psalm 18:30). Therefore, whatever decision God makes for our lives is perfect because God made it.

We may ask questions of God, certainly. In Psalm 42, the sons of Korah asked God why He had forgotten them. But they quickly followed up the question with these words: "Hope in God; for I shall again praise him" (Psalm 42:11 ESV).

It is far better for us to channel our energy into the practice of humble praise than to spend it questioning and complaining, arguing and belittling the God of the universe who loves us more than anyone else ever could.

Worship and resentment cannot coexist.

DAY 43

Job 29:21

*To me they listened and **waited**, and kept silent for
my counsel.*

There are many things to love about Job.

Near the top of that list is his transparency. He asked many of the
questions we would ask. He felt many of the emotions we would feel.
We identify with him because of his humanity.

So it makes sense for us to identify with the lessons Job learned.

 We identify with him because of his humanity.

Chiefly: God owes us nothing.

At first, it may seem mistaken—erroneous even—to say God is
not obligated to give us anything. After all, He filled His Word
with promises on which we can bank our hope. But Job, during his
conversation with the Almighty, heard these words from God: "Who
has first given to me, that I should repay him? Whatever is under the
whole heaven is mine" (Job 41:11 ESV).

So what caused Job to hope in this God who had undoubtedly
ordained the difficulty in his life? Here is what Job said: "I know that
you can do all things, and that no purpose of yours can be thwarted"
(Job 42:2 ESV).

That God's purposes cannot be altered brought Job comfort and
should reassure us as well.

Job 30:26

*When I expected good, then evil came; when I **waited** for light, then darkness came.*

Everything that happens in life has a purpose.

God is not the author of random events—He is the orchestrator of His divine plan. This should bring us comfort when we expect good and find evil, when we wait for light and meet darkness. God is not a mean or maniacal trickster interested in giving us what is harsh or painful to satisfy unholy cravings.

Yet sometimes the "all things" in Romans 8:28 includes evil. Sometimes we are called to be victims of the sinful choices of other people. But even at those times, we are being held in the sovereign fist of God, unable to be separated from the inexhaustible love of the Father.

That God had to turn His back on His Son for those excruciating hours at Calvary was evidence of His love and not His oblivion.

God is the opposite of the over-indulging Father.

That He gives us what is painful indicates He wants what is best for our lives.

Why would He do the most loving thing—send His own Son to the cross to suffer on our behalf—only to follow up that great salvation with unkind, unloving acts?

We should be so attuned to God's direct leading in our lives that we can say with Solomon, "Sorrow is better than laughter" if it is the will of God (Ecclesiastes 7:3).

DAY 45

Job 33:26

*Then he will **pray** to God, and He will accept him, that he may see His face with joy, and He may restore His righteousness to man.*

God plots for our good.

So often the response to difficult circumstances, by those who do not trust Him, is skepticism of His goodness. In the middle of catastrophe the question undoubtedly arises, "Where is God?"—as if to assume that God could not be present in the middle of someone's pain.

Many have drawn a line in the sand, separating painful experiences from pleasant—labeling one as "good" and the other as "bad"—no qualifications, no exceptions.

That God could be working, even amid unspeakable horrors, is unfathomable.

Proverbs 16:33 indicates a drastically different perspective on the goodness of God: "The lot is cast into the lap, but its every decision is from the Lord" (ESV).

What appears to us to be random, undeserved, or even senseless is still something God plans to use in our lives. Scripture is clear that God loves us. And so, by loving us, He plans to work everything for our good.

His omnipresence means He's there and His justice means He's right. *Always.*

DAY 46

Job 36:2

Wait for me a little, and I will show you that there is yet more to be said in God's behalf.

God entrusted Job with the trials in his life.

Though the events of that tragic, horrific day no doubt caught Job by surprise, they did not surprise the Lord. During the sacred conversation recorded in the first chapters of Job, God set Job in Satan's sights—pointed him out as someone worthy of testing.

"And the LORD said to Satan, 'Have you considered my servant Job, that there is none like him on the earth, a blameless and upright man, who fears God and turns away from evil?'" (Job 2:3 ESV).

God counted Job faithful. And, with everything hinging on proving God wrong, Satan went after Job with vengeance.

In a second, separate event in Scripture, God handpicked Mary to be the mother of Jesus because she found favor with Him. And while being chosen to bear the Savior of the world would go down in history as being a tremendous honor, the reality for Mary was that she was chosen to face an unwed pregnancy and the eventual pain of watching her Son be crucified on a cross.

Make no mistake. Testing is warranted by behavior.

Suffering is often endowed by God on those He trusts to prove Himself to be true.

DAY 47

Job 39:11

*Will you **trust** him because his strength is great and leave your labor to him?*

God's response to Job's asking, "Why?" is no doubt the same response He would give us.

Job asked, "Why did I not die at birth, come out from the womb and expire?" (Job 3:11 ESV).

God's answer to Job's question is a lengthy four chapters in which He revealed more of Himself to His servant. And though God never actually answered Job's question—never explained why Job had been the target of the trial—Job's response to God's explanation was one of total contentment.

At the conclusion of God's oratory on His own holiness, Job threw himself down and worshiped. Job had no idea that God would heal him and restore life to his broken, dilapidated condition, yet Job worshiped God because he had learned that God was worthy of worship even in the most dire of situations.

The lesson for us seems apparent: in times of difficulty, the goal shouldn't be finding the answer to the infamous "why" question, but rather finding out more about God. Perhaps if we sought to understand God's total character, we wouldn't need to know His individual motives.

As Elizabeth Elliot so concisely stated, "The secret is Christ in me, not me in a different set of circumstances."

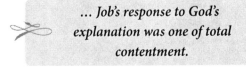

… Job's response to God's explanation was one of total contentment.

DAY 48

Job 42:10

*The LORD restored the fortunes of Job when he **prayed** for his friends, and the LORD increased all that Job had twofold.*

Friends don't always know how to respond to those who deal with crisis.

Anyone who has waded through deep waters in life can share anecdotes collected from well-meaning neighbors or nosy associates or over-ambitious friends or family.

Complete strangers approached us during our adoption to ask which one of us was infertile—as if infertility would be the only good reason we would choose to adopt. (Note: It's generally a good idea to introduce yourself before moving to the topic of infertility.)

Job certainly had his compilation of criticisms, courtesy of Eliphaz, Bildad, Zophar, and Elihu. These friends "graciously" waited until the seven days of mourning were past before visiting Job to let him know that he was in his present condition because he had sinned.

Whether or not the unhelpful responses of our brothers and sisters in Christ are intentional or naive, God is aware of them and is working on our behalf—both theirs and ours. It is interesting that God blessed Job only after Job prayed for his friends.

Would God have blessed Job if he had withheld compassion from those who had treated him poorly? The answer remains to be seen. But one thing is certain: God delighted in Job's prayer on behalf of those who had hurt him.

DAY 49

Psalm 4:1

*Answer me when I call, O God of my righteousness! You
have relieved me in my distress; Be gracious to me and
hear my **prayer**.*

Apathetic prayer is of little value to anyone.

It is not the stringing of words together that moves the heart of God.
Even the Pharisees knew how to pray (Luke 18:11), yet their prayers
were ineffective because they were not honoring God.

The prayer that honors God is the prayer that agrees with Him.
Whether communicating adoration, confession, thanksgiving, or
supplication, there is an appropriate way to pray. The prayer that takes
hold of the communicated truths of the Bible and repeats them back
to the God who inspired them is favorably received by our gracious
Father.

> **It is not the stringing of words together that
> moves the heart of God.**

David often used previous examples of God's mercy toward him to
plead his case for present favor. To put it in our words, "Lord, you
have rescued me in the past! Please be merciful to do it again!"

We must commune with God—demonstrate through our faithful,
fervent conversation—an unyielding belief that God is good and
faithful.

DAY 50

Psalm 4:5

*Offer the sacrifices of righteousness, and **trust** in the LORD.*

In the flesh, we are by nature, *not* trusting.

We are sometimes gullible, naive, too easily fooled. But trust—our complete confidence placed in someone or something outside of ourselves—is challenging. Worry, fear, and anxiety, though painful, are often preferred over trust.

There is a reason the Word of God continually reminds us to trust in God.

Trusting God is not our default reaction to life experience.

But there is hope! The fact that God tells us to trust Him means we are capable of doing it. We are equipped with everything we need to obey. At some point, trusting God with life experiences can become something we choose to do in contrast to that which comes naturally to us.

Putting the theology of Proverbs 3:5–6 into practice is difficult, yet necessary: "Trust in the Lord with all your heart, and do not lean on your own understanding. In all your ways acknowledge him, and he will make straight your paths" (ESV).

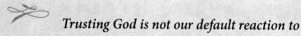

Trusting God is not our default reaction to life experience.

Here is the gospel truth: God will not disappoint those who trust in Him.

DAY 51

Psalm 5:2

Heed the sound of my cry for help, my King and my God,
*for to You I **pray**.*

God knows. That is enough.

After seventeen months of waiting for some type of word about our adoption to filter through the system and reach our ears, we were finally told that—if we didn't hear something soon—we could potentially reach out to government officials to do something for our case.

Though the prospect of involving someone bigger and stronger than we were was appealing to us, we were grateful to know that the Highest Official on earth and in heaven was already acting on our behalf. God was in control of our case all along.

King is a title for God used often in Psalms to indicate His sovereign lordship and His absolute control over the events of our lives.

If even one thing could happen outside of the absolute control of God, then God could not be sovereign and therefore completely trustworthy. It isn't enough that He can control only certain things— that His power can only extend beyond ours by comparison. He is either all-powerful—omnipotent—or He is not sovereign.

On the darkest days we have chosen to believe that "the foolishness of God is wiser than men, and the weakness of God is stronger than men" (1 Corinthians 1:25 ESV).

God knows, and for us, that is enough.

DAY 52

Psalm 5:3

*In the morning, O LORD, You will hear my voice; in the morning I will order my **prayer** to You and eagerly watch.*

Morning is a wonderful thing.

The dawn of each new day affords us the opportunity to begin again—to place at the feet of our Savior anything that hinders us from trusting Him—and to find the mercies that are guaranteed new every morning (Lamentations 3:23).

That David spoke of offering his prayer to God in the morning lends credibility to the thought that a day started with prayer is a day started well. Because peace is the product of prayer, it makes sense that a day of peace must be initiated with a morning of prayer.

Who knows what will transpire today? Maybe today the adoption agency will call or the hospital will have test results or our loved ones will suffer some unforeseen loss. Who knows what will happen?— God does. So why would we want to begin the day by discussing the possibilities with anyone else?

We would do well to say with the psalmist in 119:147, "I rise before dawn and cry for help; I hope in your words" (ESV).

> *Because peace is the product of prayer, it makes sense that a day of peace must be initiated with a morning of prayer.*

DAY 53

Psalm 6:9

*The LORD has heard my supplication, the LORD receives my **prayer**.*

Continuous trust in God is displayed by continual prayer.

God never commanded us to pray eloquently, but He did command us to pray often.

Frequently, during the long nights when we lay awake thinking about the pint-sized human being across the world who was just beginning his day—without us, once again—we were threatened by discouragement. Sometimes, after pouring out our disappointment to each other, we would bury our faces in the coolness of our pillows and cry out to God. Those petitions were no doubt some of the messiest, most inarticulate prayers—never to be printed in a book or repeated in a church service.

But God heard us when our hearts were right with Him.

And thankfully, according to Romans 8:27, we had the Holy Spirit interceding for us according to the will of God with the eloquence we could not produce.

Night often brings with it the laundry list of disappointments: sadistic reminders of shortcomings or concerns. Like a playground bully, night waits to taunt and rebuke us. But the Word of God—with its carefully outlined expectation that we would pray at all times—means we must pray at night, too.

Psalm 9:10

*And those who know Your name will put their **trust** in You, for You, O LORD, have not forsaken those who seek You.*

It is human nature to desire the path of least resistance.

We often wish our lives would travel the path that winds by stillest waters. Lives without conflict or catastrophe are most appealing to us—and if we had a choice, we would likely avoid the things that are hard in favor of everything that is simple.

But people who need nothing do not depend on anyone else—including the Lord.

Joseph, no doubt, relied on God more earnestly *while being in prison.*

David, no doubt, trusted God more fully *while fleeing from the murderous king.*

Mary, no doubt, depended on God more readily *while facing the shocking pregnancy.*

It must be real to us that God will never forsake us if we seek Him. And we must consider the possibility that our testing is not a punishment at all . . . but a gift.

"But the LORD was with Joseph and showed him steadfast love and gave him favor in the sight of the keeper of the prison" (Genesis 39:21 ESV).

DAY 55

Psalm 9:18

*For the needy will not always be forgotten, nor the **hope** of the afflicted perish forever.*

It is a good thing to be in a place where depending on God is the only option.

Early in our marriage, we learned this truth. When times were toughest and days were longest and nights were hardest, prayer and Bible reading were the natural desire of our hearts. We could breeze past the reminders at church to pray and meditate. An improved devotional life didn't show up on our yearly resolutions—it didn't have to!

One of the benefits of difficulty is the heart's bent toward deliverance.

We need someone bigger and better than us to handle the storms, and when we are traveling through them, we know inherently who that someone is.

If we respond to trials the way we were created to respond, we'll find ourselves running to our Heavenly Father instead of believing we can live without the grace that God provides us every day. It is the height of arrogance to think we can manage life on our own.

When we are afflicted and needy, we know we are dependent.

 It is a good thing to be in a place where depending on God is the only option.

DAY 56

Psalm 13:5

*But I have **trusted** in Your lovingkindness; my heart shall rejoice in Your salvation.*

Trust and joy are mutually dependent.

Trust, hope, and prayer were essentials for the psalmist. When disappointed, he prayed. By praying, he trusted. By trusting, he could rejoice in the goodness of God.

The cycle for the psalmist was constant: Disappointment led to prayer. Prayer led to trust. Trust led to rejoicing.

Expecting to find joy in the midst of difficulty is unreasonable without adding the components of prayer and trust. Rejoicing isn't the natural response to pain. We need only attend the funeral of a non-believer to understand the natural response to grief.

Grief without prayer and trust will remain grief.

Whether or not Psalm 13 was written before or after the writer received the rescue he was seeking, one thing is clear: suffering and rejoicing can happen simultaneously for the child of God.

It is possible—even expected of us—to do both at the same time.

> *The cycle for the psalmist was constant: Disappointment led to prayer. Prayer led to trust. Trust led to rejoicing.*

DAY 57

Psalm 17:1

*Hear a just cause, O LORD, give heed to my cry; give ear to my **prayer**, which is not from deceitful lips.*

Escape is appealing.

Our natural response during a season of trial is desire for its conclusion. And if we cannot secure conclusion, we at least want to be heard or understood, empathized with or sympathized for. We'd like the pain to dissipate and the disappointment to end. If life cannot go back to what it was, we'd be content if it simply got easier moving forward.

But *easy* isn't always God's plan for our lives.

Christlikeness is the goal, and satisfaction in Him is the key.

... easy isn't always God's plan for our lives.

Depending on how translators handle the text, David requests as many as seventeen things of God in Psalm 17. Most of his appeals were couched in biblical promises. He wasn't a child stomping his foot in the presence of the Almighty. He requested rescue and rest—two things God takes delight in supplying.

At the end of the chapter, David concludes with these words: "I will be satisfied with your likeness" (Psalm 17:15).

Oh, that this would be our prayer!

DAY 58

Psalm 21:7

*For the king **trusts** in the LORD, and through the*
lovingkindness of the Most High he will not be shaken.

All potential fears are futile if our faith is placed in Him.

Because God gives us everything that we need—whether we're princes or paupers—we have nothing to fear. That the lovingkindness of the Most High will not be shaken, according to the Psalms, leads us to appreciate two truths:

Fixation on circumstances will lead us to fear. Fixation on God will lead us to trust.

After many months of waiting to be united with our child, we received the phone call no adopting parent wants to get. We learned that our child's case was potentially switched with another child's case and we might not be able to bring him home after all. There was nothing we could do about the situation occurring thousands of miles away. The orphanage maintained very strict guidelines about making contact. Our hands were tied.

The choices were as real to us as if they were tangible: fixate on circumstances or fixate on God. The choice was as obvious as life and death, joy or sorrow, fear or peace.

We found comfort in the final words Moses gave to Israel: "The eternal God is your dwelling place, and underneath are the everlasting arms" (Deuteronomy 33:27 ESV).

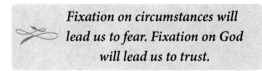

Fixation on circumstances will
lead us to fear. Fixation on God
will lead us to trust.

DAY 59

Psalm 22:4

*In You our fathers **trusted**; they **trusted** and You
delivered them.*

God uses the blessings of one generation to encourage the next.

Though Psalm 22 speaks specifically of God's rescuing the people
from slavery in Egypt, the principle applies. One generation trusting
God in difficulty is a pattern for the next.

We were encouraged by the trust our fathers placed in God. Our
decision to adopt was a third generation decision. One grandparent
adopted. Our parents adopted. And we were adopting. And though
all three situations were unique in motive and circumstance, our trust
was in the same God.

At one point we sat in the same tiny room our parents sat in thirty
years prior waiting for the same news. And Psalm 22:4 rang in our
ears. Yes, our parents trusted, and God met their needs.

As our adoption unfolded, one of our motivations for waiting correctly
became the good of our child and any future children God might give
us. Psalm 78:7 explains, "So that they should set their hope in God and
not forget the works of God, but keep his commandments" (ESV).

Our response to God during times of waiting affects more than
just us.

DAY 60

Psalm 22:5

To You they cried out and were delivered; in You they
trusted *and were not disappointed.*

There is no margin of error in the purposes of God.

We make mistakes—certainly we do. But even our sin is not outside the reaches of God's purpose. No doubt, the prodigal son found himself among the pigs as the result of his poor choices (Luke 15). Yet, had he not found himself feeding swine, he might never have come to the conclusion recorded in Luke 15:17–18: "But when he came to himself, he said, 'How many of my father's hired servants have more than enough bread, but I perish here with hunger! I will arise and go to my father, and I will say to him, 'Father, I have sinned against heaven and before you'" (ESV).

Without the pigs, there might not have been the repentance.

Without the choice to leave his father in the first place, the prodigal son might never have come to the realization that his father was good. True, the prodigal son's choices were evil, but that God ultimately used them for His glory is clear.

> *Setting aside doubts, regrets, frustrations, and failures to trust God will never result in disappointment.*

Trust enables us to fully comply with the commands of God even when our emotions are conflicted. Setting aside doubts, regrets, frustrations, and failures to trust God will never result in disappointment.

We will cry to Him and be delivered.

DAY 61

Psalm 22:9

*Yet You are He who brought me forth from the womb; You made me **trust** when upon my mother's breasts.*

God's love for us did not begin at birth.

God's love for us began before we were born and extends long after we are dead.

No matter what pain and difficulty we are experiencing now, we always deserve much worse. God's love gives us better than we deserve both now and for all eternity.

It is the unrelenting purpose of God to hold us in His hand, irremovable, unshakable, and indestructible. He may put us in the furnace, but He will walk the flames beside us. He may send us to the storms, but He will pilot the boat. He may put us in the wilderness, but He will provide the sustenance we need.

God's will is not to destroy us, but to deliver us from evil.

How do we know God is trustworthy? He has always kept His promises. And we know He is the same God today that He was when the Word was written (Hebrews 13:8).

When we are in pain, we can do what generations of believers have done before us.

"And David was greatly distressed, for the people spoke of stoning him, because all the people were bitter in soul, each for his sons and daughters. But David strengthened himself in the LORD his God" (1 Samuel 30:6 ESV).

DAY 62

Psalm 25:2

*O my God, in You I **trust**, do not let me be ashamed; do not let my enemies exult over me.*

The psalmist was honest about himself to God.

Throughout the Psalms we sense the sincerity of the writers. Dread, disappointment, discouragement, and dismay are frequent themes alongside trust and hope. The psalmists speak as much about their concerns as they do the songs that make them so well-known.

Truly, there is a Psalm for every season, so that the wounded can read about man's plight and God's commitment to save—and at any time may rejoice in the writers' God.

The same psalmist who could write about fearing no evil also asked God not to let his enemies be exalted—meaning we can find peace in the midst of life's most frustrating circumstances. We can find the means to rejoice no matter what we are facing.

Here is cause to rejoice: Undoubtedly, God leads us. And the Shepherd never leads His sheep down the wrong path.

Henry H. Barry, a nineteenth century poet, wrote, "In pastures green? Not always; sometimes He who knoweth best, in kindness leadeth me in many ways where heavy shadows be."

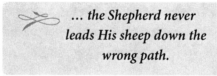

... the Shepherd never leads His sheep down the wrong path.

DAY 63

Psalm 25:3

*Indeed, none of those who **wait** for You will be ashamed;
those who deal treacherously without cause will be
ashamed.*

God's timetable is always perfect.

From our non-omniscient, non-all-knowing viewpoint, the schedule could be improved. The path could be straightened. The course we're called to endure could take a more efficient route. We would travel in the countryside, for instance, in lieu of the wilderness. We would choose the garden over the furnace.

But God's ways are not our ways (Isaiah 55:8–9).

Most often, God's plan is better understood from the tapestry-side instead of the side with the messy, crisscrossed threads that appear to move in no direction at all. God's plan for us, at times, is best read beginning with the last chapter.

If we could see what He sees, know what He knows, choose what He chooses, we would undoubtedly affirm God's ways are perfect.

Waiting is excruciating, but often waiting is necessary as a means of obedience to God.

Of waiting, C.J. Mahaney said, "The temptation is to demand that God perform for us in the present what He has promised for the future."

DAY 64

Psalm 25:5

*Lead me in Your truth and teach me, for You are the God of my salvation; for You I **wait** all the day.*

God's truth is absolute.

And here is what we know to be absolutely true: God is sovereign. Nothing happens by mishap or misfortune. Everything that transpires today will occur by God's divine appointment. Every bit of news we do or do not receive will be delivered right on time, as organized by the God who controls the universe.

The apparent lack of an answer does not mean God is not working. It means we are not yet supposed to know what God has already ordained.

We cannot confuse silence with inactivity.

Shortly after waiting on God for provision to meet a specific need in her life, Fanny Crosby put these words to paper:

All the way my Savior leads me—

Cheers each winding path I tread,

Gives me grace for every trial,

Feeds me with the living bread.

Though my weary steps may falter,

And my soul a-thirst may be,

Gushing from the Rock before me,

Lo! a spring of joy I see.

DAY 65

Psalm 25:21

*Let integrity and uprightness preserve me, for I **wait**
for You.*

Perseverance is the key.

In the language of Psalm 25:21, the continuation and protection
of uprightness is, at the core, the definition of preservation or
perseverance.

No one, during times of peace, would say that God is not good. No
one would argue that He does not love or cannot help or will not save.
But then, when cast into the furnace of trial or disappointment, men
hastily question all of the above.

How could God do this? Is God good? Will He hear?

Yet the testing of the gold requires heat.

Defeat thinks the worst of what God has planned while perseverance
holds out for the final chapter—believing God's will to be best—
holding fast the words of Psalm 145:17: "The Lord is righteous in all
his ways and kind in all his works" (ESV).

As Pastor Mark Minnick once said, "Every single virtue of the
Christian life is only as good as how long it lasts."

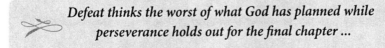

*Defeat thinks the worst of what God has planned while
perseverance holds out for the final chapter ...*

DAY 66

Psalm 26:1

*Vindicate me, O LORD, for I have walked in my integrity, and I have **trusted** in the LORD without wavering.*

God doesn't expect us to *understand*. He instructs us to *trust*.

We know this because the details of our lives—*who, how, what, why*—are often obscured from sight, while verses in the Bible abound about our responsibility to trust our Maker.

At times, we exhibit an idolatrous commitment to understand what God doesn't intend for us to know. We would rather figure things out than trust God. We would rather have our selfish questions answered than believe His purposes outweigh our own desire to know.

This worship of our own understanding is both sinful and exhausting.

We should rest in the knowledge that everything we need to know for now is found in the Bible.

In a letter to his friend, John Newton wrote the following:

How highly does it become us, both as creatures and as sinners, to submit to the appointment of our maker! And how necessary is it to our peace! This great attainment is too often unthought-of, and over looked; we are prone to fix our attention upon the second causes and immediate instruments of events; forgetting that whatever befalls us is according to his purpose, and therefore must be right and seasonable in itself, and shall in the issue be productive of good.

DAY 67

Psalm 27:14

Wait for the LORD; be strong and let your heart take courage; yes, wait for the LORD.

Is anything too difficult for the LORD? (Genesis 18:14).

As far as we know, God parted the Red Sea only one time in history—at the exact moment the Israelites needed to escape. He brought Joseph's family to Egypt to buy grain when Joseph happened to be the ruler of the land. He brought Rebekah to the well in Nahor when Abraham's servant was seeking a bride for Isaac.

So why, if God could handle the life events of Old Testament believers and cause the unlikely to happen to make the impossible a reality—do we struggle to trust Him with the events of our lives?

Hasn't He proven that He will do what needs to be done?

Moses' words to the Israelites moments before they would cross the divided sea were, "The LORD will fight for you, and you have only to be silent." (Exodus 14:14 ESV).

Meaning, in the grand scheme of life, God can take care of things by Himself. We must learn to be silent and wait for the Lord.

 We must learn to be silent and wait for the Lord.

C. H. Spurgeon said, "He turned the sea into dry land. It was no slight miracle to drive a pathway through such a sea, and to make it fit for the traffic of a whole nation. He who did this can do anything, and must be God, the worthy object of adoration."

DAY 68

Psalm 28:7

*The LORD is my strength and my shield; my heart **trusts**
in Him, and I am helped; therefore my heart exults, and
with my song I shall thank Him.*

If life were meant to be easy, the Lord would likely have used different imagery.

He might have called His Son *a summer walk* or *a gentle rain*. He might have referred to Himself as a *beautiful field* or a *perfect mist*.

But the Bible refers to the Lord as our strength, our shield, our tower, our fortress, our strong hold. If we needed any verification that life was hard or that God is good, we have it in the imagery used throughout the Word of God. Shields and bucklers aren't meant for sunny afternoons, after all.

"Incline your ear to me; rescue me speedily! Be a rock of refuge for me, a strong fortress to save me!" (Psalm 31:2 ESV)

In light of this truth, Charles Wesley penned the words that could easily be our prayer:

Other refuge have I none,

Hangs my helpless soul on Thee;

Leave, ah! leave me not alone,

Still support and comfort me!

All my trust on Thee is stayed,

All my help from Thee I bring;

Cover my defenseless head

With the shadow of Thy wing.

DAY 69

Psalm 31:6

*I hate those who regard vain idols, but I **trust** in the LORD.*

Idolatry, like an over-ambitious salesman, lingers at the door of those who are experiencing hardship. If idols are anything to which we devote ourselves more wholly than to God, then idolatry is at its most opportunistic location in a heart that is ill at ease.

When else would we be more likely to turn our attention away from God than when we believe we are not receiving from Him the things that we need?

Especially during times of waiting, the idols of understanding, relief, control, and ease are to us a golden calf worth worshiping at any cost.

> *What does this worship and trust look like?—active employment of our thoughts on God.*

But the path to idolatry is lined with counterfeit landmarks.

The unrelenting pursuit of idols will not produce peace, will not provide relief, and will not achieve favor with God.

The remedy for idolatry is worship of and trust in the right Source.

What does this worship and trust look like?—active employment of our thoughts on God. This is known as meditation and recognized as trust.

DAY 70

Psalm 31:14

*But as for me, I **trust** in You, O LORD, I say, "You are
my God."*

We cannot find comfort in something we do not believe.

God has given us incredible promises in His Word. But those promises
are only paper and ink if they remain intellectual material and are not
made personal.

As our pastor, Dr. David Doran, reminded us during our time of
testing, "You must know the Word to use it." Additionally, we know
that studying the Scriptures is of paramount importance to gaining
an eternal perspective about our pain.

There is no sudden recognition that God is bigger than any pain.
There is no lightning bolt of faith that zaps us in our sleep or leaves us
trusting unawares.

We must study the Word—find comfort in its pages—and we must
trust the Lord.

If we believe what God says to us in His Word about our suffering and
our subsequent need to wait on Him, our perspective and experience
of pain will be revolutionized.

John Wesley wrote in his notes on the Bible:

> Be this your care, to do and suffer well: He will take care of the rest.
> As unto a faithful Creator—in whose truth, love, and power, ye may
> safely trust.

DAY 71

Psalm 31:24

Be strong and let your heart take courage, all you who
hope *in the LORD.*

It is a wonderful comfort to know we will never stray from God's care.

We had a dear friend healing from her own broken heart while we were experiencing ours. As is God's perfect design (2 Corinthians 1:4), she reached out to encourage us with the comfort she had received from God. In a precious letter to us, she wrote:

It can be very easy to spout off Romans 8:28 and Jeremiah 29:11, but very difficult to make your heart truly believe them during hard times. I have often quoted those verses to myself and followed them quickly with "Lord, I believe; help Thou my unbelief!" because the unbelief feels so much more powerful than the belief right then. And sometimes my angry, willful self doesn't even want to pray for more belief; I just want the bad stuff to be over. He cares for us even in that state of mind, too.

God loves us all the time.

No difficulty can separate us from His love (Romans 8:37–39).

Lord, help our unbelief! (Mark 9:24)

DAY 72

Psalm 32:6

*Therefore, let everyone who is godly **pray** to You in a time when You may be found; surely in a flood of great waters they will not reach him.*

Crisis is a part of life.

God's plan for His children involves pain. In the words of the psalmist, floodwaters of difficulty will come.

The trials will happen. The disappointments will occur. In waiting for God to answer our requests or show Himself strong in the events of our lives, there will be long days and there will be disappointments. Too much of the Word of God teaches us how to handle trials for this not to be true.

Our confidence must be firmly rooted in God.

In nothing more. In no one else. In nothing less.

That Christ quoted Psalms on the cross should motivate us to do the same during our lesser moments of trial and pain. The Psalms were written by people who endured much and were inspired by Him who endured even more. The words of this precious Book comforted Christ in His darkest hours and should persuade us that it can do the same for us.

"My God, my God, why have you forsaken me? Why are you so far from saving me, from the words of my groaning?" (Psalm 22:1 ESV).

In the Psalms we find confirmation that the suffering of others—and ours as well—makes sense to God.

DAY 73

Psalm 32:10

*Many are the sorrows of the wicked, But he who **trusts** in the LORD, lovingkindness shall surround him.*

Blessings are found in times of testing.

When we have nowhere else to turn but to our Heavenly Father, it is then we know with certainty that He is enough. He is sufficient to love, guide, encourage, strengthen, and provide. When we trust the Father beyond human reason, his lovingkindness strengthens the relationship and makes the trial beneficial from any perspective.

Disaster is worth it if God is there.

Cancer is worth it if God is there.

Childlessness is worth it if God is there.

Many are the sorrows of wicked people because God is not with them. But for those who trust in the Lord, pain is lessened with heavenly lovingkindness and even evil is meant for good.

On some of the longest, hardest days, we found the lovingkindness of God to be the most apparent. Arms—it seemed—of comfort and peace wrapped around us in love as we pillowed our heads to wait out the night. And at those times, we found Psalm 127:2 to be true: "It is in vain that you rise up early and go late to rest, eating the bread of anxious toil; for he gives to his beloved sleep" (ESV).

When we have nowhere else to turn but to our Heavenly Father, it is then we know with certainty that He is enough.

DAY 74

Psalm 33:17

*A horse is a false **hope** for victory; nor does it deliver anyone by its great strength.*

We *will* trust *someone*.

Even the person whose life has been shattered by disappointment and who swears off trusting anyone or anything essentially trusts himself and his own opinions. It's impossible to be fully without trust.

Our loving Father intends to meet us in our need, to walk us *through* the valley, and to give us everything we need to endure. We can turn away from Him—turn to the hundreds of voices speaking to us through media or ministry who know nothing of the schedule of our suffering—and create our own refuge in lieu of God. Or we can trust the one who loves us and ordained the blueprint for our testing.

To whom we listen indicates in whom we trust.

Fact: God has never faced anything that was too hard for Him. Fact: No person, diagnosis, outcome, or test has ever been one He couldn't control. Fact: Any people on this planet we would turn to for help—doctors, counselors, parents, friends—are people God created and gifted anyway.

> *To whom we listen indicates in whom we trust.*

Yes, we should trust the doctors.

But our speaking to the doctors should not cause us to neglect speaking to the Source of wisdom, strength, and healing.

Why are we prone to put our hope in everyone other than Him?

DAY 75

Psalm 33:18

*Behold, the eye of the LORD is on those who fear Him, on those who **hope** for His lovingkindness.*

God cares.

What an incredible consideration: in a world of almost seven billion people, the eye of the Lord is on *you* if you fear Him—not just a collective "you" as in your church or your friends—but as in *you*, personally. As a devoted father is invested in the details of his child's life, so the Lord is more infinitely aware of your needs, and He exists as the all-sufficient resource for your every step. He doesn't sleep. He doesn't overlook. He doesn't lie.

What an incredible benefit for the child of God! Not only have we been saved from eternal separation from Christ, but we have also been blessed with the full attention and support of our Creator God right now. This being true, there is no earthly reason our lives should not be characterized by hope—no matter how long or dark the day may be.

Our lives must not be earmarked by loss, disappointment, or fear. Our lives must be filled with the optimism of Heavenly expectation. *Who are you?* You are not "the cancer patient." You are not "the grieving widow." You are not "the confused, bewildered, disappointed son." You are the child of God. And His eye is on *you* if you fear Him.

The pattern of every believer must be to wait for the Lord to show Himself strong, to fear Him, and to hope for His lovingkindness.

C. H. Spurgeon wrote these words about Psalm 33:18: "They who fear God need not fear anything else; let them fix their eye of faith on him, and his eye of love will always rest upon them."

DAY 76

Psalm 33:20

*Our soul **waits** for the LORD; He is our help and our shield.*

The essence of biblical waiting is believing that God will accomplish His purposes in His time and that they will be the very best thing for everyone involved.

That we belong to the Living God—were bought with a heavy price— should change the way we wait. Recognizing that we belong to Christ doesn't eliminate the pain we feel in response to suffering. But it assures us that our feet are on solid rock that will keep us from falling into despair in times of crisis.

As far as we can sink, Christ is still there.

And in the moments when we are sinking, the close presence of Jesus is real.

> *As far as we can sink, Christ is still there.*

The truth is, God has saved us and is more to us than just an eternal gift. He is the Savior to us now. Which means—in moments of pain or fear—He is our help and shield.

As Kevin DeYoung wrote in his book, *The Good News We Almost Forgot*, "God is bigger than we think—holier, more excellent, than we realize."

With this knowledge, we must wait for Him.

DAY 77

Psalm 33:21

*For our heart rejoices in Him, because we **trust** in His holy name.*

The joy is in the purpose, not the pain.

Essential to our ability to rejoice during times of testing is our recognition that our joy isn't supposed to be about our circumstances— our delight is supposed to be about our God.

James 1:2 is a common verse on which Christians linger during times of testing. It says, "Count it all joy, my brothers, when you meet trials of various kinds" (ESV).

What wonderful, wise instruction is afforded us!

But it is important to understand that this joy isn't supposed to be about the trials at all. There is no more permission given for us to trust or delight in the bad experiences—cancer, financial ruin, marital strife—than there is for us to place our hope and delight in the good things—money, friends, success.

Of James 1:2, Pastor Mark Minnick said, " 'Enjoy this' . . . is not the counsel. What it is saying is to assess this in such a way that you are rejoicing over the totality of what's going on. Count it all joy knowing the whole outcome of this thing, and the process that's involved."

That David could move seamlessly from waiting to rejoicing in Psalm 33 testifies that his trust and ultimately his rejoicing were placed in the right source: God's holy name.

DAY 78

Psalm 33:22

*Let Your lovingkindness, O LORD, be upon us, according as we have **hoped** in You.*

Hope is the untouchable gift of God.

One of the brightest threads woven throughout the tapestry of Christianity—from Old Testament believers to the martyrs of the early church to modern missionaries who face difficulty and adversity to those suffering today—is glorious, triumphant hope.

During the weightiest moments of their lives—while shackled to a Philippian prison or while staring at torturous, unmerited death sentences at the hands of Nero and the Roman Empire—Christians throughout history have been able to sing the praises of God because of hope in Him.

Hope is valuable because hope cannot be stolen. Life can be taken at the hands of someone else. Riches, happiness, and health can be removed. But hope in God is as sure as God Himself.

Hope placed in God is of more value than hope placed in relief.

Of this hope, John Piper wrote: "So the rugged hope of the believer is not that we will escape distress or peril or hunger or slaughter, but that Almighty God will make every one of our agonies an instrument of his mercy to do us good."

Hope is the untouchable gift of God.

DAY 79

Psalm 35:13

But as for me, when they were sick, my clothing was
*sackcloth; I humbled my soul with fasting, and my **prayer***
kept returning to my bosom.

One way we honor God during times of testing is by loving others.

David was a man who was concerned for people, even in the midst of his own challenges. Specifically in Psalm 35, David was concerned for those who were his enemies—people whose illnesses and deaths should have brought him relief by the world's standards.

Yet, even in the midst of his own agonies, David was concerned for those around him.

Psalm 35:13 speaks of David's sympathy for his adversaries who were sick—and his prayer was obviously more earnest than a few sentences spoken for one item on a list of random requests. He wanted these people to be healed for reasons we might not fully understand.

1 Corinthians 10:24 is unapologetic when it says, "Let no one seek his own good, but the good of his neighbor" (ESV).

Even in times of testing and difficulty—or perhaps *especially* in times of testing and difficulty—it would do us well to care about other people—perhaps even more than at other seasons of our lives.

In another biblical illustration, Job was able to love and forgive his friends whose incomprehension of what he was facing could have cut him deeply (Job 42:8).

Loving other people honors God (Matthew 25:40).

DAY 80

Psalm 37:3

Trust *in the LORD and do good; dwell in the land and cultivate faithfulness.*

God isn't naive about our faithlessness.

He doesn't chalk it up to the difficulty of our circumstances or the unfairness of our situation. Nowhere in Scripture are we invited to worry or fret because of the enormity of previous hurts.

"Surely God wouldn't do this to us again!" we cry. But we're wrong. He absolutely would allow something into our lives fifteen times in a row if it would be for our good and His glory.

In a six-month span—while we were waiting for news of our child—we buried two loved ones who died of difficult illnesses. Also during that time, the economy took a downward spike and we grew concerned about job security—especially important since an adoption relies on employment details and money to cover the costs.

And then we discovered these words by George Müller:

> Where faith begins, anxiety ends; where anxiety begins, faith ends. As long as we are able to trust in God holding fast in heart, that He is able and willing to help those who rest on the Lord Jesus for salvation, in all matters which are for His glory and their good, the heart remains calm and peaceful. It is only when we practically let go of faith in His power or His love, that we lose our peace and become troubled.

DAY 81

Psalm 37:5

Commit your way to the LORD, **trust** *also in Him, and He will do it.*

It is the natural tendency to commit to worry instead of committing to Christ.

Worry is our fingers curled around the edge of the balcony for fear that letting go will find us falling onto a busy highway instead of the sturdy, comfortable net we've been told awaits us. Worry is our manufactured confidence that somehow—some way—by thinking obsessively about our concerns, we still hold a measure of control.

All worry is useless, exhaustive creativity that excludes God's goodness.

God's command not to worry is a gift to us. Obedience to this demand frees us from the load of side effects that accompanies a worried spirit.

So maybe our adoption will be cancelled. So maybe the illness will return. So maybe the retirement fund will never rematerialize. Who cares? God cares. What will worry accomplish?

"Therefore do not be anxious about tomorrow, for tomorrow will be anxious for itself. Sufficient for the day is its own trouble" (Matthew 6:34 ESV).

Of worry, Christian counselor Ed Welch writes, "For me, knowing that there is grace for tomorrow has made the most noticeable difference on my own anxieties and fears. The hurdle that was always in front of me was that I couldn't imagine that grace, which is another way of saying that I limited God to the size of my own imagination."

DAY 82

Psalm 37:7

*Rest in the LORD and **wait** patiently for Him; do not fret because of him who prospers in his way, because of the man who carries out wicked schemes.*

Evil is not outside the purposes or plans of God.

Though God does not delight in wickedness, He is fully capable of making it profitable for those who encounter it.

In one of the most eloquent dialogues in Scripture, Joseph—after being abused by his brothers, sold into slavery, and eventually given the authority and opportunity to annihilate them—addressed them with these incredible words: "As for you, you meant evil against me, but God meant it for good, to bring it about that many people should be kept alive, as they are today" (Genesis 50:20 ESV).

Joseph confirmed that wickedness and pain are not outside the reaches of God's omnipotence.

But there is another, more powerful illustration of this truth.

No doubt the most evil deed ever committed in human history occurred the day the created killed their Creator. Yet God, in His unfathomable lovingkindness used even that malevolence for our good.

The vices at Calvary assured our victory for all eternity.

 No doubt the most evil deed ever committed in human history occurred the day the created killed their Creator.

DAY 83

Psalm 37:9

*For evildoers will be cut off, but those who **wait** for the LORD, they will inherit the land.*

God is in control.

If we feel like we can't accomplish something—cannot complete a task or finish the race—we are right. In and of ourselves, we can achieve no good thing. Yet being preoccupied with our human limitations is at best deconstructive, and at worst, egocentric and insulting to our Creator God.

Because, when we fixate on our shortcomings, we are still consumed with ourselves.

The subject of our preoccupation should be Christ and His inexhaustible strength.

God is in control. Evil will fail. Good will prevail. There is a resolution to our current disappointments—in either this life or the next—and God is at the center of it all.

 In and of ourselves, we can achieve no good thing.

Therefore we can pray the words of 1 Chronicles 29:11: "Yours, O Lord, is the greatness and the power and the glory and the victory and the majesty, for all that is in the heavens and in the earth is yours. Yours is the kingdom, O Lord, and you are exalted as head above all" (ESV).

DAY 84

Psalm 37:34

*Wait for the LORD and keep His way, and He will exalt
you to inherit the land; when the wicked are cut off, you
will see it.*

Trials aren't always as they appear.

Sometimes the method of grace God seeks to use in our lives is the
object we're kicking against. Take for instance the story of Jonah.
After disobeying God, he was thrown overboard by the ship's crew to
appease the storm.

> *Sometimes the painful incident in our lives is actually the
> kindest thing God could do.*

Why didn't he drown?—because God's plan involved a merciful
intervention with a fish.

It is no accident Jonah survived the experience. It was God's plan
to send him to Nineveh all along. For three days and nights Jonah
lingered inside the belly of the fish until, convicted of his disobedience,
he repented.

Trials aren't painful experiences for pain's sake—they are the gracious
working of God in our lives to mold us further to Christlikeness.

Sometimes the painful incident in our lives is actually the kindest
thing God could do.

Left to the natural consequences of our choices, perhaps we'd drown.

DAY 85

Psalm 38:15

*For I **hope** in You, O LORD; You will answer, O Lord
my God.*

Unbelief is at the root of every wrong reaction.

Failing to believe that the Bible is true or that God intends to keep
all His promises or that Christ is truly aware and committed to our
circumstances, leads us to compromise.

When we don't believe He is strong enough, we seek strength
elsewhere.

When we don't believe He is listening, we talk to everyone but Him.

When we don't believe He is capable, we take matters into our own
hands.

Like the childhood song that establishes the consequences of the house
built on the sand versus the house built on the rock, we are building
our hope on a foundation that will make a world of difference when
the rain falls. And the foundation is built via belief.

Belief that Christ hears our prayers and will intercede for us will lead
us to the psalmist's conclusion: *For I hope in You, O Lord.*

Herein is the conflict. We cannot believe what we do not believe. But
if we know we should believe something—as outlined in the Word of
God—we can ask God to expand our belief until we believe (Mark
9:23–24). And if the belief pleases Him, it will grow immeasurably.

Arriving at trust in God has all the security of weathering a storm in
concrete quarters.

DAY 86

Psalm 39:7

*And now, Lord, for what do I **wait**? My **hope** is in You.*

Hope in anything or anyone that cannot conquer death is insufficient to save.

The Lord is true and trustworthy—capable of accepting, entrusting, and exceeding the expectations of men. He will bring all genuine hope to fruition in His perfect timing.

In lieu of the best or wisest men, Christ must be the sole source of our hope.

Hope—in biblical terms—is unique to the child of God. It is a gift from God that we are able to hope in Him on the worst of days in the worst of circumstances.

So let us use this gift of hope from Him—not leaving the check uncashed in our moment of need. Christ has given us everything we need to trust Him.

The source of our hope, now and forever, is Christ.

C. H. Spurgeon says of Psalm 39:7 in *The Treasury of David:*

> Away from sand to rock let all wise builders turn themselves, for if
> not today, yet surely ere long, a storm will rise before which nothing
> will be able to stand but that which has the lasting element of faith
> in God to cement it. David had but one hope, and that hope entered
> within the veil, hence he brought his vessel to safe anchorage, and
> after a little drifting all was peace.

DAY 87

Psalm 39:12

*Hear my **prayer**, O LORD, and give ear to my cry; do not be silent at my tears; for I am a stranger with You, a sojourner like all my fathers.*

God gladly hears the cries of His children.

No verse in Scripture gives any indication that God listens to our prayers in the spirit of obligation or duty. What we do, as believers, we often call "responsibility." What Christ does for us, He always calls "love."

That He listens to our prayer and gives ear to our cry is yet another demonstration that He loves us more than anyone ever could.

The honest questions that pour from our broken hearts do not touch cold, uncaring ears.

If we are going to be overwhelmed by anything during our time of trial—and there are plenty of things that threaten to engulf us—we should be overwhelmed by this: God loves us. And in addition to that, He longs to hear from us.

Truly, that fact is inconceivable.

"And this is the confidence that we have toward him, that if we ask anything according to his will he hears us" (1 John 5:14–15 ESV).

> *That He listens to our prayer and gives ear to our cry is yet another demonstration that He loves us more than anyone ever could.*

DAY 88

Psalm 40:1

*I **waited** patiently for the LORD; and He inclined to me
and heard my cry.*

That's what it is to pray well—to make our petitions known and to
wait patiently for the Lord.

Psalm 40:1 implies endurance.

Endurance in a culture that prizes immediacy is not a comfortable
task. We can heat up meals in thirty seconds, can shoot an e-mail to
another country with a click, and can conduct an entire day's business
from our phones (while lying on the couch, no less!)

So when the Bible commands that we wait patiently for the Lord—
even when it feels like Heaven is stonewalling us—we are not in our
comfort zone to do so.

It is much easier for us to scale Mount Everest, swim the English
Channel, or build a pyramid with our hands than to endure the task
of waiting. Endurance implies the undertaking of a marathon and not
a sprint—it is a challenge of longevity.

But it's a race that is won sitting still.

At times, our solitary assignment is to wait for the Lord.

His mercy to us is great, His goodness to us is infinite, and our
fellowship with Him will be eternal. So "let us run with endurance the
race that is set before us" (Hebrews 12:1-2 ESV).

DAY 89

Psalm 40:3

*He put a new song in my mouth, a song of praise to our
God; many will see and fear and will **trust** in the LORD.*

Joy that results from trust during trials is contagious.

Who isn't encouraged when the widow testifies of God's faithfulness?
Who isn't buoyed by the confident hope of him who has endured
much?

The new song that David sings in Psalm 40:3 is not "new" in the way
our songs are new. He has not just been to church where he learned
the latest melody or downloaded the latest album. Instead, David has
found a new reason to praise God, and his song comes from a heart
that is overflowing with a rejuvenated desire to praise the Lord.

That he has found God to be completely trustworthy prompts him to
share his song so that others will see and trust in the same unfailing
source.

One way that we can magnify our God in the middle of our difficulties
is by giving verbal declarations of honor and admiration to Him who
has saved us from so much. Praise that honors God is not silent.

"The LORD is my strength and my
shield; in him my heart trusts, and
I am helped; my heart exults, and
with my song I give thanks to him"
(Psalm 28:7 ESV).

> *Praise that honors God is
> not silent.*

DAY 90

Psalm 40:4

How blessed is the man who has made the LORD his
trust*, and has not turned to the proud, nor to those who*
lapse into falsehood.

Lapsing into lies is a threat to every hurting Christian.

Unless we maintain—*guard, protect, ensure*—a biblical perspective about God and His promises to us, we will buy the lies that entice us to bail on God in our moment of crisis.

We've watched friends walk away from God in the midst of pain. Late one night we listened to a lifelong friend pour out his heart to God over an agonizing piece of news he received from home. We wept with him. We carried his burden to God as if it were our own. But within months, we learned that this friend began denying any relationship with a God who could allow such disappointment.

Our friend bought the lies.

Ironically, bailing on God in crisis is more damaging to the soul than any earthly calamity ever could be.

In *Waiting on God*, Andrew Murray wrote, "The message comes to us, 'Above everything, when you wait on God, do so in the spirit of abounding hopefulness. It is God in His glory, in His power, in His love longing to bless you that you are waiting on.'"

Waiting is the antithesis of bailing.

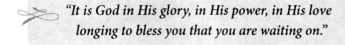
"It is God in His glory, in His power, in His love
longing to bless you that you are waiting on."

DAY 91

Psalm 41:9

*Even my close friend in whom I **trusted**, who ate my bread, has lifted up his heel against me.*

We cannot rely on anyone else for the things that God alone can give us.

Though friends are meant to be iron for us—and us for them (Proverbs 27:17)—they cannot meet all of our needs in this life.

At times, we cannot depend on our friends to be what we need them to be. At other times, we are not sufficient to meet the needs of those we love.

God will always be worthy of our trust.

That He promises to meet our needs means He will give us everything we need to endure trials and difficulties correctly. So in the moments of difficulty and discouragement, we must turn to Him—not our companions in this life—for what only He can provide.

Our friends cannot achieve the perfection of God. God will not exhibit the limitations of men. Keeping these truths straight will save us additional heartache in the valley.

Truth: Christ will never forsake those who place their trust in Him.

"He who did not spare his own Son but gave him up for us all, how will he not also with him graciously give us all things?" (Romans 8:32 ESV).

DAY 92

Psalm 42:5

Why are you in despair, O my soul? And why have you become disturbed within me? **Hope** *in God, for I shall again praise Him for the help of His presence.*

Why?

It isn't an uncommon question for those who experience difficulty. In the waiting room of life, *"Why?"* is as common as air. *Why this illness? Why this death? Why this disappointment?*

Many wise have said, "We cannot know the mind of God."

But, though we do not know His thoughts, we do have glimpses into His perspective from the Bible and the plethora of examples of what motivates Him. Jeremiah 29:11 is one such insight: "For I know the plans I have for you, declares the LORD, plans for welfare and not for evil, to give you a future and a hope" (ESV).

It is important to understand that our good and God's plans never contradict.

Ultimately, as the Scottish pastor Alexander Maclaren said, "The aim of God is the production in us of a God-pleasing character."

 It is important to understand that our good and God's plans never contradict.

DAY 93

Psalm 42:8

*The LORD will command His lovingkindness in the daytime; and His song will be with me in the night, a **prayer** to the God of my life.*

That the psalmist meditated on songs does not indicate pleasure so much as peace.

Songs aren't meant just to be expressions of happiness, enjoyed when life is good. Sometimes they are sermons of the soul, meant to communicate difficult truths in an aesthetically pleasing way.

One night when the waves of circumstance were particularly high, we lay awake, motionless, staring at the ceiling. At some point—because words failed to articulate what we were thinking or what we needed— we reached for the headphones, each took one half, and listened to this old hymn, by Karolina W. Sandell-Berg, until sleep came:

Day by day, and with each passing moment,

Strength I find to meet my trials here;

Trusting in my Father's wise bestowment,

I've no cause for worry or for fear.

He, whose heart is kind beyond all measure,

Gives unto each day what He deems best,

Lovingly its part of pain and pleasure,

Mingling toil with peace and rest.

Psalm 42:11

Why are you in despair, O my soul? And why have you become disturbed within me? **Hope** *in God, for I shall yet praise Him, the help of my countenance and my God.*

Talking to yourself is a good idea.

D. Martin Lloyd Jones, in an explanation of Psalm 42:11 said, "The main art in the matter of spiritual living is to know how to handle yourself."

He went on to explain that the believer must be able to talk himself out of unbiblical and harmful thinking—*Why are you in despair, O my soul?*—and talk himself into the assurance of hope—*Hope in God!*

That God wants us to meditate on His Word is not just something He wants us to put on a to-do list to check off every day. Bible reading, as a rule, is less about fulfilling a duty and more about nourishing our hope. Reading the Bible is our recognition that we need the comfort and counsel of Scripture to inform our thinking when we are disquieted.

Scripturally-informed thinking produces Scripturally-conformed behavior.

On the afternoons when we struggle the most to believe the right things about God and His plans for us—when our soul is disturbed with doubts consistent with our human weakness—it is then we most need to read the Word.

We cannot manufacture the true hope that we need. This hope comes from Him.

As Dr. Sam Horn said, "It's the Word that waters the soul."

Psalm 43:5

Why are you in despair, O my soul? And why are you disturbed within me? **Hope in God,** *for I shall again praise Him, The help of my countenance and my God.*

Our feelings are indicative of what we believe.

Sometimes we irrationally conclude that God alone is responsible for how we feel about what we experience. If we are disturbed—to use the language of the psalmist—then we believe it is God's responsibility to fix things so that we can be happy and hopeful again.

It is surely easier to justify how we feel if how we feel is not our fault.

Psalm 43:5 indicates we have the opportunity to talk truth to ourselves when we are in despair. This would mean, at least in part, we are accountable for our outlook on our circumstances.

What separates useful talk from useless chatter is constructive truth.

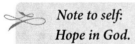

Note to self:
Hope in God.

Paul Tripp asked the following:

> How wholesome, faith-driven, and Christ-centered is the conversation that you have with you every day? Do you remind yourself of your need? Do you point you, once again, to the beauty and practicality of His grace? Do you tell yourself to run toward God in those moments when you feel like running from Him?

Note to self: Hope in God.

DAY 96

Psalm 44:6

*For I will not **trust** in my bow, nor will my sword save me.*

The strongest man doesn't stand a chance in a wrestling match with God.

Our intelligence, strength, creativity, and wisdom are not to be compared with the Creator. We must abandon any thought that we are strong enough to solve our problems on our own or with the creative mechanisms of man.

On one particular Sunday afternoon when we were praying to God to do specific things for our adoption, it occurred to us slowly and powerfully—if God always did what we wanted Him to do simply because we wanted Him to do it—wouldn't that make us God and Him servant to us?

He doesn't operate that way, and we cannot expect Him to.

He is God. We serve Him. We must keep this truth straight in times of waiting.

If there is one thing we should want more than what we ask, it should be what God wants. No instrument can save us—only Him (James 4:15).

"The king is not saved by his great army; a warrior is not delivered by his great strength" (Psalm 33:16 ESV).

Our loyalty to God is demonstrated by our trust in Him and nothing else.

If there is one thing we should want more than what we ask, it should be what God wants.

DAY 97

Psalm 52:8

*But as for me, I am like a green olive tree in the house of
God; I **trust** in the lovingkindness of God forever and ever.*

The children of God will flourish during difficulty to the degree that
they depend on God.

Often the Bible uses the image of a tree to represent security. Psalm
1:3 is perhaps the greatest illustration of this: "He is like a tree planted
by streams of water that yields its fruit in its season, and its leaf does
not wither. In all that he does, he prospers" (ESV).

Through his illustration of the olive tree in Psalm 52, David affirms
that the person who trusts in the lovingkindness of God will be
secure.

Though not stated outright, this verse insinuates endurance.

A tree has roots that go deep into the ground. Trees weather the
brutality of storms and the abuse of extreme seasons and harsh
temperatures. But because of its anchorage several feet below the
surface, the tree is not in danger of being uprooted when the rain,
snow, and heat arise.

And, in fact, given time, the tree will produce fruit.

Like the olive tree, the believer who endures may find longevity,
security, and fruitfulness in the season so appointed by God. As the
last verse of *How Firm a Foundation* reads:

The soul that on Jesus hath leaned for repose,

I will not, I cannot, desert to his foes:

That soul, though all hell should endeavor to shake,

I'll never—no, never, no, never forsake!

DAY 98

Psalm 52:9

*I will give You thanks forever, because You have done it, and I will **wait** on Your name, for it is good, in the presence of Your godly ones.*

God commands us to be thankful in every situation (1 Thessalonians 5:18).

It is important to understand that *happy* and *thankful* are not the same. *Happy* feels what *thankful* knows. We are not instructed to be happy for happiness' sake. We don't need to cheer over the loss of a loved one, the loss of a job, or the dissolution of a relationship—but we are commanded to rejoice that God is in control.

We know that the final chapter has not been read in thorny situations. If, this side of heaven, something is not solved, we know it will be resolved on the other side. We may not receive what we want right now—but in time, we will want something radically different.

We will want to be with God for eternity.

While we wait, we must live with certainty that this life and these cares are not God's final word.

This is more than psychology's power of positive thinking—this is God's peace within believers. Peace is the outworking of deep-seated belief.

It is our privilege to prove, by our gratitude, that God is good.

DAY 99

Psalm 54:2

*Hear my **prayer**, O God; give ear to the words of my mouth.*

Confidence is critical in the practice of prayer.

Our prayers must be earnest and fervent before God when we have something we need Him to hear.

That David was confident in his prayer demonstrates that he knew on whom his welfare depended. He had no other options when it came to his protection or provision. On one hand, God was David's refuge by process of elimination—no one else could do for David what God promised to do.

But though God was David's only hope, He was also David's greatest hope.

So it is for us—though our need isn't always as obvious.

Our life may not hang in the balance, but our soul certainly does.

Absolute dependence on God, which results in confident prayer, is a gift to those who wait on God.

Suffering affords us seasons of growth in godliness through the recognition of our necessary dependence on God.

Let us confidently address our needs to Him who encourages us to pray.

> *Absolute dependence on God, which results in*
> *confident prayer, is a gift to those who wait on God.*

DAY 100

Psalm 55:1

*Give ear to my **prayer**, O God; and do not hide Yourself
from my supplication.*

Jesus Christ understands betrayal.

Jesus was betrayed by Judas in the Garden of Gethsemane for thirty
pieces of silver (Matthew 26:14–16).

Nothing could be more repulsive than the decision Judas made.

In Psalm 55, David pours out his heart to God after the betrayal of
someone he cared about. Students of the Bible believe the betrayer
may have been Absalom, David's own son.

Betrayal hurts.

Everyone has felt betrayal's sting at some point. During times of crisis,
betrayal from those in our inner circle is heightened.

Friends might sell us out for the opportunity to have the best goods
at the rumor mill. Loved ones might speak rashly about things they
should know would hurt us.

They are sinners as we are sinners.

Regardless of the extent of the betrayal, we must rest in the knowledge
that—though people hurt us, God permits it.

This pain is always and somehow for our good.

DAY 101

Psalm 56:3

*When I am afraid, I will put my **trust** in You.*

Fear and faith do not coexist.

They can alternate, but they cannot be present simultaneously. This is the reason we are called to abandon worry and distress: when we are anxious, we do not believe that God is in control.

Worry is blind to the goodness of God. It does not reflect back on God's promises or previous examples of His goodness. It doesn't dwell on prayers answered or needs met. It overlooks years of blessings to fixate, instead, on current dilemmas. And most often, it leaves God entirely out of the picture.

The solution to uncertainty is always the same: trust God's goodness; obey God's Word.

As children, we learned that *obedience is the very best way, to show that you believe.*

As adults, we are expected to live as if we believe what we've learned.

Hebrews 11:8 says, "By faith Abraham obeyed when he was called to go out to a place that he was to receive as an inheritance. And he went out, not knowing where he was going" (ESV).

Worry is blind to God. Trust is blind to worry.

> *... obedience is the very best way,*
> *to show that you believe.*

DAY 102

Psalm 56:4

*In God, whose word I praise, in God I have put my **trust**; I shall not be afraid. What can mere man do to me?*

Trust in God is a decision made with the mind and not the emotion.

The fear of man, mentioned in Psalm 56, quickly becomes an emotional entanglement. The *what ifs* and the *why dids* and the *how dares* go to battle with the logic that says, "You won't figure people out and it doesn't really matter."

The only thing we can rest securely on when it comes to the intentions of men is what the Bible says. Jeremiah 17:9 assures us: "The heart is deceitful above all things, and desperately sick; who can understand it?" (ESV).

The reality of Psalm 56:4 is simple: Men will disappoint because they are sinful. God will satisfy because He is good.

That God is true and trustworthy means we can logically trust in Him at all times—whether or not we feel like trusting anyone. The logic with which we choose to trust God must be different from that logic we use to trust men. We trust men when they prove themselves.

God has proven Himself a thousand times over.

That God is true and trustworthy means we can logically trust in Him at all times—whether or not we feel like trusting anyone.

DAY 103

Psalm 56:11

*In God I have put my **trust**, I shall not be afraid. What can man do to me?*

No man has the ability to do anything to us outside of God's sovereign design.

God is not intimidated by anything. So if God is not afraid of man and we put our trust in God, we have no reason to be troubled by anyone.

Psalm 46:1 is an encouragement to many who face fears : "God is our refuge and strength, a very present help in trouble" (ESV).

Of this verse, C.H. Spurgeon wrote:

> He is more than "present," He is very present. More present than the nearest friend can be, for He is in us in our trouble; more present than we are to ourselves, for sometimes we lack presence of mind. He is always present, effectually present, sympathetically present, altogether present. He is present now if this is a gloomy season. Let us rest ourselves upon Him.

To believe that others have control over us is to believe that God doesn't have control over them, which is to make a critical error in terms of God's omnipotence.

Trust in God eradicates fear of man.

DAY 104

Psalm 61:1

*Hear my cry, O God; give heed to my **prayer**.*

Encouragement often comes in unusual ways.

After receiving difficult news one afternoon, we picked up the phone to make a completely unrelated call across town. After being put on hold by the store manager, words flooded our ears from none other than the "hold music"—and the song was about finding peace from God in the midst of life's storms.

Call it a *happy accident* or *the way the cookie crumbles*, it makes no difference to us. We were encouraged by the reminder that God is our strength. And we were comforted that the reminder came from an unsuspecting place when we most needed it.

But here is the truth about encouragement.

Without being paired with endurance, encouragement is little more than a short burst of adrenaline that fades, like a Fourth of July firework, only moments after it occurs. Encouragement and endurance are a double prescription during times of difficulty.

One without the other makes the trial very difficult.

Need encouragement? Here it is: God hears our prayers. And sometimes He delights to answer them in ways we least expect.

DAY 105

Psalm 62:1

*My soul **waits** in silence for God only; from Him is my salvation.*

That we trust God with the future of our soul should enable us to trust Him with the events of today.

Think of it. If we can go to bed at night and not fear the eternal condemnation of hell or the holy wrath of God, why would we worry that our Heavenly Father cannot handle the details of our day? Either we have no idea from what we've been saved, or we are mistaken about our Savior.

Salvation in the Scriptures is used to describe more than just our eternal destiny.

God's salvation includes all of life—today, tomorrow, forever. We are already in His hands (John 10:27-30).

On one particular morning when we anticipated news, but were not sure if the news would be good, bad, or non-existent, we were encouraged by the well-timed admonition of a friend to "Hold on to the awesome truth that God already knows the outcome of today!"

And so we did. And we still do.

God's salvation includes all of life—today, tomorrow, forever.

DAY 106

Psalm 62:5

*My soul, **wait** in silence for God only, for my **hope** is from Him.*

Waiting signifies silence.

In waiting for God to give us the answers we need for the dilemmas we face, we must search the Bible and wait in silence for Him to show us—in His recorded Word—what He wants us to do.

It is essential for us to understand that true hope comes only from God. Though good books, kind people, and encouraging music can be tools of the Father to fashion hope in our lives, it is impossible for us to find true hope by avoiding God or His Word.

Whether God's words are written, spoken, or sung, ultimately His recorded truth produces hope in our lives.

Silencing our troubled thoughts to read God's Word is a stabilizer for us in difficult seasons.

Stand in strength.
Wait in silence.
Hope in God.

Of Psalm 62:5, C. H. Spurgeon once said in a sermon, "It is a hard matter to be calm in the day of trouble; but it is a high exercise of divine grace when we can stand unmoved in the day of adversity."

Stand in strength.

Wait in silence.

Hope in God.

DAY 107

Psalm 62:8

Trust in Him at all times, O people; pour out your heart before Him; God is a refuge for us. Selah.

God, alone, should be our refuge.

Choosing to take safety in anyone other than God is a critical and costly mistake, because finding refuge in anyone else means we are finding refuge outside of God.

And finding refuge outside of God is unbiblical and unwise.

What does taking safety in oneself look like? *I can do this. I need to toughen up. I must find the strength inside myself to make this happen. I just need to pick myself up by the bootstraps and do this.*

This kind of thinking is more than afternoon-talk-show rhetoric or positive self-speak. This kind of talk is dangerous because it makes no mention of God.

To reach inside ourselves and find the strength to endure hardship is to leave God out of the equation. It is to enter battle without our shield, to face our enemy with our hands tied behind our back, and to join the debate with our strongest advocate locked in a closet.

We are not our own best refuge.

> *God, alone, should be our refuge.*

Psalm 62:10

*Do not **trust** in oppression and do not vainly **hope** in robbery; if riches increase, do not set your heart upon them.*

Emotions are fickle masters.

While they are certainly real in their impact on us, emotions lack the fortitude needed to aid us in making good decisions.

Like the pilot who experiences spatial disorientation in the midst of a difficult flight, so we experience confusion when we encounter the blizzards of trial and circumstance.

The psalmist's admonition to avoid trusting in worldly things is wise.

We will never regret replacing skewed emotional realities with solid biblical truth. We will be safest in our flight when we rely upon the compass of God's Word when the storms are raging.

God's truth is always dependable.

When we are on the mountain top—confident of God's grace displayed in our lives—God's truth is trustworthy. When we are in the valley—unsure of God's favor—God's truth is equally trustworthy.

Keep your eye on the instrument of God's Word and the spatial disorientation will quiet.

God's mercies are new every morning regardless of how we feel.

DAY 109

Psalm 65:2

*O You who hear **prayer**, to You all men come.*

We have no greater privilege than to talk to and be heard by God.

Social workers and government officials are difficult people to reach. If you learn anything in the process of adopting overseas, you will learn that much quickly. These workers have many responsibilities in their charge, not to mention the number of people who are clamoring (as we were!) for their attention.

It struck us one day, as we were trying in vain to reach one such individual across town, how amazing it is that we can reach God's ears in a split second. (Even with all the people clamoring for His attention!)

Psalm 65:2 refers, in part, to the future millennial kingdom when all who have been saved will unite to worship and praise the Lord. What an incredible thought—that all of us who have waited through the centuries will one day converge to praise God together!

And more amazing still, we will continue to be heard by God. Those of us who know Him will never be outside the reaches of His hearing.

> *We have no greater privilege than to talk to and be heard by God.*

Psalm 65:5

*By awesome deeds You answer us in righteousness, O God
of our salvation, You who are the **trust** of all the ends of
the earth and of the farthest sea.*

What God promises to do for us is awesome.

But what God *has done* for us is awesome.

What Christ did for us at Calvary is our secret to being content in the
difficult seasons of life. If we cannot appreciate what God has done for
us in salvation, we know nothing of the gospel or God's saving grace.
Christ's death provides us with the greatest reason to hope.

At times during our trial, we were encouraged by well-meaning people
to "consider the worse situations of others." Indeed, we thought about
people with all kinds of difficult illnesses, heard stories of those whose
adoptions failed in the final hours, read about horrible accidents, and
were reminded that bad things happen to people every day.

And they do.

But while various stories moved us to pray or cry, they didn't ultimately
give us peace or grant us permanent satisfaction. Comparing
ourselves, or our situation, with others isn't the final answer.

What our sin put Christ through on the cross makes our worst
situations pale by comparison. And comparing our current situation
to what we deserve is cause for contentment.

And still, in spite of what He's already done, God has a plan for us that
defies our imagination (1 Corinthians 2:9).

DAY 111

Psalm 66:19

*But certainly God has heard; He has given heed to the voice of my **prayer**.*

God delights to give us joy that is greater than the depths of our suffering.

We have all met people who are experiencing enormous struggles yet seem to possess an unusual, inexhaustible amount of joy in the process. It would seem we hurt for them and their situations more than they do. And, perhaps, we do.

This is what it means to experience God's grace.

Grace is the goodness of God that keeps us afloat in times of suffering. It is the source for the unexplainable strength that God gives—always in the right proportion to our needs—that allows us to know that the trial will amount in the end to something good and God-glorifying.

"But he said to me, 'My grace is sufficient for you, for my power is made perfect in weakness.' Therefore I will boast all the more gladly of my weaknesses, so that the power of Christ may rest upon me. For the sake of Christ, then, I am content with weaknesses, insults, hardships, persecutions, and calamities. For when I am weak, then I am strong" (2 Corinthians 12:9–10 ESV).

Grace that amounts to joy is possible in times of trial because of the expected outcome—God's power made perfect in our weakness.

Psalm 66:20

*Blessed be God, Who has not turned away my **prayer** nor His lovingkindness from me.*

"He gives to His beloved sleep" (Psalm 127:2 ESV).

We can rest in God because we are secure in Him.

The wording of Psalm 23:2 is interesting: "He makes me lie down in green pastures" (ESV). Our Father knows we need rest. He knows if we have our choice, we will choose worry, work, or worse over the quiet solitude of respite. So in the moments of our need, He gives us everything necessary to rest in Him.

One of His great lovingkindnesses to us is His provision of our rest in the middle of storms or valleys or shadows of death.

Those who do not know the Savior wonder if the storm is the end of the story or if provision in the valley is even a possibility. But those who know Christ understand that His power enables Him to silence the storm with words from His mouth (Mark 4:39). They are strengthened to say with David in Psalm 3:5, "I lay down and slept; I woke again, for the LORD sustained me" (ESV).

If we are not resting, it is not because God has not given us everything we need to do so.

So let us rest.

 If we are not resting, it is not because God has not given us everything we need to do so.

DAY 113

Psalm 69:3

*I am weary with my crying; my throat is parched; my eyes fail while I **wait** for my God.*

The Bible is clear: suffering is not likely; it is certain.

St. Augustine correctly said, "God had one Son on earth without sin, but never one without suffering."

To what degree we are called to endure hardship, we will not know until life is finished. But we do know that there will be days when we experience difficulty, days when we are weary with our crying while we wait for our God.

Herein is a valuable lesson that we would do well to learn: The most joyful people are not those who are free from pain or suffering. The happiest people are free from worrying that difficulty will happen and are instead content to rest in the goodness of God.

The most joyful people believe the Bible.

And what does the Bible make clear?—that God will never allow difficulty into our lives without simultaneously strengthening us with the grace to endure (2 Corinthians 12:9).

Part of believing the Bible means accepting the reality that difficulty will come and recognizing that we can rest in God while waiting.

"Come to me, all who labor and are heavy laden, and I will give you rest" (Matthew 11:28 ESV).

DAY 114

Psalm 69:6

*May those who **wait** for You not be ashamed through me,*
O Lord GOD of hosts; may those who seek You not be
dishonored through me, O God of Israel.

How we respond in times of testing doesn't just affect us.

The psalmist understood that his response to situations could cause other believers to stumble. Keeping in mind that other people aren't always privy to the details of our testing—or to the grace that God gives us while we are experiencing the nuances of our situation—it is paramount that we sift our speech through the filter of godliness.

How we feel is not the most important part of the equation.

That God be glorified—and not dishonored—is of supreme importance.

When James 1:2 tells us to "Count it all joy, my brothers, when you meet trials of various kinds" (ESV), he isn't telling us to force some type of irrational glee onto our face or into our lives. The instruction to count it joy isn't centered upon the difficulty—but upon the knowledge that God is working in us through the situation.

We should count it joy that our Father is creating in us more of His likeness.

During our time of testing, we were surrounded by a tight-knit group of friends and family who prayed with us over the details of our struggles, encouraged us in the moments of our weakness, and shared with us in the blessings of our God.

And, Lord willing, those who watched us wait were not ashamed.

DAY 115

Psalm 69:13

*But as for me, my **prayer** is to You, O LORD, at an acceptable time; O God, in the greatness of Your lovingkindness, answer me with Your saving truth.*

God is an unstoppable force for good in our lives.

He is right 100 percent of the time, even when evil appears to triumph and goodness never seems to have its day. That is why we can pray to the Lord with confidence.

Because we believe God's guarantee that He only does good things, we don't need to gauge the outcome or impact of a situation based on what we feel or how it appears.

We can be confident that God has our very best in mind.

Additionally, we can rest confidently that our current testing is not the result of our Christian performance. For if that were the case, it would mean we are ultimately in control.

Here is what we know to be true: God is committed to the task of making sure everything turns out exactly as it should. He is as devoted to our present salvation as He is our future salvation.

We can say with Paul in Philippians 1:6, "And I am sure of this, that he who began a good work in you will bring it to completion at the day of Jesus Christ" (ESV).

This is saving truth.

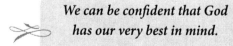

We can be confident that God has our very best in mind.

DAY 116

Psalm 71:5

*For You are my **hope**; O Lord GOD, You are my confidence from my youth.*

God longs to replace our ineffective coping mechanisms with hope in Him.

Temporary distractions from waiting on God can be attractive and effective for awhile, but in the end, they do little to lessen the pain.

Some people become workaholics while others abuse medications or relationships to escape the current assignment of waiting. Entertainment is particularly attractive to someone who wants to think about anything other than the task at hand.

An excessive hunt for knowledge in a crisis, or denial that the crisis exists at all, are both coping strategies.

No matter the means of escape, the truth is the same. Only hope in God sustains us in crisis.

God has given us prayer and His Word to help us manage the ups and downs of waiting. Replacing these instruments of grace with anything else will be futile and frustrating. We should say with the preacher, Edward Mote:

My hope is built on nothing less
Than Jesus' blood and righteousness;
I dare not trust the sweetest frame,
But wholly lean on Jesus' name.

DAY 117

Psalm 71:14

*But as for me, I will **hope** continually, and will praise You yet more and more.*

One Sunday afternoon we pulled Spurgeon's tiny paperback *The Practice of Praise* off the shelf. We had picked it up at a summer rummage sale and put it aside, unread. When we opened the book, a sentence highlighted by the book's previous owner beamed off the page at us: "See well to your faith and your hope, for otherwise God will be robbed of His praise." The reference attached to the thought was Psalm 71:14.

And we were reminded in a poignant way that there is a good and holy way to experience pain.

For the psalmist, suffering and praise happened simultaneously. He did not wait for God to fix everything before offering God the honor He deserved. To put it in a modern context, the psalmist offered the praise before the prayer request was answered. He did not sit back to see if God would answer before arriving at the conclusion that God was good. The psalmist knew with certainty that God was worthy of praise.

God *is* good. Let us hope in Him continually.

"Therefore let those who suffer according to God's will entrust their souls to a faithful Creator while doing good" (1 Peter 4:19 ESV).

 ... the psalmist offered the praise before the prayer request was answered.

DAY 118

Psalm 84:8

*O LORD God of hosts, hear my **prayer**; give ear, O God of Jacob! Selah.*

Trusting in our prayers isn't praying correctly.

The only prayer that pleases God is the prayer that displays trust in Him.

During our wait, we would often pray together as a couple. And during these times, questions would abound. *Were we praying correctly? Did we need to ask more people to pray with us? What if we were inadvertently leaving something important out of the formula? Were we not receiving the desire of our hearts because of something we were or weren't saying when we talked to God?*

We tried all of the approaches, including boldness, brokenness, silence, transparency, and regularity. We were careful to pay attention to the model for prayer in Luke 11.

And still we watched the weeks pass without any sign of the answer we sought.

In the meantime, we were reminded that while the Bible does demand various dispositions in the presence of God, it never invites us to trust in the prayer itself.

The instructions to us were simple: Trust God. Pray to Him. Wait.

> *The only prayer that pleases God is the prayer that displays trust in Him.*

DAY 119

Psalm 84:12

*O LORD of hosts, how blessed is the man who **trusts**
in You!*

Trials are meant to bless.

We are at our peak condition in this life when we trust God, when our hearts are more pliable to His leadership, and when our gaze is fixed entirely on Him.

During periods of testing, these activities are often what we crave: prayer, Bible reading, and music. They are the necessary food groups in the diet of the suffering. At few other times in our lives can we say with confidence that we crave the presence of the Lord above anything else.

One way that trials are meant to bless is that they prompt us to reflect on truths we often neglect, such as the reality of evil and the hope of heaven. The darkness of our present circumstances makes heaven a little brighter and that realization is a gift.

Broken hearts should more readily accept that God alone is good and gracious. Trial is to the heart what cultivation is to the soil (James 1:3). Trials enliven us to grow in grace. Believing this allows us to say with the psalmist, "I am blessed when I trust God!"

Hugh MacMillan, a Scottish minister who lived in the nineteenth century, wrote, "Amidst my list of blessings infinite stands this the foremost, that my heart has bled; for *all* I bless thee, most for the *severe*."

Psalm 86:2

*Preserve my soul, for I am a godly man; O You my God, save Your servant who **trusts** in You.*

The real enemy in crisis is bitterness.

One way we preserve our souls during difficult periods of waiting is by disallowing bitterness into our lives. Additionally, we must recognize that rejecting bitterness during seasons of distress must be done every day, and sometimes every hour!

When new pains crop up, so do new opportunities to grow angry. And really, bitterness is only fermented anger or nourished self-pity.

The hurts may go deep. But bitterness always runs the risk of going much deeper.

At each turn of our adoption—each hint that yet something else was not going to go as we had planned—we were given the unmistakable opportunity to grow bitter by our problems. There were very definitely things done to us, or not done for us, by people who held great sway in our process.

And, as far as we know, we were never to blame for the carelessness or inconsideration.

But almost like a whisper in our ear, we heard the question after each obstacle, "Are you going to get bitter this time?" To which we always took care to respond, "Lord, preserve our souls! We are trusting You!"

DAY 121

Psalm 86:6

*Give ear, O LORD, to my **prayer**; and give heed to the voice of my supplications!*

There is something very right about begging.

One practical reason why prayer is a delight to God is that when we pray we are acknowledging that our dependence is on Him.

In our culture, the concept of nagging, begging, urging, or petitioning is impolite. Good manners suggest we ask for something once and then let the request drop. This pattern of thinking is so ingrained in us that we would hardly ask for a glass of water in someone's home without following the request with an apology or concession.

God wants us to address Him very differently.

God wants us to plead with Him for the things we need. "Supplication" in Psalm 86:6 carries with it the image of a beggar, not the illustration of a guest in the home of a new acquaintance.

 ... when we pray we are acknowledging that our dependence is on Him.

That God calls the prayers of the saints "golden bowls of incense" (Revelation 5:8) indicates that He doesn't regard our prayers in the way Miss Manners regards uncivilized behavior.

Throughout the Scriptures, the message is clear: Ask! Ask again! Ask again after that!

We must never stop pleading with God.

DAY 122

Psalm 88:2

*Let my **prayer** come before You; incline Your ear to my cry!*

Prayer sets in motion the providence of God.

Though we do not understand the intricacies of prayer—why the Lord listens to us at all being one of the great mysteries—we know He does. And we know He wants us to pray.

When we pray, we acknowledge our insufficiency and His sufficiency.

The right kind of prayer, therefore, is humility in action. By praying, we recognize that there is nothing we can do and everything for Him to do if He is pleased to do it.

Our days of difficulty must concurrently be our days of prayer.

In a very real way, we came to understand our total powerlessness through our adoption. Figuratively speaking, a high, impenetrable wall existed around the officials who were responsible for making our adoption successful. Any time we wanted to talk to someone, we had to go through mediators and translators. And there were scores of rules that kept us from picking up the phone, shooting off an e-mail, or boarding a plane to talk to people. We virtually had to be invited to communicate with the decision-makers. So for months at a time, we could do little.

But for months at a time, there was also much we could do because of prayer.

Praying prompts God's providence. It's the way He designed it. Thankfully, with Charles Wesley we can learn to say, "Jesus, my strength, my hope, on Thee I cast my care; with humble confidence look up, and know thou hear'st prayer."

DAY 123

Psalm 88:13

*But I, O LORD, have cried out to You for help, and in the morning my **prayer** comes before You.*

No one stumbles into a habit of prayer.

Praying consistently and correctly, specifically during times of waiting, is hard work.

It is a danger to believe that we can ever achieve a level of spirituality that will make the Christian disciplines effortless or innate. Though our hearts, motivated by the ebb and flow of life, are sometimes bent to pray or praise, they are not permanently fixed to those actions.

Most often, we are one situation, conflict, or disappointment away from running in the wrong direction if our habits of prayer, Bible reading, and trust in the Lord are not secure.

As the Apostle Paul learned to be content in whatever situation he found himself (Philippians 4:11), so we must learn to pray no matter the circumstance. Contentment is largely achieved by prayer.

The disciples were wise enough to ask Christ to teach them to pray (Luke 11). We must also be wise enough to learn from Christ's response. Through the schooling of God's Word, we must discover how to pray passionately and persistently.

God graciously allows difficulties into our lives to teach us that we must rely on Him.

No one stumbles into a habit of prayer.

Psalm 91:2

*I will say to the LORD, "My refuge and my fortress, my God, in whom I **trust**!"*

We will take refuge in something. We will go somewhere for help.

As human beings, we are made to share our sufferings. But it is imperative that we understand something: God is the only one who is capable of being our perfect place of safety. Too often we look to people around us to be for us what God alone can be. And then we are disappointed when people don't match up to God's goodness.

One of our favorite verses is one we often find ourselves sharing with those who experience hardship: "The Lord is good, a stronghold in the day of trouble; he knows those who take refuge in him" (Nahum 1:7 ESV).

There is nothing better than to be known and loved by God.

We must resist the temptation to doubt that God is enough. We must flee from the suggestion that anyone or anything else can be our refuge. We must trust in Him.

More than anything in this world, we need Christ.

> *There is nothing better than to be known and loved by God.*

DAY 125

Psalm 102:1

*Hear my **prayer**, O LORD! And let my cry for help come to You.*

God takes note of our tears.

One of the great reasons our God is good is because He exists to be more than an instrument of change in our lives. While He is fully capable of taking the scalpel and carving out the disease in our character, He is also compelled to care about our cries.

This is incomprehensible love.

Christ gave us insight into this component of His character in John 11 when He responded to the sisters who notified him of the death of their brother, Lazarus. Knowing the outcome of the situation—that He would raise Lazarus from the dead and cause incredible rejoicing for this man's friends and family—Christ still had compassion on the grieving sisters. He didn't encourage them to "stop crying" or "wait and see."

Instead, in one of the most famous verses in the Bible, "Jesus wept" (John 11:35 ESV). He cried with them because He understood and empathized with their suffering.

That Jesus shed tears with these sisters indicates that He is not removed from our grief. Our tears do not escape the Almighty, even though He holds in His hands all the answers to our suffering.

This is mighty affection.

Psalm 102:17

*He has regarded the **prayer** of the destitute and has not despised their **prayer**.*

God hears us in our helplessness.

We waited nearly eighteen months before we received word that news was right around the corner. We were actually given a date and told to check our e-mail.

The night before we knew the e-mail would be in our inbox, we finally allowed ourselves to start planning the things we wanted to do when our son got home.

There would be places to visit and people to introduce him to and lots and lots of bonding.

And then the e-mail arrived.

After eighteen months of waiting, the only thing we learned in that "all-important e-mail" was that we would likely need to wait for several more months. Nothing had been done on behalf of our case for almost a year.

In a twenty-four-hour period, we went from songs to sadness—both of which are mentioned in James 5:13. And as thousands of believers have done for thousands of years, we turned to Psalm 46 to settle our spirits.

"The LORD of hosts is with us; the God of Jacob is our fortress" (Psalm 46:7 ESV).

And all we could do was pray.

DAY 127

Psalm 104:27

*They all **wait** for You to give them their food in due season.*

We are dependent on God for everything we have (Matthew 6:25–34).

By the command of our good God, His creation is fed (Psalm 104:28), dies (Psalm 104:29), and lives (Psalm 104:30). Nothing escapes God's good provision (Matthew 6:26).

If we ever think we are the exception to God's promises, we fool ourselves.

When there is nothing left for us to do except wait for God and pray to Him, we are in the best possible position in life. For though all of God's children are exhorted to live in this way, our obedience—our dependence on God—is the most natural path if we submit to what God has chosen for us.

And while we could turn our car around on the road of life and insist on driving against the flow of traffic on the one-way street, it would be harder and less advantageous for us to do so.

God made our dependence on Him more apparent by obliterating other options, and that is a gracious act of our good God. Because, in reality, we are always dependent on Him, only in this season of waiting and praying we know it more readily.

With these truths in mind, we must cast ourselves and all of our cares on the loving mercy of our Heavenly Father, waiting patiently with God's creation for our sustenance in due season.

Andrew Murray wrote of waiting, "It is in the course of our feeble and very imperfect waiting that God Himself, by His hidden power, strengthens us and works out in us the patience of the saints, the patience of Christ Himself."

DAY 128

Psalm 106:13

*They quickly forgot His works; they did not **wait** for His counsel.*

Despair ensues when incorrect conclusions are drawn about God.

Many have endured times of testing without experiencing despair, while others have encountered despair at the first sign of trouble. The difference between the two is not the severity of the situation, but rather the conclusion about the Lord.

The quickest route to despair is to disregard the things God has already done. Psalm 106 tells of the Israelites wandering in the wilderness, so consumed by what they wanted to eat and drink that they actively forgot what God had already provided for them. As a direct result of their decision not to trust God, God gave them what they wanted, and it ended up making them sick.

The Israelites, through their decision not to wait for God, must teach us two truths about Him: First, we must want God more than we want anything else. Second, we must recognize that we couldn't make our situation any better if we were given the opportunity to change God's will for our lives.

Our perspective is limited. God's point of view is perfect. This should incline us to say with Paul in 2 Corinthians 4:8: "We are afflicted in every way, but not crushed; perplexed, but not driven to despair" (ESV).

First, we must want God more than we want anything else.

DAY 129

Psalm 109:4

In return for my love they act as my accusers; but I am
*in **prayer**.*

God's truth is no less true when we experience doubts.

The promises in the Bible remain viable and available to us even when we are in the depths of disappointment.

Which is why our hearts are anchored—steadfast—when we trust in Him.

Which is why our hearts are *only* anchored—steadfast—when we trust in Him!

When we hit the nineteen-month mark of our adoption and were still facing roadblocks and speed bumps, frustrations, and disappointments, there were people who encouraged us to consider quitting. "God could have made the adoption happen by now," one person said to us.

And true, He could have.

But He didn't—and that didn't make His promises any less true.

We didn't disparage these accusers. It was likely their concern for us that compelled them to counsel in this way. But we didn't doubt God's sovereign control of the situation either.

And we didn't doubt that it wasn't meant to happen at all, because it didn't happen quickly.

God doesn't move. We move. God doesn't become less trusting. We trust less.

DAY 130

Psalm 112:7

*He will not fear evil tidings; his heart is steadfast, **trusting** in the LORD.*

There really are only two ways to respond to testing: correctly and incorrectly.

The correct response is a biblical one that recognizes God's sovereign goodness in our lives. The incorrect response is a fleshly one that wants only to have the trial finished and the difficulty placed securely in the past.

But removing our suffering isn't the only way God shows us He is good. If we view God's goodness to be His unscrambling our difficulty and "straightening things out," we don't understand God's goodness.

Our desire should not just be for the removal of the pain. It should be for Christ's purposes to be accomplished in our lives.

After many months of waiting and praying and pouring out our hearts before God for Him to bring our adoption to a resolution, we found ourselves heavy with sorrow. The rest of our life wasn't stopping while we waited; and so, in the process of trying to complete a difficult process, we also buried two loved ones who died of difficult diseases. We weathered the storm of the plummeting economy. We watched family and friends encounter dark days and long nights.

And our prayer, over time, became this: "Lord, if Your goodness and mercy will be demonstrated in our lives most remarkably through our weakness, then help us want what you want for us more than what we currently desire."

Our goal was to remain steadfast, trusting in the Lord.

DAY 131

Psalm 115:9

*O Israel, **trust** in the LORD; He is their help and their shield.*

Israel had every reason to trust in the Lord.

As the chosen people of God, Israel had a long history of God's providential provision. Yet, as the Bible records, the nation still struggled with unbelief at various times in her tumultuous history.

One of the most insightful passages about God's love for His people is recorded in Nehemiah 9. The chapter lists several of the Israelites' offenses against God, including the infamous worship of the golden calf, and then says:

> You in your great mercies did not forsake them in the wilderness. The pillar of cloud to lead them in the way did not depart from them by day, nor the pillar of fire by night to light for them the way by which they should go. You gave your good Spirit to instruct them and did not withhold your manna from their mouth and gave them water for their thirst. Forty years you sustained them in the wilderness, and they lacked nothing. Their clothes did not wear out and their feet did not swell." (Nehemiah 9:19–21 ESV)

Even during the Israelites' suffering in the wilderness—for evil choices that they made—God took care to provide them with what they needed. If ever we wanted proof that God is a good God who acts, in love, like a Father to His children, we need only turn to Scripture and the surplus of examples in which He cared for those He loved, even in their struggles.

"Nevertheless, in your great mercies you did not make an end of them or forsake them, for you are a gracious and merciful God" (Nehemiah 9:31 ESV).

We have every reason to trust the Lord—even in our wilderness moments.

Psalm 115:11

*You who **fear** the LORD, **trust** in the LORD; He is their help and their shield.*

We trust God because He is good.

History bears witness to dozens of leaders who have achieved loyalty or obtained a following because they were angry, dictatorial, or superficial. These leaders amassed their followings because people were afraid, coerced, or naive.

Our God's leadership is not like the flawed leadership of men.

"The Rock, his work is perfect, for all his ways are justice. A God of faithfulness and without iniquity, just and upright is he" (Deuteronomy 32:4 ESV).

We trust God because He is faithful to fulfill the promises He has made (Psalm 117:1-2).

There is nothing in God's holy character that prevents Him from giving us what we request. He is not belligerent, harsh, malevolent, or mean. If He has not yet given us what we have asked for, it is because He is good and knows what is best for our lives. And what we have asked for is not yet the very best thing—even if its absence currently causes us pain.

The Puritan preacher, Thomas Watson, wrote: "If we have not what we desire, we have more than we deserve. For our mercies, we have deserved less; for our afflictions, we have deserved more."

When we are struggling under the weight of our trials and disappointments, which tend to come in waves and not in isolation, we must fear the Lord and keep this truth in focus: Our good God loves us.

DAY 133

Psalm 118:8

*It is better to take refuge in the LORD than to **trust**
in man.*

We do not have an unsympathetic Father.

Though we can't be sure, there were times during our adoption process that we felt taken advantage of. We were in a precarious place for much of our wait—forced to pay whatever was asked of us, forced to fill out and re-fill out paperwork, forced to make drives, answer questions, and take tests. Our emotions were raw and people didn't always care.

That is the simple reality of it.

But God cared.

> *We do not have an
> unsympathetic Father.*

And if it wasn't enough for us that God cared, it was doubly encouraging that He understood what it was to wait: "For we do not have a high priest who is unable to sympathize with our weaknesses, but one who in every respect has been tempted as we are, yet without sin" (Hebrews 4:15 ESV).

We were comforted by the reality that God understood the pain of adoption. He went through more than we did when He adopted us. Anything we experienced as we waited to meet our child was less than what He endured at the cross.

And that resulted in deeper appreciation for our Father.

DAY 134

Psalm 118:9

*It is better to take refuge in the LORD than to **trust**
in princes.*

God will always be worthy of our trust.

One of the remarkable characteristics of humanity is our ability to trust untrustworthy people, "untrustworthy" referring, in this context, to individuals who haven't earned the trust as opposed to those who have broken it.

Many today will go under the knife for various operations without doing a moment's research on the surgeon. Many today will go on blind dates, will pass credit cards across a counter, or will leave their children in daycares full of workers they've never met.

Yet, when it comes to our relationship with God, at times we more readily trust politicians, or "princes" in the language of Psalm 118, than we do the Lord.

Countless times during our adoption, we were told to expect something. We would run to our e-mail, watch for the mailman, listen for the telephone call—and often, nothing would happen. Yet, each time we responded the same way.

Of course, we will hear something! We were told to expect it.

So why is it hard to trust the Lord? God is not like man. What He pledges to do for us, He always does. Here is the question: What does God need to do that He hasn't already done to make me believe that He is trustworthy?

We have been given so much from Him. How do we believe so little?

DAY 135

Psalm 119:42

So I will have an answer for him who reproaches me, for I **trust** *in Your word.*

The best answer in a moment of crisis is a biblical one.

Whether we are responding to an antagonist or our own adversarial doubts, the best answer in a difficult situation comes straight from the Word.

God and His Word are completely good—responsible for salvation and reliable for life.

During times of testing, we often spend too much time asking questions that have no immediate answers. We believe, somehow, that knowing why something happened—or didn't happen—will alleviate the pain or cause us to further trust the Lord in the midst of grief.

Really?

Could the loss hurt less? Would cancer be easier to accept if we heard a heavenly voice say, "It is the result of a fallen world"? (Though, in one sense, we have already been given that in Romans 5:12.) What answer do we want when we ask the difficult questions?

What answer would be sufficient? Perhaps this: "For to this you have been called, because Christ also suffered for you, leaving you an example, so that you might follow in his steps" (1 Peter 2:21 ESV).

It is biblical.

 God and His Word are completely good—responsible for salvation and reliable for life.

DAY 136

Psalm 119:43

*And do not take the word of truth utterly out of my
mouth, for I **wait** for Your ordinances.*

Grumbling is not God's desire.

No matter how legitimate the complaint or frustration may appear to
be, a critical spirit is not a biblical response. God wants us to speak
His truth while we wait for Him.

As A. W. Tozer said, "Among those sins most exquisitely fitted to
injure the soul and destroy the testimony, few can equal the sin of
complaining."

Admittedly, there were times during our difficulties that we wanted to
erect a billboard and proclaim to others the obvious unfairness of our
situation. Indeed, we experienced some bizarre treatment at times,
and it occurred to us that perhaps we would feel better if people
understood our authenticity and other's duplicity.

It's true. The human heart takes comfort in receiving empathy in
times of injustice.

But the comfort is short-lived. And God is not pleased.

Like feasting on fast food, grumbling satisfies a short-term need and
leaves the heart in want of something better, more wholesome, and
truly satisfying.

One way that we obey God and wait correctly is by forgiving people
who have hurt us and refusing to complain about them.

God's Word remains the greatest solution for the hurting heart.

DAY 137

Psalm 119:49

Remember the word to Your servant, in which You have made me **hope.**

God calls us to do more than "hang in there"—to endure with a type of stamina that the saved and unsaved alike can muster. God wants us to persevere—to live with patient confidence that what He promised will happen (Revelation 3:10).

On difficult days, this task seems impossible.

When God appears to be unresponsive, this calling feels unfeasible.

If, during times of waiting on God, our perseverance were reliant on our own strength, we would be in serious trouble. But thankfully, we have a God who doesn't faint or falter.

The same God who commands us to persevere, empowers us to do so. He has not set us in motion like a child sets a spinning top, then sits back to watch it spin on its own.

He has enabled us, entrusted us, and now He expects us

> *The same God who commands us to persevere, empowers us to do so.*

to persevere on the path He has called us to travel. And for our good and His glory, He travels with us.

"Have you not known? Have you not heard? The LORD is the everlasting God, the Creator of the ends of the earth. He does not faint or grow weary; his understanding is unsearchable" (Isaiah 40:28 ESV).

DAY 138

Psalm 119:74

May those who fear You see me and be glad, because I
wait *for Your word.*

The more we delight in God, the more we will pray.

Throughout the Word of God, we read the exhortations to come to God with bold requests (Matthew 7:7; 1 John 5:14). It hardly feels right to us as mere human beings to bring petitions to the Almighty. Perhaps, like the ill-mannered child making requests of his father, we are fearful that God will be angry or insulted or uninterested.

Surely, from our view and with our mindset, we would be annoyed with us if we were God. We know the many ways in which we fall short.

But for reasons that make little human sense, God delights in us. And He wants us to delight in Him by means of prayer.

It is vital that we understand that we are never a nuisance to God when we bring our cares and concerns to Him. It is impossible for us to bother God when we talk to Him in the way He invites us to pray.

Here is the fuel for our confidence in prayer: Our Heavenly Father cares for His children.

And just as He has cared for His children through the ages, He will care for us now while we wait for Him.

"Humble yourselves, therefore, under the mighty hand of God so that at the proper time he may exalt you, casting all your anxieties on him, because he cares for you" (1 Peter 5:6–7 ESV).

DAY 139

Psalm 119:81

*My soul languishes for Your salvation; I **wait** for
Your word.*

"Whoever has the Son has life" (1 John 5:12 ESV).

We can want or have any number of positive things in this world—the
comfort of a good job, the security of a strong marriage, the enjoyment
of a beautiful home, or the satisfaction of a healthy child—but none
of these things promise life.

It is easy to feel like they do, especially if we are in the process of
losing one or wanting another, but the good things of this world do
not guarantee life.

He that has the Son has life.

We should be able to reverse the truth. In other words, not being in
possession of good things—such as health, wealth, or happiness—
does not rob a man of his life. To have nothing in this world but Jesus
still guarantees life.

To have nothing in this world but Jesus means we are still capable of
experiencing joy.

We can say with Psalm 73:26, "My flesh and my heart may fail, but
God is the strength of my heart and my portion forever" (ESV).

Our soul may languish, but we wait with joy if God waits with us.

> *He that has the Son has life.*

DAY 140

Psalm 119:114

*You are my hiding place and my shield; I **wait** for Your word.*

God Almighty protects those that belong to Him.

At a certain point in our adoption process, we encountered a series of incredibly maddening experiences. In addition to being pointless for us to list the problems here in this book, it would also read like very bad fiction.

Surely, fiction wouldn't allow for so many crushing blows to pummel one character!

In a two-week span it felt like every person on the planet wanted to halt our process. And, while we know that is not true, it seemed like barely an exaggeration at the time. We wanted nothing more than to meet our son, yet obstacle after disappointing obstacle stood in the way.

Professionals' oversights threatened to cost us lots of time and lots of money.

Then one night, reflecting on the truth that God is our hiding place, we read Psalm 23. And though it is one of the earliest Psalms we had ever put to memory, it was to us one of the sweetest ever written. With new perspective and eyes that were weary with tears, we read: "The LORD is my shepherd; I shall not want. He makes me lie down in green pastures. He leads me beside still waters. He restores my soul. He leads me in paths of righteousness for his name's sake" (ESV).

And we knew with certainty—whatever the outcome of our adoption—that we would dwell with our Lord forever. And to us, that brought tremendous peace.

DAY 141

Psalm 119:116

*Sustain me according to Your word, that I may live; and do not let me be ashamed of my **hope**.*

God's Word sustains us in times of testing.

Not only did the psalmist understand God's Word in relation to his survival, but Jesus Christ also demonstrated the Word's power when He was led away to be tempted by Satan (Matthew 4:1–11).

Interesting to note—Satan tempted Christ with a shortcut out of His suffering—an opportunity to bypass the difficult path of obedience to God and get what He wanted with less pain.

Jesus, weakened physically by forty days of fasting, was no doubt hungry. And Satan presented to Him a well-crafted alternative to what He was experiencing: "Command these stones to become loaves of bread" (Matthew 4:3 ESV).

Satan's offer to give Jesus what the Father already planned to give Him—but without experiencing death on the cross—was undoubtedly an attractive offer to a physically-weakened Christ. What appeal would death on the cross proffer?

Often our greatest temptations involve shortcuts out of endurance.

Christ endured by quoting Scripture (Matthew 4:10).

And so should we.

God's Word sustains us in times of testing.

DAY 142

Psalm 119:147

*I rise before dawn and cry for help; I **wait** for Your words.*

We can most readily observe our priorities in prayer when we are crying out to God for help.

What we ask for indicates what we really value.

What we ask for indicates what we think we need.

What we don't ask for indicates what we don't believe God can really do.

Do we want relief and release above everything else? If so, we know that our desires are for this life and not the next. Do we want to glorify God and endure as Christ endured? If so, we know that our desires are for eternity.

While we were in the midst of our own trek through the valley, our pastor reminded our church family that a whole lot of our praying is for things that won't matter when we're dead.

And he was absolutely right.

Though God wants us to bring our needs and anxieties to Him, we should be concerned when the largest portion of our praying is for things that won't be of consequence in heaven.

The Lord does not honor ill-motivated prayers (James 4:3).

> *What we ask for indicates what we really value.*

DAY 143

Psalm 119:166

*I **hope** for Your salvation, O LORD, and do Your commandments.*

"Just put one foot in front of the other."

There were several times during our testing that we were encouraged by the simple instruction to just do what was expected of us next. It was easy to be overwhelmed by the host of items on our to-do list.

We often explained our international adoption case to friends as an enormous Rubik's cube—the 3-D puzzle that requires each row to be aligned in order for the whole to be complete. Our adoption was an integral web of matching dates with paperwork and permissions and fees—all against a running clock. When one set of paperwork expired, we had to realign the row.

The biggest challenge was that each row relied on other people to do their portion.

But, even with our pressures, we had no rights that other believers didn't have. We didn't have permission to lose our temper or criticize God's plan for us. Even when we were weary from the trek, we knew it was our responsibility to place one foot in front of the other and do the next right thing.

"And this is love, that we walk according to his commandments; this is the commandment, just as you have heard from the beginning, so that you should walk in it" (2 John 1:6 ESV).

While we wait for God, we must remain active in our obedience to Him.

Our challenges do not exempt us from God's commandments.

DAY 144

Psalm 125:1

*Those who **trust** in the LORD are as Mount Zion, which cannot be moved but abides forever.*

God remains unwavering.

His working in our lives means we can be steadfast, too.

Just as our faith can move mountains (Matthew 17:20), our trust in God makes us unmovable and our faith unshakable. When everything else is crashing down around us, our faith remains intact. When nothing is happening and we are forced to continue to wait, our faith still remains whole.

God is our only and all-sufficient stability.

We learned over time that the difficult issue is relating to God correctly when we don't receive a response when we feel we should have one. It's one thing to pray and receive a clear answer—even if it wasn't the answer being sought. A house doesn't sell, for instance, or the job is offered to someone else. God is clearly at work in those situations.

In some ways, it's easier to praise God for the *no* than the *nothing*.

But when months of praying and waiting yield little visible result, it is challenging to relate to God in the way He requires. It is tough to believe that God is still just as involved in the situations where we receive the instruction to "wait."

But He is.

"How precious to me are your thoughts, O God! How vast is the sum of them!" (Psalm 139:17 ESV). The true test is how we relate to God when we're waiting and not receiving.

DAY 145

Psalm 130:5

*I **wait** for the LORD, my soul does **wait**, and in His word do I **hope**.*

Endurance is not a natural-born characteristic.

Fighting is natural. Worrying is normal. Running from difficulty is customary.

But waiting for the Lord over a long haul—and trusting in His Word without doing the math or calculating the human odds—is a work of grace. The challenge is to wait fervently and patiently.

It is the kindness of God that He filled His Word with the stories of real people. The Psalms, for instance, trace many of the difficulties of David as he cried out to the Lord. In the space between Genesis 3 and Revelation 20, there are very few recorded stories without the element of tremendous heartache or loss. And, for our own edification, we are invited to learn from those who endured and those who quit.

C. H. Spurgeon said of God's Word: "This volume is the writing of the living God. Each letter was penned with an Almighty finger; each word in it dropped from the everlasting lips."

And though writers labored over what to put on the page, we know it was God that inspired each word, each story, and each lesson to be included (2 Peter 1:21).

It is God who strengthens us to endure by giving us His Word in which to hope.

> *It is the kindness of God that He filled His Word with the stories of real people.*

DAY 146

Psalm 130:6

*My soul **waits** for the LORD more than watchmen for the morning; indeed, more than the watchmen for the morning.*

The morning is coming!

"Weeping may last for the night, but a shout of joy comes in the morning" (Psalms 30:5).

This is the confident promise for the children of God—we may be in the midst of a dark night, but morning is coming!

One thing we learned from fellow believers who were experiencing painful circumstances at the same time we were: The pain is intense, but so is the joy. To be satisfied with the goodness of God is the best kind of delight—yes, even better than before the trial existed.

This kind of joy is bizarre, eccentric, extraordinary, which is why Philippians 4:7 says, "And the peace of God, *which surpasses all understanding,* will guard your hearts and your minds in Christ Jesus" (ESV).

We weren't meant to understand the interworking of peace and how it dialogues with our weary soul, but we were meant to experience it.

Peace, at its most basic level, is the satisfaction God gives us that we are safe with Him.

> *We may be in the midst of a dark night, but morning is coming!*

DAY 147

Psalm 130:7

*O Israel, **hope** in the LORD; for with the LORD there is
lovingkindness, and with Him is abundant redemption.*

True hope is unique to believers.

What we experience in trials—the feelings, the questions, the
anguish—is not unique to us as Christians. Watch a nation experience
a catastrophe and many of the same questions will arise, though they
are seldom met with the correct answers about God.

But while personal tragedy is not unusual, true hope is a uniquely
Christian experience.

Psalm 130:7 is considered to be a "song of ascent," sung by the children
of God on their way up to Jerusalem. Though only a handful of Psalms
are classified this way, all of the songs of ascent are characterized as
hopeful.

Hope is a truly remarkable gift, given to God's children to sustain
them in darkness.

There was hope among the people of God that they would be redeemed
as a result of their trust and obedience. This faith, no doubt, caused
many to persevere.

So it is in our trials that we should exhibit true hope in darkness. Our
God is rich in lovingkindness. With Him is abundant deliverance
from whatever we are facing.

Imagine receiving these words when they were given in Zephaniah
3:17: "The Lord your God is in your midst, a mighty one who will
save; he will rejoice over you with gladness; he will quiet you by his
love; he will exult over you with loud singing" (ESV).

DAY 148

Psalm 131:3

*O Israel, **hope** in the LORD from this time forth
and forever.*

We do not need to live defeated lives, no matter how bleak our current situation.

Experiencing hardship can turn from being a bitter to a beneficial circumstance with one word:

Hope.

David experienced extreme situations that caused him both to rise to the heights and sink to the depths. He both conquered Goliath and lost sons. He both reigned as a king and ran for his life. He was called *a man after God's own heart* (Acts 13:22), and he was rebuked by Nathan for the murder of Uriah (2 Samuel 12).

Yet in Psalm 131:3—despite his cyclical relationship with grief and glory—he challenged his nation to hope in the Lord based on his own experience with God's mercy.

The verse directly preceding Psalm 131:3 begins: "But I have calmed and quieted my soul" (Psalm 131:2 ESV).

Powerful, isn't it?—to hear someone who experienced so much pain praise the Lord.

That David could tell the people to hope in God means that we, too, should encourage those around us to trust in God's faithfulness. And we, ourselves, should always hope in God.

Our situation may be exhausting, but our hope is rejuvenated because of the goodness of the Lord.

DAY 149

Psalm 141:2

*May my **prayer** be counted as incense before You; the lifting up of my hands as the evening offering.*

Prayer is worship.

Though we have been granted access to pray any time and about any need or concern, we must be careful to recognize that talking to God is much different than just chatting with a friend over coffee.

Prayer is more than conversation—it is communion.

Prayer is never less than talking to God, and acceptable prayer is always more than conversation.

When we see Christ in the Garden, praying before His death, we do not see banter or chat—and neither do we find hysteria or stoicism. For though the Son of God knew what He was about to endure, He approached His Father earnestly, intensely, and reverently.

His prayer should be for us an example of how to approach God in the most trying of situations. We will never experience painful circumstances to the degree in which Christ did.

Christ's words demonstrate His posture in the presence of God: "Father, if you are willing, remove this cup from me. Nevertheless, not my will, but yours, be done" (Luke 22:42 ESV).

If anyone, from our perspective, had the right to talk to God as an equal, it was Jesus Christ. Yet, even Christ approached the throne of grace with humility, reverence, and worship.

We must offer our prayer as incense to God who is worthy of our praise.

DAY 150

Psalm 143:1

*Hear my **prayer**, O LORD, Give ear to my supplications!*
Answer me in Your faithfulness, in Your righteousness!

What Christ did for us at Calvary was extraordinary.

That all of Christ's suffering can be directly linked to our sin should prohibit us from ever throwing the "unfair" card at God. It is tempting during trials to ask, "Why me?" But the greater question should be— "Why *not* me?"

Why, for all I have done against Christ, should I be exempt from suffering?

Yes, difficulties will occur. Sadness will come. Pain will ensue.

Life doesn't take care to deal disappointments in equal proportions. Some people appear to scoot through life with relative ease while others face enormous loss.

But God is faithful. And even in the difficulties, here is what is most alarming: "For Christ also suffered once for sins, the righteous for the unrighteous, that he might bring us to God" (1 Peter 3:18 ESV).

That He is faithful to us when we are unfaithful to Him is unreasonable. We deserve no such love. Yet He loves us.

God has proven Himself faithful. It is our turn to prove ourselves trusting.

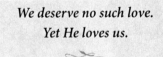

We deserve no such love.
Yet He loves us.

DAY 151

Psalm 143:8

Let me hear Your lovingkindness in the morning; for I
trust *in You; teach me the way in which I should walk; for*
to You I lift up my soul.

There is nothing better than the mercy of God in the morning.

It was always on the day when we anticipated some new bit of news or movement in our adoption case that anxiety, like an unwelcome, over-assuming guest, seemed to invite itself to our breakfast table and volunteer to follow us to work.

Anxiety arrived whenever medical test results were due.

Anxiety arrived when two of our loved ones were dying many miles away.

Anxiety arrived when important paperwork deadlines loomed.

We actively—and often—had to battle our unease with the precious promises of God.

Isaiah 41:10 (ESV) reads, "Fear not, for I am with you; be not dismayed, for I am your God; I will strengthen you, I will help you, I will uphold you with my righteous right hand."

That God promises to uphold us means that—though anxiety persistently knocks on our front door— God's presence and grace in our lives will be there to answer it.

Though it may not be God's immediate plan to remove our distress, neither is it His will for us to battle anxiety. This is why His mercy is new every morning.

DAY 152

Psalm 146:3

*Do not **trust** in princes, in mortal man, in whom there is no salvation.*

God is just.

Though at times it may feel like evil is prevailing—and maybe we wonder where God's justice dwells—we can be confident of this: our emotions are not the standard for what is right and wrong in the world. God, alone, knows what is best.

During our time of testing, we learned to look for God's fingerprints in the details of our situation. When extra costs accrued, that we had to pay because of someone's oversight or error, we learned to look for how God planned to meet the need. When our hearts were troubled by a setback or disappointment, we looked for how God would give us peace. When the injustice came, we looked for how our just God would intervene.

And when, all at once, we would be reminded of a verse, find extra money in a pay check, or experience unexplainable joy on a long afternoon, we would know with certainty that God does what is right.

What God does is always right.

> *... our emotions are not the standard for what is right and wrong in the world.*

Our good and just Father intervenes with mercy so that we will trust in Him and not the people on this earth, with whom there is no salvation.

DAY 153

Psalm 146:5

*How blessed is he whose help is the God of Jacob, whose **hope** is in the LORD his God.*

We must believe that God is capable of doing profound and incredible things!

When we stop believing that God is able to do for us what we need Him to do, we will stop seeing His hand in the details of our lives. We will pat ourselves on the back for things we have no business taking credit, and we will miss the blessing that exists in our dependence on our Heavenly Father.

Hope is believing that God is able to do more than we could ever imagine.

A verse of comfort we discovered during our time of need was 2 Corinthians 9:8 which says, "And God is able to make all grace abound to you, so that having all sufficiency in all things at all times, you may abound in every good work" (ESV).

When we were first matched with our child, we were told that a "worst case scenario" would mean that we would travel in October (nineteen months after beginning the process) to meet him in the country of his birth. When October came and went, we were grossly disappointed. When we found out via an e-mail that it looked like we wouldn't even meet him by the end of the year, we were confounded.

Somehow it didn't seem right that we would celebrate another holiday season without the child we loved and longed to meet. It didn't seem right that we would close out another year without him.

What did seem right to us was believing that God could still do whatever He wanted to do on our behalf. We leaned on the certainty that God's will would be accomplished in God's way at God's time— with or without the consent of those working on our case.

God does whatever He pleases (Psalm 115:3).

DAY 154

Psalm 147:11

*The LORD favors those who fear Him, those who **wait** for His lovingkindness.*

God is the creator of all things—the pain and the pleasure—and all creation serves Him.

As much as His creation pleases Him, His true enjoyment is in His children who acknowledge His power and authority and situate their hope and trust in Him.

"Behold, the eye of the LORD is on those who fear him, on those who hope in his steadfast love" (Psalm 33:18 ESV).

One of the reasons that the Psalms are some of the best-loved pages in the Bible is because of the forthrightness of the writers. The book brims with candid conversation, and we are invited to eavesdrop on some of the most intimate conversations that the psalmists have with God. And, in many instances, we hear our own thoughts echoed by someone else who has more confidence to say what we only think.

There is much to learn from the Psalms: sincerity, transparency, trust.

Though the Psalms are earnest, and in some cases frank, it is important to note that they are not left in their natural, unfiltered state. Even the most painful complaints that the psalmist expresses to God have been put through the sieve of God's unyielding truth.

At the end of pouring out his heart, about whatever the difficulty or hardship involves or whether or not there is immediate light at the end of the tunnel, the psalmist always concludes that God is in control. And so we must accept the pattern of the psalmist and say, "Yes, right now I am perplexed and disappointed, but God, I trust that You are good."

DAY 155

Proverbs 3:5

Trust in the Lord with all your heart and do not lean on your own understanding.

David did not stand confidently in the Valley of Elah with any delusion that he was strong enough to kill a giant. One-hundred-year-old Abraham did not anticipate the birth of his son with any ignorance about his wife's inability to bear children. Noah did not build an ark because of any prior understanding or experience with floods. These individuals, and scores of others like them, trusted God's promises to them for one reason: They knew God.

For them, the key to trusting God came from knowing Him. Yet, how can we trust someone with whom we have no familiarity? Knowing God is not the direct result of refining any spiritual gimmicks or honing in on innovative techniques in prayer or worship, but of studying God's Word and believing what it says, especially when the belief is unaccompanied by sight. Trusting God has little to do with understanding His motive and everything to do with resting in His sufficiency. This kind of trust leads to the only productive change in our lives.

Knowing and trusting God are vitally connected.

If we know Him, we will trust Him. And as we know Him better, we will trust Him more fully with the details of our lives—however lacking in our human logic they may appear to be.

Abraham's response to Sarah's pregnancy serves as an example for us today. Romans 4:20 says, "No distrust made him waver concerning the promise of God, but he grew strong in his faith as he gave glory to God" (ESV).

DAY 156

Proverbs 8:34

*Blessed is the man who listens to me, watching daily at my gates, **waiting** at my doorposts.*

We must wait on God expectantly.

The imagery of Proverbs 8:34 is that of a maid, a butler, or a servant who is waiting, hand and foot, on the master. "Watching daily at my gates" is not a casual observance, but rather it carries the idea of someone whose livelihood depends on not missing the appearance of someone or something important.

We must wait on God, and subsequently wait for His wisdom, in this way.

Practically speaking, we should want to hear the words of God more than anything else. We should want to speak to God and ask for His guidance before we speak to anybody else. When He moves in our lives, we should recognize the movement as belonging to Him.

God walks with us, granting us His wisdom on our journey to heaven.

If we do not have the necessary wisdom to make a decision, the solution is simple. "If any of you lacks wisdom, let him ask God, who gives generously to all without reproach, and it will be given him" (James 1:5 ESV).

How many times we begged the Lord for wisdom during our adoption experience. Very often, we knelt by the bed of our son and begged God to give us what we needed.

With wisdom, we wait expectantly to see what our good God will do.

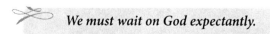
We must wait on God expectantly.

DAY 157

Proverbs 10:28

*The **hope** of the righteous is gladness, but the expectation of the wicked perishes.*

The righteous can rejoice in any season.

Discontentment can hover like a solitary rain cloud over an individual whose expectations aren't being met. The nagging voice of missed opportunity or lost dreams rarely stops chattering. The visitors of doubt or desperation come calling at all hours of the night.

Words like, "By now we should have" . . . are minefields of the heart.

We were just beginning our twentieth month of waiting when we received news that close family members were expecting a baby. By their admission, the pregnancy was a surprise.

We were thrilled. Make no mistake. We rushed to the store to buy that first gift for the baby we had never met but already loved.

Admittedly, though, our tears were mixed—joy with confusion.

Thank you, Lord, for blessing them. Now, why not us? We long to meet our son.

Those who are the children of God can have hope that others cannot understand. We can have joy, not in the situations we face, but in the God who controls all things. We can rejoice when others are blessed by God. And we absolutely should!

Jeremiah Burroughs, a Puritan preacher, wrote about this "jewel of Christian contentment." He said, "It is a sweet, inward heart thing. It is a work of the Spirit indoors. It is a box of precious ointment, very comforting and useful for troubled hearts in times of troubled conditions. It is the inward submission of the heart."

Contentment is possible because satisfaction is found in Christ.

DAY 158

Proverbs 11:28

*He who **trusts** in his riches will fall, but the righteous will flourish like the green leaf.*

Trusting God is infinitely wiser than trusting man.

One morning, while driving, we were considering ways we might reach out to our caseworker in a new or creative way. The e-mail, "Heard anything yet?" was getting old, no doubt for us and for her. We thought of ways we might involve other people who might do something to help us with our stagnant case. Maybe we could reach out to Embassy officials. They had powers, no doubt.

And then an eighteen-wheeler pulled in front of us. And in the thick layer of dust on the back of the cab where obscenities or silly messages were usually written for the entertainment of passersby, we saw these words, "Just trust God!"

Really? Whose conscience has ever been convicted by the back of a truck?

It isn't enough just to trust. We must *trust God.*

Trust in anything or anyone else is inadequate by comparison.

During hard times it can be tempting to trust in people who are doing the most to help. For us it was friends, family, or those who took pity on our case and gave us advice or encouragement. Solomon trusted marriage, treaties, and a large army. King Asa of Judah trusted in the King of Syria (1 Kings 15:18); Sennacharib put his trust in past victories (2 Kings 18–19).

We were reminded by words scrawled in the dust on an eighteen-wheeler: All trust is futile unless our trust is placed in God.

Proverbs 13:12

Hope deferred makes the heart sick, but desire fulfilled is a tree of life.

Valleys are lonely places.

 The valley isn't lonely if we meet God there.

Private heartache and disappointment are ghost towns of the soul.

We spent many years labeled "childless." We lived in a void neither as "young married" nor as "parents" while we waited to adopt our son. We didn't talk much about this disappointment with our friends—it didn't feel right to do so—certainly not with those who accepted us as we were, and never with those who didn't.

And we learned quickly that the fastest route to frustration was traveled on the highway of introspection.

Why is it taking so long? Should we have made different choices? Is this somehow our fault? How can we make this situation better? What if . . . What if . . . What if . . .

It takes very few introspective questions to spiral into the black hole of guilt, doubt, and blame. This is, perhaps, the reason God wants us to look outside of ourselves and fix our gaze on Him for the hope that we need.

That the Bible commands us not to place our hope in men means we cannot place our hope, or our constant search for it, in ourselves.

The valley isn't lonely if we meet God there.

Proverbs 15:8

*The sacrifice of the wicked is an abomination to the
LORD, but the **prayer** of the upright is His delight.*

It is not enough to do the right things outwardly.

If the heart is corrupt with bitterness, anger, and resentment, then our
worship is revolting to the Lord.

During times of difficult, drawn-out waiting, our posture before the
Lord must reflect a heart that is willing to do what He wants us to do,
when He wants us to do it.

Even though the wait is excruciating.

We must adjust our responses so that they are biblical. Instead of
lashing out against God and charging Him foolishly, we must come
to Him with a humble spirit, knowing that "the sacrifices of God
are a broken spirit; a broken and contrite heart, O God, you will not
despise" (Psalm 51:17 ESV).

John Wesley wrote in his *Notes on the Bible*, "A broken spirit—this is
of more value than many sacrifices."

During our time of waiting, we filled our lives with many good things.
We taught Sunday School to a group of teenagers we really enjoyed.
We participated in youth group and counseling opportunities. We did
a lot of *upright* things.

Yet, the task of keeping an upright heart before God is the most
significant duty we have.

> *"A broken spirit—this is of more
> value than many sacrifices."*

DAY 161

Proverbs 15:29

*The LORD is far from the wicked, but He hears the **prayer** of the righteous.*

God is generous with His children.

For one, He gives us life eternal. For another, He hears our prayers. What amazing gifts!

From the beginning of time, God's children have experienced great difficulties. We live in a world that stands in stark contrast to the heaven that is to come. Paul referred to God's creation as "groaning." Even Adam and Eve were not exempt from heavy sorrow and agonizing grief. Every family since the first has had its share of pain and disappointment. Yet, God has always responded to the cries of His children.

One afternoon, after receiving difficult news about our adoption—which happened so often we cringed when we saw our agency's number on the phone—a song came on the radio. The words, written many years ago by Horatio Spafford stopped us in our complaints. And, with tears falling, we realized, no matter how difficult the events of this life at times may be, God is still generous with us.

When peace, like a river, attendeth my way,
When sorrows like sea billows roll;
Whatever my lot, Thou has taught me to say,
It is well, it is well, with my soul.
But, Lord, 'tis for Thee, for Thy coming we wait,
The sky, not the grave, is our goal;
Oh trump of the angel! Oh voice of the Lord!
Blessed hope, blessed rest of my soul!

God is generous with His children. Because of His goodness, it is well with our soul!

Proverbs 16:20

*He who gives attention to the word will find good, and
blessed is he who **trusts** in the LORD.*

Everything in our lives must be adjusted to the truth of God.

Long before the canon was complete or God's purposes for the
events of human history were unfolded, David, Abraham, Noah, and
a host of other well-loved biblical personalities knew enough about
God to trust Him to the full extent of His Word. And they were not
disappointed.

In the words of Proverbs 16:20, God's people who give attention to
God's Word find good and are encouraged to trust in the Lord.

Whether, for the individuals in biblical history, God's Word was
revealed audibly through a prophet, or in some written form, God's
people knew to trust what He said. Failure to do so always resulted
in the most egregious consequences, whereas refuge in God always
resulted in the highest good.

"But let all who take refuge in you rejoice; let them ever sing for joy,
and spread your protection over them, that those who love your name
may exult in you" (Psalm 5:11 ESV).

We have in our hands today God's written Word—His gift to us which
offers lasting and enduring hope to anyone who reads and trusts. If
we struggle to find hope, or complain that we cannot hope, we admit
that we are not giving enough attention to God's Word.

Because anyone who trusts God's Word will find good.

We must trust our good God.

DAY 163

Proverbs 20:22

*Do not say, "I will repay evil"; **wait** for the LORD, and He will save you.*

Evil begs to be repaid. Injustice demands to settle the score.

Ignorant questions. Hurtful comments. Careless oversights. Sometimes these things happen innocently—other times they are the cruel choices of those who would call themselves our friends. Yet the Bible is clear that we are not to repay unkindness with unkindness.

No matter how much it hurts.

What comfort, then, to know with confidence that "No temptation has overtaken [us] that is not common to man. God is faithful, and he will not let [us] be tempted beyond [our] ability, but with the temptation he will also provide the way of escape, that [we] may be able to endure it" (1 Corinthians 10:13 ESV).

We had strangers ask us why we didn't have children. We had well-meaning friends assume we didn't want "a family." Our second miscarriage came on the heels of the hurtful actions of a man we trusted and loved.

But no matter. It is not ours to repay. John Wesley said it best:

Let us receive every trial with calm resignation, and with humble confidence that He who has all power, all wisdom, all mercy, and all faithfulness, will support us in every temptation; so that in the end all things shall work together for good, and we shall happily experience that all these things were for our profit, that we might be partakers of His holiness.

DAY 164

Proverbs 22:19

*So that your **trust** may be in the LORD, I have taught you today, even you.*

Trials are personalized, sacred assignments from God.

Asking the wrong questions during trials will lead us to confusion, despair, and bitterness. On the other hand, asking the right questions will lead us to trust the Lord further and be taught in the classroom of suffering. One good question to ask is, "Why are trials necessary?"

"Count it all joy, my brothers, when you meet trials of various kinds, for you know that the testing of your faith produces steadfastness. And let steadfastness have its full effect, that you may be perfect and complete, lacking in nothing" (James 1:2–4 ESV).

God's Word, as seen in this Scripture, indicates that trials are necessary for our growth.

Of James 1, Dr. Mark Minnick said:

> What clearly is being indicated is that there will be no such thing
> as the Christian maturity and completeness that God intends for
> any one of us unless He makes use of the shaping of trials—in the
> multiple, "trials" plural—and of diverse character, various in their
> nature, in their length, and in their severity.

In promising to meet our needs, God supplies us with the trials necessary to fashion us to greater Christlikeness.

DAY 165

Proverbs 23:18

*Surely there is a future, and your **hope** will not be cut off.*

Our biggest obstacle is always unbelief.

The Bible has given us all we need to have hope and to endure correctly. Verse upon verse assures us that God is in control, ordaining each event in our lives for our good and His glory. And yet, we struggle to believe there is a future; we struggle to have hope.

We were reminded during our time of waiting that to be like Christ, we must learn to endure difficulty with Him, His way, and "share in suffering as a good soldier of Christ Jesus" (2 Timothy 2:3 ESV).

Immediately, the natural response to a statement like that is, "Why must Christians suffer? Why would God want to put His children through warfare to the neglect of those who have no desire to know Him? Wouldn't it make more sense for nonbelievers to do battle while believers enjoy God's peace?"

But we know that theirs is a battle still to come. And it will be longer and worse than any we will ever know in this life. For now, we rest in the knowledge that the testing of our faith proves the authenticity of our hearts (James 1:3).

To enjoy peace, we must conquer unbelief.

If ever we are tempted to envy the lives of our unregenerate counterparts who appear to live lives of ease while we endure difficulty, we must remember this: Those who do not know Christ will not succeed forever.

Mercy in this life is a gift for us all.

Proverbs 24:14

Know that wisdom is thus for your soul; if you find it, then there will be a future, and your **hope** *will not be cut off.*

The need for wisdom is a common denominator for those who experience difficulty.

At any point in any trial, the need for wisdom to determine the next step is imperative.

What to do? Who to talk to? What to say? When to stop? These are the questions that often need answers. Because this is true, asking God for wisdom during difficulty is our wisest response to the trials in our lives.

When we don't know what to do next, we must ask God for the wisdom that we need.

"If any of you lacks wisdom, let him ask God, who gives generously to all without reproach, and it will be given him" (James 1:5 ESV).

Good thing for us, God is not stingy with dispensing wisdom. He gives it openhandedly.

But it is important to note: the not-so-secret key to receiving God's wisdom is asking for it. God could have designed it so that we receive wisdom instantly. Perhaps at salvation we could have been granted the wisdom we needed for all of life.

But that was not God's plan. And God's plan is always perfect.

God has ordained that we humble ourselves and ask for the help that we need for any and every situation. God commands we ask, but He promises that when we do, we will receive.

DAY 167

Proverbs 28:25

*An arrogant man stirs up strife, but he who **trusts** in the LORD will prosper.*

The correct responses to God and to others are born out of worship.

When we have spent time with God—poured out our hearts to Him as David did throughout the Psalms, and asked Him to intercede in the events of our lives—we are best poised to respond appropriately to the situations of life.

On the days when we spent our mornings in prayer and Bible reading, we were well-equipped to handle the difficult phone calls, the disappointing news, and the unresponsive caseworkers. On the days when we shortened our worship to move on to other things, it was more of a challenge to be the one who "trusts in the Lord" as opposed to the one who "stirs up strife."

Worship generates trust.

A lack of worship never leads to good fruit.

We tend to associate the word *prosperity* with monetary terms. However, as Proverbs 28:25 says, we can prosper in many other ways than just fiscal gain.

We can flourish spiritually, relationally, and emotionally when we trust the Lord the way in which the Bible commands. And trusting the Lord during seasons of waiting is vital.

Trust, not arrogance, is the key to prosperity.

> *When we have spent time with God—we are best poised to respond appropriately to the situations of life.*

DAY 168

Proverbs 28:26

*He who **trusts** in his own heart is a fool, but he who walks wisely will be delivered.*

At the heart of discontentment is the conclusion that God hasn't given us the right things.

Preoccupation with the timetables that we have created, along with the sneaky, subtle comparison of ourselves with others, feeds the disgruntlement that grows out of a septic, human heart. And all of it essentially leads us to trust in ourselves, which is "foolish" in the words of the Proverbs.

It is by trusting God that our trust in God is strengthened. It is by hoping in Him that our hope in Him is reinforced. Waiting until our emotions prompt us to do what God has commanded is trusting in our own heart. And it is naive.

As Proverbs 28:26 makes clear, "He who trusts in his own heart is a fool." But the flipside of the verse says, "he who walks wisely will be delivered."

If the heart of discontentment is a belief that God has given us the wrong things, then the heart of contentment is a realization that God has given us all we need and more than we deserve.

"He who did not spare his own Son but gave him up for us all, how will he not also with him graciously give us all things?" (Romans 8:32 ESV).

At the very least, we know that we have never given to God more than He has given to us. We would be wise to trust in Him.

> *It is by trusting God that our trust in God is strengthened.*

DAY 169

Proverbs 28:9

He who turns away his ear from listening to the law, even
*his **prayer** is an abomination.*

It is in our power to make our suffering worse.

Difficulty is bad enough on its own. Whatever we are waiting for right now is challenging enough without adding the dimensions of increased struggle or frustration. But according to the Bible, there are abundant ways we can pour salt into the wound of our suffering. And one of them is by worshiping externally while possessing a sinful heart.

We have the ability to complicate our suffering by sinning in our worship so that God is not pleased with our prayer. That God would not listen to us at a time when we most need and want Him to hear our cries should motivate us to worship with sincerity.

While we don't have control over our situation, we have been placed in charge of our responses. And how we respond can make a world of difference in our distress.

Disobedience to God puts us at risk for faulty worship. Specific to Proverbs 28, one way we impair our worship is by doing it externally, while internally we are not worshiping God at all. Perhaps we're angry, bitter, or resentful at what He has brought into our lives.

Not helpful.

During seasons of suffering, we are most at risk for external worship. It's not always the easiest thing to sing songs about the joy of the Lord or to listen to people talk about the rich blessings they are experiencing while we feel like we are missing out on something from heaven. But it's imperative that we meet with God in honesty, reverence, and love.

The key to worshiping correctly during times of trial is living submissively to God's authority—remembering who He is and who we are.

DAY 170

Proverbs 29:25

*The fear of man brings a snare, but he who **trusts** in the LORD will be exalted.*

Worry indicates we don't know God as well as we think we do.

Fear over the potential outcome of a situation that is not in our control signifies that we are not trusting in the Lord fully. No matter how confidently we believe that we are trusting God, if we are still wrestling over unanswered questions or consumed with finding solutions, we are not waiting correctly.

The solution to worry is trust.

We must believe whole-heartedly that God is committed to our good and His glory.

Our trust in God cannot be linked to getting what we want when we want it. It must be linked to the wisdom of God and wanting what He wants in His time. When we don't have something we request, God is still good and He is still trustworthy. Worry indicates we do not believe the best about God.

He knows infinitely better than we do what is best for our lives (Psalm 33:11).

It looked to us like a clear answer: our son should be growing up in a home with parents who love him instead of in an orphanage surrounded by hundreds of children whose needs were as significant as his own.

But God knew better and we trust Him.

So with everything in us, we refused to worry.

DAY 171

Ecclesiastes 9:4

*For whoever is joined with all the living, there is **hope**;*
surely a live dog is better than a dead lion.

We are ignorant to the blueprints of God.

Even those of us who want to please Him are not privy to the plans of God for our lives. At best, we go to His Word, claim the promises, and try to piece together an explanation for why He might be allowing something painful into our lives. It is natural to ask certain questions of God. And, in response, we know certain truths: We know He wants us to be more like Christ. We have been given that certainty.

But why God chooses a particular circumstance, illness, loss, or grief, to be the instrument of our shaping or fashioning, we do not know.

There comes a point when we all must acknowledge that we are blessed and have hope simply because we are still alive to experience God's blessing. Even in the most difficult circumstances, God has granted that we remain bless-able on earth.

In Ecclesiastes 9:4, the lion exists as a strong animal and the dog as a scavenger. The lion is the more desirable imagery, yet the dog that is alive is always better than a lion that is dead.

We might say it this way, "As long as I'm alive, I have something for which to praise God!" We had a grandfather who, when asked how he was doing, would respond, "I'm still alive!"

We know this much to be true: God's hope trumps our disappointment.

And His grace will always triumph.

DAY 172

Isaiah 12:2

*Behold, God is my salvation, I will **trust** and not be afraid; for the LORD GOD is my strength and song, and He has become my salvation.*

We must ask God to protect us from ourselves.

Our own worst enemy in times of waiting is often the person staring back at us in the mirror. Our thoughts can be toxic. Our faith can be weak. Our resolve can be short-lived.

Sadly, it doesn't take much time for the pendulum to swing from delight to despair.

In a culture that values enjoyment over endurance, it is easier at times to view death as more appealing than discomfort. As a culture, we are not equipped with fortitude.

We were asked the following questions an alarming number of times: Why on earth would you put yourself through an adoption that has so many complications? Are you sure you really want to do this? Have you considered walking away?

Thankfully, the success of God's perfect plan does not depend on man. Or we would be in trouble on the day of testing.

Writing of trusting God during difficulty, Os Guinness said, "As believers, we cannot always know why, but we can always know why we trust God who knows why, and that makes all the difference."

God is our strength and our salvation!

> *Thankfully, the success of God's perfect plan does not depend on man.*

DAY 173

Isaiah 25:9

*And it will be said in that day, "Behold, this is our God for whom we have **waited** that He might save us. This is the LORD for whom we have **waited**; let us rejoice and be glad in His salvation."*

We must be careful not to confuse the truth with what we want the truth to be.

God wants us to rest and wait. It is we who prefer stress to stillness and activity to respite. The Bible says, "Those who seek the Lord lack no good thing" (Psalm 34:10 ESV), yet we prefer searching for the good things ourselves.

Waiting for God requires trust that His schedule is better than ours, and an acceptance that we may never know the items on His agenda, but they are perfectly ordered.

We can never blame God for our anxiety. Choosing stress is always our decision.

When things got quiet in our adoption, the temptation to start doing things increased immensely. If we didn't know what was happening, it was easy to assume nothing was happening at all! The sound of silence truly is deafening!

"But they who wait for the Lord shall renew their strength" (Isaiah 40:31 ESV).

"It is in vain that you rise up early and go late to rest, eating the bread of anxious toil; for he gives to his beloved sleep" (Psalm 127:2 ESV).

"Do not be anxious about anything" (Philippians 4:6 ESV).

We learned, in time, to fill the silences with prayer.

To live at peace in this world, we must fix our eyes on Christ, look beyond the immediate disappointment, and see the invisible hand of God who is orchestrating each day and detail to work for our good and His glory.

DAY 174

Isaiah 26:3

The steadfast of mind You will keep in perfect peace,
*Because he **trusts** in You.*

Waiting on God requires a conscious and deliberate decision to take our attention off ourselves and to place it fully and wholly on Christ. Though the concept of trust is a frequent theme in the Bible, and consequently, a popular subject in Christian literature and music, it is not without its struggle for the child of God.

After beginning our adoption process, a friend of ours sent us some encouragement that we printed and taped in a conspicuous spot in our home. On the tiny square of paper are these words:

1. God's love for me is unchanging.

2. God's purpose for me is Christ-likeness.

3. God's grace is sufficient.

In the long days that stretched between conversations with our agency when we wondered if we would meet the child we had already come to love, we clung to the scriptural truth on that little piece of paper. No matter what, God's love for us is unchanging. Regardless of what happens in the future, God's purpose for us is Christ-likeness. And in spite of any present disappointment or pain, God's grace is sufficient.

Waiting on God requires a conscious and deliberate decision to take our attention off ourselves and to place it fully and wholly on Christ.

DAY 175

Isaiah 26:4

Trust in the LORD forever, for in GOD the LORD, we have an everlasting Rock.

It is good to trust the promises, but better to trust the Promiser.

When we place the totality of our trust in the promises, we run the risk of being utterly disappointed when the promise doesn't yield what we expect. We can misapply God's guarantees, confuse needs and wants, or believe that whenever we knock that the door of opportunity will be opened to us.

When we apply the promises to our lives, the variable is "we."

We don't always know enough of God's perspective to get it right.

But if we trust the one who gave the promises, believe that God will never fail us or abandon us (Hebrews 13:5), we will find Him to be our everlasting Rock.

Instead of viewing God through the lens of whether or not we think the promise held true, we will view the promise through the lens of whom we know God to be. And we know God cannot lie.

If we trust the Lord forever, we will find His promises to be wholly trustworthy.

"The Lord is faithful in all his words and kind in all his works" (Psalm 145:13 ESV).

So let us trust Him.

DAY 176

Isaiah 26:8

*Indeed, while following the way of Your judgments, O LORD, we have **waited** for You eagerly; Your name, even Your memory, is the desire of our souls.*

We must remember what God has done in the past.

Isaiah 26:8 reveals the key to deliverance for God's people is waiting on God.

The key to waiting on God is remembering what He has done in the past and what He is capable of doing in the future.

Three tiny words with enormous implication:

He is able.

Very little in the world beats watching a child sing about God's ability to carry us through testing. We enjoy the motions and smile at the refrain. Children can be hearty singers.

But it is interesting to note that the song rehearses what God has done in the past. What He has done gives us hope for our future. God designed it that way.

In our time of testing, we didn't doubt that God could do the very best thing. God can do whatever He chooses (Psalm 115:3). The temptation was to doubt whether He would do the very best thing *for us*.

Our own faithlessness considered, why would God act on our behalf?

Sometimes there is a disconnect between the reading of incredible stories in the Bible—with fantastic conclusions wrought by God—and what we think He can do for us in our situation.

But He is able to carry *us* through . . . anything.

DAY 177

Isaiah 26:16

*O LORD, they sought You in distress; they could only whisper a **prayer**, Your chastening was upon them.*

It is often the hard sovereignties in our lives that drive us to call upon God.

Trials have a way of revealing our inadequacies. We learn that our bank accounts are exhaustible, our strength expendable, our possessions consumable, and our health disposable.

Perhaps most distressing, we learn that our wisdom is insufficient for life. Most of our education stands speechless in the moment of crisis.

What do we say? What can we do?—this is not the stuff of classroom instruction.

But our shortfalls are not all bad. It is in those moments of staring at the loss, the lack, or the letdown that we identify with clarity the one true need of our hearts: God.

"But for me it is good to be near God; I have made the Lord GOD my refuge, that I may tell of all your works" (Psalm 73:28 ESV).

When we are struggling under the weight of tremendous pressures and conflicts, we must remember our goal: "Indeed, I count everything as loss because of the surpassing worth of knowing Christ Jesus my Lord. For his sake I have suffered the loss of all things and count them as rubbish, in order that I may gain Christ" (Philippians 3:8 ESV).

Knowing Christ more fully is the greatest possible outcome of facing our own insufficiency.

DAY 178

Isaiah 30:15

For thus the Lord GOD, the Holy One of Israel, has said,
"In repentance and rest you will be saved, in quietness and
***trust** is your strength." But you were not willing.*

We can choose to make our waiting worse.

Isaiah 30:15 offers strategies for endurance—repentance, rest, quietness, and trust—and as evidenced in Isaiah 30, the Israelites wanted nothing to do with them. Perhaps they were unwilling because they trusted in their own strength. Or maybe they simply wanted nothing to do with the encouragement of God.

The words, "But you were not willing," put the Israelites in a world of hurt.

The imagery of a parent hanging over the backseat of a car, one finger wagging in the face of a child, while the parent says the infamous words, "We are on vacation and you will enjoy it!" is not the way God intends us to view our trials.

He has never commanded us to enjoy the pain.

But God has offered us the means to improve our situation—to save us from suffering more than is necessary. If we choose to disregard this grace, we cannot blame Him.

In the moments when we were dizzy with discouragement, we were encouraged by Psalm 116:7 (ESV): "Return, O my soul, to your rest; for the LORD has dealt bountifully with you."

Remembrance of what God has done in the past, as well as meditation on what He promises to do in the future, will enable the soul to be at rest once more.

And that is the best place to be.

DAY 179

Isaiah 30:18

*Therefore the LORD longs to be gracious to you, and therefore He **waits** on high to have compassion on you. For the LORD is a God of justice; how blessed are all those who long for Him.*

Faith doesn't always feel good. But faith is always good.

Throughout the first nineteen months of what we learned to call "hard waiting," one question seemed to constantly re-appear:

Is God enough if your circumstances never change?

The question seemed to materialize in different ways and different wording whenever we were in the midst of praying about a long list of needs.

We needed a clean bill of health. We needed financial provision. We needed the understanding support of our friends and family. We needed assurance that we were making the right decisions.

But then, all at once we would arrive at the same conclusion: all we really need is God.

Faith is not a feeling, a mood, or an emotion. Faith in God is the confidence that our Heavenly Father is sufficient. *Sans the clean bill of health. Sans the financial provision. Sans the understanding support of anyone.*

We must have faith that God is doing more behind the scenes than we can imagine.

John Piper once wrote, "God never does only one thing. In everything He does He is doing thousands of things. Of these, we know perhaps half a dozen."

DAY 180

Isaiah 33:2

*O LORD, be gracious to us; we have **waited** for You. Be their strength every morning, our salvation also in the time of distress.*

God's care for us is perfect.

> *God actively, daily, lovingly shepherds His people.*

There is no way around it. The analogy of the Shepherd and His sheep is precise because, like the wandering, confused, indecisive animal, we need the loving care of an all-knowing guide.

Though there are many times we may think we know best the path our life should take, our Savior is painstakingly committed to what is right, even when what is right isn't what we want.

God actively, daily, lovingly shepherds His people.

As Isaiah 33:2 indicates, the Lord is gracious to us. He is our strength every morning and our rescue in moments of misery. Because of these truths, we can rest in His presence, regardless of where the path takes us.

We may be called to walk on thorny, messy, tricky paths, but our Savior walks with us.

"Even though I walk through the valley of the shadow of death, I will fear no evil, for you are with me; your rod and your staff, they comfort me" (Psalm 23:4 ESV).

It is not without significance that the trek through the valley of the shadow of death is walked—not run or rushed—and that comfort exists on the journey. Psalm 23 makes no mention of hysteria.

The Shepherd is there. And all is well.

DAY 181

Isaiah 38:18

*For Sheol cannot thank You, Death cannot praise You; those who go down to the pit cannot **hope** for Your faithfulness.*

The worst part of hell isn't the fire.

The worst part of hell isn't even the separation from those we loved on earth.

The worst part of hell is the absence of hope. In the act of being permanently separated from God, there is no hope of reconciling the situation. As Isaiah 38:18 makes clear, "Those who go down to the pit do not hope for your faithfulness" (ESV).

So if hopelessness is the worst kind of hell, then the acquisition of hopefulness should be the best gift to us in this life and the next.

There are times in this life when our circumstances and their obstacles may feel like torment. We puzzle over verses like 2 Corinthians 4:17 that refer to our troubles in this lifetime as "light" or "momentary." Grief and loss are anything but easy.

Written in the margin of our Bible are these words: "For those who trust God, earth is the closest to hell they'll ever get; for those who do not know God, earth is the closest to heaven."

And we read 2 Corinthians 4:17 with new perspective: "For this light momentary affliction is preparing for us an eternal weight of glory beyond all comparison" (ESV).

Paul could call affliction "light" and "momentary" because he fixed his gaze on glory.

The reality of heaven, and what awaits us, is a source of endurance.

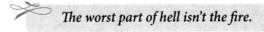
The worst part of hell isn't the fire.

DAY 182

Isaiah 40:31

*Yet those who **wait** for the LORD will gain new strength;*
They will mount up with wings like eagles, They will run
and not get tired, They will walk and not become weary.

Waiting requires us to stand still.

Perhaps this is why waiting is such a challenge. As people, we are made to move, to fix, to work, to do, but our loving God has ordained that our strength be acquired by waiting on the Lord. Not surprising at all—is it?—that the production and allowance of strength has nothing to do with us and everything to do with God.

And so we must learn what it is to wait so that we can do it correctly.

In a message preached from Isaiah 40:31, Dr. Alan Cairns said, "To wait upon the Lord is to wait, as children, upon a father, to do him honor, and to render obedience unto him."

Just as a father knows which of the child's requests should be granted and which should be denied, so does our Heavenly Father carefully dispense what is best for our lives. And He expects us to wait on Him in the process.

Tired? Weary? Worried? Weak?

Wait upon God and your strength will be renewed.

> *"To wait upon the Lord is to wait, as children,*
> *upon a father, to do him honor, and to render*
> *obedience unto him."*

DAY 183

Isaiah 42:17

*They will be turned back and be utterly put to shame,
who **trust** in idols, who say to molten images, "You are
our gods."*

In times of trial, idolatry is a threat to the soul.

Shortly before we began the adoption process, we had the opportunity
to work with the children in our church and teach them parts of the
Westminster Catechism, full of stabilizing truths for the Christian life.
In doing so, we studied its 450-year-old counterpart, the Heidelberg
Catechism.

Question 95 of the Heidelberg catechism asks, "What is idolatry?"

The answer: "Idolatry is instead of, or besides, that one true God, who
has manifested Himself in His Word, to contrive or have any other
object in which men place their trust."

Idolatry really is that simple. It's anything that replaces our worship
of God.

Suffering affords us seasons of self-focus if we so choose. Generally
speaking, suffering happens because we have lost something—a
person, an object, or an ideal—and it is easy to believe that whomever
took it from us owes us something in return.

But replacing worship of God with self-pity is, essentially, idolatry.

Gritty resolve to seek relief, comfort, payback, or control above the
resolution to love and honor God is a type of worship, because, at the
heart of it, is love and service to self.

The remedy for idolatry is total preoccupation, or worship,
of God alone.

Isaiah 49:23

*Kings will be your guardians, and their princesses your nurses. They will bow down to you with their faces to the earth and lick the dust of your feet; and you will know that I am the LORD; those who **hopefully wait** for Me will not be put to shame.*

Hope is the trademark of trust.

Throughout the Bible, there are illustrations of men and women who displayed their hope in Christ with remarkable trust in Him.

Joseph did not lose courage in prison. Abraham raised his knife-wielding hand, prepared to sacrifice his only son. Moses led the people into the roaring waters of the great Red Sea. David dared to fight the Philistine. Esther risked her life to save her people.

On and on the narratives go—and what do they have in common?

In calamity, which is plentiful in the Scriptures, there are equally extraordinary displays of hope. That men and women could endure inconceivable pain and still trust God is evidence of His goodness.

Perhaps one of the kindest things God did when He inspired the Bible was allow us to get a glimpse of the sorrow and tragedy that transpired over the biblical timeline. We aren't made to believe that Old or New Testament believers lived lives of comfort and ease.

God used forty individuals from widely assorted backgrounds over a period of roughly sixteen hundred years to record the words that sustain us in our hardest moments.

Repeatedly we see that hope sustains in moments of crisis.

Hope is the natural result of trust in God.

DAY 185

Isaiah 50:10

*Who is among you that fears the LORD, that obeys the voice of His servant, that walks in darkness and has no light? Let him **trust** in the name of the LORD and rely on his God.*

We are at God's mercy.

We depend on God whether we want to or not. He is the giver of life, the author of our faith, the maker and sustainer of the universe. With a nod of His head or a blink of His eye, He is powerful enough to blot us out of existence.

We might do well to question whether or not activities like the earth's rotation or the changing of the seasons or the rise and fall of day are truly perpetual—or whether God is simply faithful to continue speaking them into obedience. He is certainly capable of putting an end to it all—and we are, as a result, utterly dependent upon Him.

"And he is before all things, and in him all things hold together" (Colossians 1:17 ESV).

But more than dependence by compulsion, we should *want* to rely on God.

Reliance on Him means we run straightway to the throne of grace to find help when we need it—before running to everyone else. Reliance on Him means we trust though we can't see.

We should be at God's mercy because it's the very best place to be.

Matthew Henry wrote, "God has wisely kept us in the dark concerning future events and reserved for Himself the knowledge of them, that He may train us up in a dependence upon Himself and a continued readiness for every event."

Isaiah 51:5

*My righteousness is near, My salvation has gone forth,
And My arms will judge the peoples; the coastlands will
wait for Me, and for My arm they will wait expectantly.*

God is the only one who makes and keeps His promises perfectly.

We can wait on God with confidence because His promises endure forever (Isaiah 40:8).

It is tempting to wonder if God is near during seasons of waiting. There were weeks when we prayed for the same specific request continually and didn't have any reason, apart from the Word of God, to believe our prayers were being heard.

Waiting without discernible reassurance is agonizing.

But waiting without discernible reassurance proves the genuineness of our faith.

When things don't go as we have planned, it is natural for us to call out as Mary did when Jesus arrived to see Lazarus, "Lord, if you had been here, my brother would not have died" (John 11:32 ESV).

That is how it feels, isn't it?—that if God were near, things wouldn't be as difficult? If God were interested in our lives, we wouldn't be experiencing so much difficulty.

To believe this common misperception about God, that He would never allow something bad to happen, is to grossly miscalculate the Almighty. For to believe that He would never intentionally allow something bad into our lives is to believe that there are a great many things more powerful than He is. And if that is the case, we are all in danger of damnation.

So we must believe that God is near. And we must wait expectantly.

"For we walk by faith, not by sight" (2 Corinthians 5:7 ESV).

DAY 187

Isaiah 56:7

*Even those I will bring to My holy mountain and make them joyful in My house of **prayer**. Their burnt offerings and their sacrifices will be acceptable on My altar; for My house will be called a house of **prayer** for all the peoples.*

Joyful worship is the greatest remedy for a broken heart.

Sacrifice has always been an important part of God's economy. At one point in history, the sacrificial offering of animals was necessary to fulfill the law. But even in the Old Testament—and especially today—God's interests primarily lay in His children's willingness to offer their lives to Him.

"I appeal to you therefore, brothers, by the mercies of God, to present your bodies as a living sacrifice, holy and acceptable to God, which is your spiritual worship" (Romans 12:1 ESV).

It is the privilege of those of us who love God to worship Him. At the worst of times and with the heaviest of hearts, we do well to praise our Creator. Worship is motivated by the mercy of God, of which those who endure difficulty know well.

God wants us to pray to Him. So much so that He established a "house of prayer."

Of Isaiah 56:7, Matthew Henry wrote:

> Three things are promised. Assistance: I will not only bid them welcome, but incline them to come. Acceptance. And Comfort: though they came mourning to the house of prayer, they shall go away rejoicing. They shall find ease by casting their cares and burdens upon God. Many a sorrowful spirit has been made joyful in the house of prayer.

 Joyful worship is the greatest remedy for a broken heart.

DAY 188

Isaiah 57:10

*You were tired out by the length of your road, yet you
did not say, "It is **hopeless**." You found renewed strength,
therefore you did not faint.*

Hope unto itself is not the end goal.

We must hope for the right outcome, hope with the right strength,
and hope in the right Source. At first glance, Isaiah 57:10 could be a
life verse, the type that sustains us in struggle.

Finding renewed strength is the goal, after all.

But in context, the Israelites found renewed strength to pursue the
wrong things.

Idol worship, for the Israelites, was not benefiting them in any way. No
surprise, really. Yet they continued after their adoration of the wrong
gods with zeal. When they should have given up on their idolatry,
they caught a second wind to endure with enthusiasm.

Amazing, isn't it, that if we pursued God with the same eager
determination that we pursue the quick fixes of this world, we would
find the renewed strength that we are trying to manufacture? Hours
spent reading self-help literature could be invested in Bible reading
with greater results. Time spent talking to counselors could be spent
talking to God with better outcomes. Complaints could be replaced
with promises, grumbling exchanged for prayer.

The dedication of the Israelites was on target. But their aim wasn't
God.

And God makes all the difference.

"But they who wait for the LORD shall renew their strength; they shall
mount up with wings like eagles; they shall run and not be weary;
they shall walk and not faint" (Isaiah 40:31 ESV).

Isaiah 64:4

*For from days of old they have not heard or perceived by ear, nor has the eye seen a God besides You, Who acts in behalf of the one who **waits** for Him.*

When we wait for God, we do not run the risk of waiting in vain.

Waiting on God is not like waiting for the end of a book or movie in which we find out if we wasted our time by reading or watching. Waiting on God, per the promise of the Scriptures, is always a valuable exercise that yields more than we could ever imagine.

While we wait, it is only and ever God behind the scenes of our lives, constructing the events that will make us more like His Son.

When we recognize the goodness of God in our lives and understand that the details never escape His almighty attention, then we can do nothing other than praise Him.

No doubt, when we stand in heaven and see our lives for what they were, and understand that God allowed what He did because of love, we will stand slack-jawed, without the means or methods to show sufficient gratitude for these difficult days of waiting. Our praise and thanksgiving for all eternity will be our best efforts to provide return on His investment.

At times during our adoption wait, we questioned whether or not our humanity—which so often stood opposed to what God designed—could possibly thwart what God had planned for us. *What if we said the wrong thing? What if we didn't ask the right questions? What if we needlessly offended someone by our urgency to meet our child?*

Through studying God's Word, we came to understand that God knows best how to weave even our failures into His plan for our lives, which is only and always good.

While we wait, we recognize that we know the end of the story and it is perfect.

Jeremiah 14:22

*Are there any among the idols of the nations who give
rain? Or can the heavens grant showers? Is it not You, O
LORD our God? Therefore we **hope** in You, for You are the
one who has done all these things.*

We must never become accustomed to the fact that God loves us.

The most inconceivable truth in the entire Bible is this: "For God so
loved the world, that he gave his only Son, that whoever believes in
him should not perish but have eternal life" (John 3:16 ESV).

Some would translate the beginning of the verse to read, "For this
is how God loved the world." And this is how God loves the world
even now: God gives good gifts to His children, and the greatest gift
is Himself.

His first great gift was life. His second
great gift was Christ. His third great
gift is sustenance. For we truly have all
that we need when we have Him.

> *... we rest in the truth
> that God loves us.*

"If you then, who are evil, know how to give good gifts to your
children, how much more will your Father who is in heaven give good
things to those who ask him!" (Matthew 7:11 ESV).

God is the one, in the words of Jeremiah 14:22, who has done all these
things. No other god can do for us what God has done or plans to do.
Just as the false prophets discovered in Elijah's day, the only giver of
gifts is the one true God.

So while we wait for Him, we rest in the truth that God loves us.

DAY 191

Jeremiah 17:5

*Thus says the LORD, "Cursed is the man who **trusts** in mankind and makes flesh his strength, and whose heart turns away from the LORD."*

The war isn't primarily fought externally.

A battle as real as any being waged in the deserts of the Middle East rages in the minds and hearts of all believers over the answer to one question: In whom will you trust?

Answer: God. Of course God.

Five seconds in a Sunday School classroom for five-year-olds will yield that response.

Theologically we know that the answer is God. But what is the point of theology if it doesn't change how we live? If, in the moment of desperation, we question God's motives and doubt His goodness, and instead trust anyone and everyone else—then we do not trust in God.

As excruciating days, weeks, months, and years passed while we waited to hear about our son, we came to believe wholeheartedly that our greatest battles were fought internally. Externally, we could do the right things.

Internally, we battled a mind that was hard-wired to sin.

In Andrew Murray's book, *Waiting on God*, he writes: "Seek not only the help, the gift, seek Himself; wait for Him. Give God His glory by resting in Him, by trusting Him fully, by waiting patiently for Him. This patience honors Him greatly. It leaves Him, as God on the throne, to do His work. It yields self wholly into His hands. It lets God be God."

God cares for those who trust Him.

DAY 192

Jeremiah 17:7

*Blessed is the man who **trusts** in the LORD And whose
trust is the LORD.*

We will never find joy apart from Jesus Christ.

We were excited whenever we received news about our son. We were
thrilled whenever it looked like our case was beginning to move.

*He had a good doctor's appointment. He is healthy. His favorite
word is "dog."*

You'd think each notification we received—each detail we learned
about our little boy—was of national or even global significance. We
certainly celebrated as if that were the case.

But each piece of good news lasted only long enough for us to want
the next piece of good news and the next. Sadly, if our lives had risen
and fallen on news of our adoption, we would have spent the better
part of two years depressed.

The words "Contact us again next week" became our least favorite.

And then we discovered Paul's words in Philippians 4:11, "For I
have learned in whatever situation I am to be content" (ESV). And
we understood, perhaps better than any other time in our lives, that
contentment is a learned behavior.

Paul's sense of security had nothing to do with his circumstances.
The entirety of Paul's contentment originated and continued in his
relationship with Christ.

Because of Christ, joy is absolutely possible in any situation.

DAY 193

Jeremiah 17:13

*O LORD, the **hope** of Israel, all who forsake You will
be put to shame. Those who turn away on earth will be
written down, because they have forsaken the fountain of
living water, even the LORD.*

Trusting anything apart from God is idolatry.

Though at times it can be tempting to trust many things other than
God, it is always wrong to do so.

For us, we were tempted to trust social workers, government officials,
economic stability, savings accounts, and political peace. Though we
would never have said we trusted these things, the true test of our
trust lay in what it took for us to feel hopeless.

If we were tempted to despair—when the social worker was at a
loss to help us or the government officials returned our documents
incomplete or the economy nose-dived or the savings account
dwindled, or the uprising overseas heightened (which it all did)—
then that was where our hope was anchored.

If we weathered the disappointments with holy confidence that God
was in control, we knew our trust was safely in Him.

As Christians, we are tempted to think that it is no big deal to put
our trust in something else, but God takes it seriously. There are far-
reaching theological consequences to trusting the wrong source. To
trust in anyone or anything apart from God is to be put to shame.

God Himself is unchanging. God alone is trustworthy.

"It is better to take refuge in the LORD than to trust in man" (Psalm
118:8 ESV).

Jeremiah 29:11

*"For I know the plans that I have for you," declares the LORD, "plans for welfare and not for calamity to give you a future and a **hope**."*

God has a plan for our lives that is far beyond our imagination.

C.S. Lewis, wrote of this idea:

> It would seem that Our Lord finds our desires not too strong, but too weak. We are half-hearted creatures, fooling about with drink and sex and ambition when infinite joy is offered us, like an ignorant child who wants to go on making mud pies in a slum because he cannot imagine what is meant by the offer of a holiday at the sea. We are far too easily pleased.

Without a doubt, we are too easily satisfied if we want an outcome—a better diagnosis, a baby, a job—instead of God's glory and goodness for our lives.

The truth is, if we love God, and if we love God's Word, we should therefore learn to love His plans for us, no matter how obscured from our view they currently seem to be.

A dear family friend was dying of cancer; someone we would have longed to introduce our child to. Upon visiting her in the hospital, we noticed an index card tucked in her Bible with Jeremiah 29:11-13 written in careful penmanship. She gave us the card, and it is now displayed in a place in our home where we can daily be reminded: "For I know the plans I have for you, declares the LORD, plans for welfare and not for evil, to give you a future and a hope. Then you will call upon me and come and pray to me, and I will hear you. You will seek me and find me, when you seek me with all your heart" (ESV).

DAY 195

Jeremiah 29:12

*"Then you will call upon Me and come and **pray** to Me, and I will listen to you."*

Prayer equips us to wait correctly.

The Bible makes it clear that if we are not praying diligently, we are not equipped to handle what God has called us to endure. Like a vehicle sputtering along the highway on an empty gas tank, our own strength is futile in the race that is our lives without the power of prayer.

God has graciously invited us to participate in His divine plan for our lives through prayer. Instead of arguing over the parts of our lives over which we have no control, we must avail ourselves of the means God has given us to contribute to His plan.

Jeremiah 29:12 is a gift. God could have commanded us to pray and told us nothing more about it. Yet He gave us the insight to understand that He does listen. Can we truly comprehend it? God of Glory listens to *us*.

We couldn't reach the embassy of our son's country if we tried, yet we could reach God's ears in a heartbeat. God tells us that He is a God who hears. He listens to our requests and answers them according to His will.

Jeremiah 29:13 declares, in no uncertain terms: "You will seek me and find me, when you seek me with all your heart" (ESV).

Refusing to seek God demonstrates disinterest in finding Him.

And refusing to use the resources that God has provided us is nothing but our own fault. It is choosing to run on an empty gas tank when all the necessary fuel is at our disposal.

DAY 196

Jeremiah 31:17

*"There is **hope** for your future," declares the LORD, "And your children will return to their own territory."*

God always keeps His promises.

That said, we must accept that it's not always God's plan to remove our pain in this life.

Jeremiah 31:17 must have seemed like an odd declaration at the time it was said. The words were delivered to a people who were on their way to exile. Like a convict being led to the gas chamber and hearing, "You still have hope," the Israelites were given the promise of hope in extremely dreary circumstances.

Yet the promise was delivered by a loving God with an eternal perspective, unlike ours.

The truth we sometimes fail to recognize is that God's promises do not need to be fulfilled on our timeline or even in our lifetime for them to be perfect. Yet what God promises to do, He will absolutely do because His name is at stake.

No matter how permanent or perplexing our present circumstances are, we can hope in God. If God says everything will work together for our good, we can bank on it.

During the time of our testing, we understood that God gives grace, but He doesn't promise us tomorrow's grace before tomorrow's need. Nor does He withhold today's grace from us when we need it today. So when the picture of our future is bleak, we can still trust that God is in control and we can still have hope.

We can say with Paul, "But he said to me, 'My grace is sufficient for you, for my power is made perfect in weakness.' Therefore I will boast all the more gladly of my weaknesses, so that the power of Christ may rest upon me" (2 Corinthians 12:9 ESV).

DAY 197

Jeremiah 39:18

*"For I will certainly rescue you, and you will not fall by the sword; but you will have your own life as booty, because you have **trusted** in Me," declares the LORD.*

Trusting God is always the command.

Trusting God in spite of our questions is the difficulty.

Most often in waiting, there are questions: *Why this? Why now? Why me?*

Questions for the Lord are not of themselves a bad thing. As He was dying on the cross, Christ called out to His Father, "Eli, Eli, lema sabachthani?"

"My God, my God, why have you forsaken me?" (Matthew 27:46 ESV).

Yet none would doubt that Christ trusted His Father. We know Christ trusted God perfectly because Christ was sinless and trust in God is always the command, in spite of the questions.

Trusting God is always of significant benefit to the believer in times of testing. In addition to experiencing the precious, inimitable presence of the Lord, there is often the added benefit that accompanies obedience.

Sometimes we receive answers. Sometimes we receive deliverance.

Ebed-melech trusted God in Jeremiah 39 and chose to be kind to the prophet Jeremiah, even when his life was on the line. Because of this, God spared Ebed-melech from the siege that cost the king his family and eyesight.

No matter what the outcome of our testing—whether we are called to endure testing or receive deliverance—trusting God is always our assignment.

DAY 198

Lamentations 3:18

*So I say, "My strength has perished, and so has my **hope** from the LORD."*

An obstacle-free life warrants no trust.

We would know nothing about God's sustaining grace—or His power in our weakness—accessible to us if we know Him, if we did not experience difficulty.

As much as the idea of a trial-free life appeals to us, there are precious dimensions of God's character that we would know nothing about if we were not made to travel with Him through difficulty.

We would not know God to be our Shepherd and would not relate to Him as our Sustainer; we would not know Him to be our Rock or refer to Him as our Stronghold. Like the spoiled child who always receives what he wants from his indulgent dad, we would relate to God as a vending machine—asking and receiving—but never strengthening a relationship that was built to last for eternity.

All of that in exchange for an easy existence on earth would hardly be worth it.

In Lamentations 3, the prophet has reached the end of his rope. His heart cry is similar to Job's in Job 17:15 (ESV), "Where then is my hope? Who will see my hope?"

God was gracious to include these bitter moments in the Bible. For one, we observe the humanity of men and women we greatly respect. We recognize that people like David, Abraham, Moses, and Gideon were equipped with the same flawed hearts that exist within us.

For another, we recognize the roadmap to finding relief from God.

By Lamentations 3:21, the prophet reached the destination we all desire: hope in God.

DAY 199

Lamentations 3:21

*This I recall to my mind, therefore I have **hope**.*

Hope in God is healing.

The book of Lamentations was written in a landscape that offered little encouragement. The very name *Lamentations* is indicative of grief. So it is—in the midst of this heavy text—that a light shines through as bright as the morning sun: Hope is the bright spot in Lamentations.

Jeremiah, who had previously been a man crying out in anguish, recalled the goodness of God and recognized it as hope for his life.

We must do the same thing when we are parched. Waiting can leave us weary.

But God is unfathomably and perfectly good.

God has saved us and is more for us than a Savior when we die. He is our Savior now—in this life. The same hope that we have in this life will be the hope we have for all eternity.

This we recall to mind. *This* gives us hope. What God promises to be for us in this life and in the next should make us hopeful people.

God is bent on finishing the work in us that He began.

Here is our hope: "The LORD will fulfill his purpose for me; your steadfast love, O LORD, endures forever. Do not forsake the work of your hands" (Psalm 138:8 ESV).

> *God is bent on finishing the work in us that He began.*

DAY 200

Lamentations 3:24

"The LORD is my portion," says my soul, "Therefore I have **hope** *in Him."*

No matter how bad life gets, we have the capacity to trust in the Lord.

If we do not trust God, it is not God's fault.

Lamentations 3 was written at a time when Judah was experiencing God's holy judgment. Yet, even in the midst of God's righteous wrath, God demonstrated His love by empowering His children to trust in Him.

God always empowers His children to trust Him.

Doubting that God will do what He says is the root of all insecurity in Christ.

"For the one who doubts is like a wave of the sea that is driven and tossed by the wind. For that person must not suppose that he will receive anything from the Lord; he is a double-minded man, unstable in all his ways" (James 1:6–8 ESV).

Hoping in God, therefore, has implications for all of life.

Thomas Manton, a seventeenth-century English Puritan, wrote:

> Men deceive themselves when they think they doubt because they know not the will of God: their main hesitancy is at His power. Look, as in the case of conversion, we pretend we cannot, when indeed we will not, so oppositely, in the case of faith, we pretend we know not God's will when we indeed we doubt His can. Therefore the main work of your faith is to give Him the glory of His power, leaving His will to Himself.

"Leaving His will to Himself" and glorifying Him for who He is—that is the challenge.

DAY 201

Lamentations 3:25

*The LORD is good to those who **wait** for Him, to the person who seeks Him.*

We like to ascribe good things to God: God provided money for the bills. God spared the soldier's life. God saved the agnostic neighbor.

It is true that those good things belong to God. But it is far more difficult for us to ascribe the difficult things—the trials, adversities, disappointments, pain—to the same good God.

Perhaps our view of God's sovereignty isn't always the issue at stake. Maybe our understanding of what is "good" causes us trouble. Scripture is clear that God wants what is good for His children.

"For the LORD God is a sun and shield; the LORD bestows favor and honor. No good thing does he withhold from those who walk uprightly" (Psalm 84:11 ESV).

Meaning what is painful isn't always bad.

In fact, the difficult experience we are facing must be a very good thing.

God's purpose for us is always good because God is always good.

> *Scripture is clear that God wants what is good for His children.*

Lamentations 3:26

*It is good that he **waits** silently for the salvation of
the LORD.*

God's got it all under control.

For sanctified sinners, the road between devotion and despair is
very short. The Lord does something for us—answers our prayer,
perhaps—and we tell everyone how good He is. Days later, we find
out the answer to another prayer is not what we wanted and we doubt
His goodness.

As Lamentations exhorts, it is good to wait silently for God's
salvation.

Lashing out at our Heavenly Father is synonymous with saying He
is not good. Ultimately, when we accuse God of faulty timelines or
misappropriated power or lack of effort on our behalf, we are saying
that He is not who He says He is.

But God is only good and only does good.

God has everything under His control.

Though not the most well-known verse in *Be Thou My Vision*, the
third reads:

Be Thou my battle Shield, Sword for the fight;
Be Thou my Dignity, Thou my Delight;
Thou my soul's Shelter, Thou my high Tower:
Raise Thou me heavenward, O Power of my power.

It is good to wait for God's deliverance!

DAY 203

Lamentations 3:56

You have heard my voice, do not hide Your ear from my
prayer *for relief, from my cry for help.*

God is a proven stronghold (Nahum 1:7).

Though we do not understand why God allows various events to unfold in our lives or in the lives of those we love, we know that He can only do good. So when we observe difficult things and are tempted to believe the worst about a situation or outcome, we must rest assured that God is still our good and faithful God.

The author of Lamentations has seen the effects of God's judgment on the people of Israel, yet he still sees God as his rescuer. He knows that despite his circumstances, God is his only hope, so his prayers continue.

Even in challenging circumstances, we can experience God's goodness to us through His willingness to hear our prayers for relief.

The overwhelming truth is that man's deepest lows do not prevent him from reaching God in Heaven by prayer. No pit, no valley, no foxhole, or no cave can bar a man from communing with Christ in prayer.

God is our everlasting fortress, our garrison, our citadel.

Jonah discovered God's accessibility from the belly of a fish. Paul and Silas found God to be reachable from prison. David communed with God while hiding in caves from his enemies.

God will not close His ears to the prayers of His children, no matter the depth of their location or situation.

DAY 204

Daniel 3:28

*Nebuchadnezzar responded and said, "Blessed be the God of Shadrach, Meshach and Abed-nego, who has sent His angel and delivered His servants who put their **trust** in Him, violating the king's command, and yielded up their bodies so as not to serve or worship any god except their own God."*

Testing is not an indication that God is displeased with us.

In addition to the well-known example of the young men from Judah who were brought into the court of King Nebuchadnezzar—refusing to worship anyone but the true and living God—and were thrown into the blazing furnace as a result, we have a second powerful illustration.

Matthew 3:17 (ESV) said of Christ, "And behold, a voice from heaven said, 'This is my beloved Son, with whom I am well pleased.'" The verse immediately following reads: "Then Jesus was led up by the Spirit into the wilderness to be tempted by the devil" (Matthew 4:1 ESV).

Though we know that Jesus never sinned, it is profound that these two verses would appear side by side in the Bible. God expressed His delight in His Son and then ordained His wilderness testing immediately thereafter. Perhaps the biblical order was meant to further indicate that God's testing does not suggest certain dissatisfaction by the Father.

We know Job was selected to suffer *because* he was righteous (Job 1:8).

God ordains the method and the means of our service in suffering for Him. Both Job and the young men in King Nebuchadnezzar's court in addition to Jesus Christ in the wilderness would, by their example, testify to the reality that God is the only one in whom we can trust.

Our response to difficulty must be the same as Christ's reply to Satan.

We must worship God alone, trusting that He knows best what we need (Matthew 4:10).

DAY 205

Daniel 6:10

*Now when Daniel knew that the document was signed,
he entered his house (now in his roof chamber he had
windows open toward Jerusalem); and he continued
kneeling on his knees three times a day, **praying** and giving
thanks before his God, as he had been doing previously.*

Trials tempt us to question our allegiance to God.

Daniel's commitment to pray and trust the Lord even when his life
was on the line was a testimony to those who were watching.

Difficulty will yield clarity of purpose and strength of resolve.

Trials will either confirm what we already know to be true about God,
or trials will convince us that what we thought we knew we never
knew at all.

Those who trust God will find God to be more than enough. Those
who do not trust God will drift from any religious pretense.

And those who remain steady on the course will be a testimony to
those who watch.

Ninety-nine people could make the right decisions—to love and trust
the Lord in good times—but the one-hundredth person who does
so in the midst of difficult circumstances is of more value than the
ninety-nine to the non-converted masses who are watching.

For to trust in trial is to prove that He is true.

C. S. Lewis said it best: "God whispers
to us in our pleasures, speaks in our
conscience, but shouts in our pains; it is
His megaphone to rouse a deaf world."

> *Difficulty will yield
> clarity of purpose
> and strength of
> resolve.*

DAY 206

Daniel 6:23

> *Then the king was very pleased and gave orders for Daniel*
> *to be taken up out of the den. So Daniel was taken up*
> *out of the den and no injury whatever was found on him,*
> *because he had **trusted** in his God.*

Trust in God does not always mean escape from difficulty.

Many godly men and women have lost their lives for faith in Christ. Indeed, the apostles faced persecution while exhibiting tremendous trust in God.

On one hand, that the godly suffer persecution should encourage us that maltreatment is not the chastisement of our good and loving Father. On the other hand, it should remind us that trust in God during trials, regardless of any potential outcome, is of paramount importance.

As Daniel demonstrated before being thrown into the den of lions, trusting God means doing what God has explicitly told us to do and then believing that He will take care of us in the midst of it.

Those who obey do not weigh odds or consult probabilities before choosing to act.

Daniel was delivered because God believed Daniel's life better glorified Him at that moment in history than Daniel's death. But for Christians before and after Daniel's experience with the lions, that hasn't always been the case.

Our faith must be biblically-informed—substantiated by the Scriptures, and fortified by prayer.

> *Those who obey do not weigh odds or consult probabilities before choosing to act.*

DAY 207

Daniel 9:3

*So I gave my attention to the Lord God to seek Him
by **prayer** and supplications, with fasting, sackcloth
and ashes.*

It is impossible for us to manipulate God.

It is easy to try to transform our behavior for the purpose of getting what we want. Perhaps if we can perfect the externals of trust, hope, and prayer, then we can convince God to give us what we request.

But if we trust, hope, and pray the way God designs, then we will not primarily be concerned with the outcome of our situation. We will be more concerned with the condition of our hearts. We will want God's glory more than want His gifts.

We should be motivated by love for God to trust, hope, and pray, leaving the formula of our behavior and His blessing to Him.

Christ was gracious to set an example of enduring difficulty and obeying perfectly without manipulating His Father.

"For to this you have been called, because Christ also suffered for you, leaving you an example, so that you might follow in his steps. He committed no sin, neither was deceit found in his mouth. When he was reviled, he did not revile in return; when he suffered, he did not threaten, but continued entrusting himself to him who judges justly" (1 Peter 2:21–23 ESV).

Prayer is not simply a tool for getting what we want from God. Daniel 9:3 is the opening to a heartfelt and humble acknowledgment of the sins of a nation and a pleading for forgiveness and restoration.

It is impossible to deceive God.

Daniel 9:4

*I **prayed** to the LORD my God and confessed and said,
"Alas, O Lord, the great and awesome God, who keeps His
covenant and lovingkindness for those who love Him and
keep His commandments."*

Gratitude to God stems from loving Him.

If we are not adequately thankful for what He has done, it is, at least
in part, due to our not adequately loving who He is.

That Daniel loved God fueled his gratitude which sustained him for
the periods of waiting that God would call him to endure.

Daniel's prayer, recorded in Daniel 9:4, instructs us on how we should
pray: we must humble ourselves and extol the goodness of God. It is
both that simple and that difficult.

To truly humble ourselves—enough to admit that what God is
choosing to do right now is absolutely right—and to extol His
goodness —even when we do not always recognize it as readily as we
should—is the believer's twofold objective.

We must be more than grateful for what God gives us.

We must be grateful for who God is.

Waiting requires us to pray in the way Daniel prayed, by viewing our
God and ourselves correctly.

"Know therefore that the LORD your God is God, the faithful God
who keeps covenant and steadfast love with those who love him and
keep his commandments, to a thousand generations" (Deuteronomy
7:9 ESV).

*... we must humble ourselves and extol the goodness of
God. It is both that simple and that difficult.*

DAY 209

Daniel 9:17

*"So now, our God, listen to the **prayer** of Your servant and
to his supplications, and for Your sake, O Lord, let Your
face shine on Your desolate sanctuary."*

If God is in the midst of the storm, why would we want to be anywhere else?

The Bible is clear—God is our help in trouble and not our escape out of it (Psalm 46:1).

If we believe, even momentarily, that our difficulty is evidence that Christ is not nearby us as He promised to be, then we do not understand the love of God.

God is with us in the difficulties. He doesn't expect us to travel alone.

If we knew with certainty that our best communion with God would happen in the midst of waiting, would we accept it more patiently, endure it more willingly, and embrace it more wholeheartedly?

Or would we still want it to be over at the first opportunity?

We were faced with this question late into our wait. After recognizing that we had grown closer to the Lord—understood parts of His Word and the anatomy of our own souls better than before—we came to Paul's conclusion in Philippians 3:8 and 10: "Indeed, I count everything as loss because of the surpassing worth of knowing Christ Jesus my Lord. For his sake I have suffered the loss of all things and count them as rubbish, in order that I may gain Christ . . . that I may know him and the power of his resurrection, and may share his sufferings, becoming like him in his death" (ESV).

Unlike us, God's primary focus in giving gifts is not the happiness of the recipient but the righteous glory it brings Him. Daniel sought the restoration of Israel for the glory of God.

We pray for the gift of our son if it would bring God the most glory.

DAY 210

Hosea 12:6

*Therefore, return to your God, Observe kindness and justice, and **wait** for your God continually.*

We must believe that God loves us supremely and only wants what is best for our lives.

All temptation on earth, beginning with Satan's lie to Eve, entices us to believe that God doesn't really love us enough.

Isn't that the difficulty? At the root of our failure to trust God and wait for Him correctly is a struggle to accept that everything God does for us is done in love.

"If God loved me, He would give me what I want" must be replaced with "Because God loves me, He withholds what I do not currently need."

We cannot doubt His love.

"Greater love has no one than this, that someone lay down his life for his friends" (John 15:13 ESV).

"For God so loved the world, that he gave his only Son, that whoever believes in him should not perish but have eternal life" (John 3:16 ESV).

When we believe God loves us and has our best interest in mind, we will *wait well.*

Loving God is evidenced by our obedience.

DAY 211

Jonah 2:1

*Then Jonah **prayed** to the LORD his God from the
stomach of the fish.*

What God does for us may not be punishment at all. It may be the
kindest thing.

When Jonah prayed to God from the stomach of the fish, he had
no way of knowing that God would give him another chance. Most
remarkable, then, is that Jonah's prayer was one of thanksgiving and
not one of deliverance (Jonah 2:9).

From inside the fish, Jonah recognized that God had spared him from
drowning and therefore identified this astonishing survival as God's
hand on his life. What was uncomfortable for Jonah could have been
much worse.

What we learn from Jonah's trial is simple: God ordains the means as
well as the end of our journey through suffering.

God doesn't just allow us to face difficulties in the process of
transforming us to Christlikeness—He decrees the means of our
transformation. He places the fish in the right spot, He sends most
of the army home, and He allows the wine at the wedding feast to
run dry.

And what looks from every angle to be the makings of a disaster is
really only God preparing to do something extraordinary.

What God does for us is not about retribution. It's for His glory.

DAY 212

Jonah 2:7

*While I was fainting away, I remembered the LORD, and my **prayer** came to You, Into Your holy temple.*

Our praying should reflect that we are desperate for the Lord's help.

The world provides many options in which we can take refuge during times of difficulty. Entertainment, shopping, eating, relationships, and music have been used by refuge-seeking people for centuries.

And if we are honest, they work . . . for an afternoon.

We get caught up in the euphoria of an experience, and we forget our pain for a moment.

While we were waiting for news about our adoption, we would often receive the encouragement from a pitying friend to try a specific restaurant or watch a particular movie. Our friends wanted for us what we wanted for ourselves, an oasis from the discouragement.

Indeed, we needed an escape. There was no question about it.

But God designed a perfect sanctuary that He knew would encourage those who were prone to faint. God gave us the refuge of Himself, accessible by prayer at any time. And His refuge was built for eternity.

There is no question about it, we need God every day. But on days when we are fainting away, we know most acutely that we do.

We feel our need for God when we are exhausted, and it is kind that God enables us to feel this need for Him.

"God is our refuge and strength, a very present help in trouble" (Psalm 46:1 ESV).

Jonah 4:2

*He **prayed** to the LORD and said, "Please LORD, was
not this what I said while I was still in my own country?
Therefore in order to forestall this I fled to Tarshish, for
I knew that You are a gracious and compassionate God,
slow to anger and abundant in lovingkindness, and one
who relents concerning calamity."*

Shame on us for forgetting how much God loves us.

It is easy in times of testing to criticize the pain or stress over the losses. But when we do, we fail to recognize that God is allowing each complexity, each disappointment to make us more like Him. Waiting on God is itself an exercise of becoming more like Christ.

God loves us infinitely and perfectly.

In Jonah 4:2, the prophet was displeased that God was willing to forgive the people of Nineveh. They had sinned greatly against the Lord, and yet God was willing to love and forgive. This angered Jonah so much so that in his prayer, in which he lashed out at his Creator, he told the Lord that he fled to Tarshish for this very reason: *God is gracious and compassionate.*

And, on one hand, Jonah was right. The Bible makes it clear that God is a good and loving God who is rich in love and mercy.

What Jonah failed to recognize, however, is that the same compassion God demonstrated to the people of Tarshish, He also demonstrated to Jonah.

And the love that God bestowed to Jonah, He now lavishes on us.

"For great is his steadfast love toward us, and the faithfulness of the LORD endures forever. Praise the LORD!" (Psalm 117:2 ESV).

DAY 214

Micah 7:7

But as for me, I will watch expectantly for the LORD;
*I will **wait** for the God of my salvation. My God will*
hear me.

The God who created us knows best how to comfort us.

Micah 7 opens on a dreary scene where Micah is visibly a man in misery. Searching for righteousness and finding only evil, he is desperately in need of confirmation that God is still in control. The situation all around him is bleak at best.

Occasions exist in every season of testing where God's people seek evidence of His involvement. We want to believe—don't we?—that God is aware and attentive to our plight. Even when times are tough, we want to see evidence of God's concern.

Nothing is more terrifying than believing that God has left us alone to figure things out.

Thankfully, for the child of God, we need not fear His lack of interest.

Verses like Hebrews 13:5 remind us that we have all we need to live satisfied lives: "Keep your life free from love of money, and be content with what you have, for he has said, 'I will never leave you nor forsake you'" (ESV).

Though the beginning of Micah 7 records the laments of a miserable man, the chapter concludes with words about the faithfulness of God.

"You will show faithfulness to Jacob and steadfast love to Abraham, as you have sworn to our fathers from the days of old" (Micah 7: 20 ESV).

On our hardest days of waiting, we will still find God to be faithful to His Word.

DAY 215

Zephaniah 3:2

*She heeded no voice, she accepted no instruction, she did not **trust** in the LORD, she did not draw near to her God.*

We must draw near to God.

Zephaniah 3:2 speaks of a time in Jerusalem's history when she would learn the hard way that disobeying God, by refusing to trust or listen to His voice, leads to God's chastisement.

Unlike the Psalms or Proverbs where personal application beams off the page, the passage from Zephaniah isn't the easiest passage to identify with until you read the last eight words: "She did not draw near to her God."

Sadly, we can identify with this when God's wisdom doesn't seem wise to us and when we are prone to doubt His involvement in the details of our lives.

It is safe to say that we make our difficulty worse when we refuse to draw near to God. We were made for a relationship with Him. Our salvation is about so much more than rescue from hell or entrance into heaven. While we have the Scripturally-identified benefit of missing hell eternally if we are God's child, we also have the greatest benefit of experiencing everlasting communion with our Father.

We need not wait for eternity to draw close to Him.

In times of waiting, we must learn to say with the writer of Psalm 73:28: "But for me it is good to be near God; I have made the Lord GOD my refuge, that I may tell of all your works" (ESV).

 We need not wait for eternity to draw close to Him.

DAY 216

Matthew 5:44

*But I say to you, love your enemies and **pray** for those who persecute you.*

We must resist the temptation to respond to those who hurt us by sinning against them.

It is a challenging yet indispensable task that we pray for those who discourage us. Included in the Sermon on the Mount, spoken by Christ Himself, were these words: "But I say to you who hear, Love your enemies, do good to those who hate you, bless those who curse you, pray for those who abuse you" (Luke 6:27–28 ESV).

In the task of waiting, we encounter all kinds of people—those who understand and empathize with the assignment, those who haven't necessarily experienced great lengths of waiting but offer their support nonetheless, and those who for reasons unknown to us are callous or uncaring—and all of them need God's love.

We need God's love. Christ also said in His sermon, "And as you wish that others would do to you, do so to them" (Luke 6:31 ESV).

And so, with that in mind, we must model for those who are watching us—whether they are for us or against us—that we are satisfied in the all-sufficiency of God. We should pray for them. We should love them. When they encounter periods of difficult waiting, we should assist them.

> *It is a challenging yet indispensable task that we pray for those who discourage us.*
>
>

And we should want the same profound contentment for their lives that we have found.

DAY 217

Matthew 6:5

*When you **pray**, you are not to be like the hypocrites; for they love to stand and **pray** in the synagogues and on the street corners so that they may be seen by men. Truly I say to you, they have their reward in full.*

To live in private what we believe in public, we must pray with persistence.

In Matthew 6:5, Christ was not condemning all public prayer— certainly He prayed publicly at times (Luke 9:16)—but He was advising against prayer that was offered to gain the approval of men. Certainly prayer prayed for the praise of men is not intended for the ear of God.

Thus the Bible says that hypocritical public prayer has its reward in full.

Sometimes the sweetest times of prayer are the private times of pleading, or the joyful expressions overflowing from a heart that is thrilled with God's compassion.

The Bible brims with examples of believers who were equipped to complete their assignments through the exercise of private prayer: Jabez, David, Hannah, Hezekiah, Abraham, and a host of others met God privately. Their lives reflected the benefits of doing so.

We bear hundreds of burdens that friends may know nothing about. So it should be our delight to meet with God alone, to speak to Him *who knows.*

We should pray for God's deliverance.

We should pray for God's grace.

We should pray for the private, weighty burdens of our heart.

And in meeting God alone, we will cherish Him even more, share the experience of walking a difficult road with Him, and know in the end that He alone equipped and sustained us for the task.

DAY 218

Matthew 6:6

*But you, when you **pray**, go into your inner room,*
*close your door and **pray** to your Father who is in secret,*
and your Father who sees what is done in secret will
reward you.

It is our privilege to address God as "Father."

After nearly twenty months of waiting to receive word about our adoption, we were given the rare opportunity to address the director of our son's overseas orphanage through an e-mail.

Imagine our dilemma. We had many things we wanted to say—"Please let us come and get our child!"—being at the top of the list. But this was the orphanage director, a key participant in the success of our adoption. We knew that when we addressed her, what we asked for, and how we presented ourselves could have a lasting effect on our ability to bring our son home.

Saying the wrong thing, or even the right thing in the wrong way, could be damaging.

In many respects, we should be afraid to talk to God. He is the Ruler of the world, the Maker of the universe, and the King of kings. He is *the* key participant in the events of our lives.

And yet, we have the privilege of calling Him, "Abba, Father."

"See what kind of love the Father has given to us, that we should be called children of God; and so we are" (1 John 3:1 ESV).

We closed our e-mail to the director with these words, "Please know that, when we adopt our child, we will teach him about your kindness to us and your work on our behalf."

The same—and so much more—could be said of our Heavenly Father.

DAY 219

Matthew 6:7

*And when you are **praying**, do not use meaningless
repetition as the Gentiles do, for they suppose that they
will be heard for their many words.*

There is a difference between repetition and persistence when it comes
to prayer.

Prayer is not meant to be ritualistic or punitive.

Those who pray, repeating things dozens of times and keeping careful
count so as to reach a specified number, miss the point entirely.

Herein is the formula for prayer: we bring our requests to God and
God does what He sees fit.

For over twelve months, we did not receive any positive news about
our adoption. Twelve long months, to us, felt like a lifetime to wait.
Each e-mail, phone call, or letter was filled with more disappointing
news.

When we eventually received some information that wasn't necessarily
negative—news we clung to like children cling to their mothers to
avoid going to the nursery—our elation was short-lived. Days later,
we received the worst report we had received all along.

It was easy to begin using prayer as an ordering service. Fairly quickly
into our adoption experience, we found ourselves praying, ". . . and
we need . . . and please give . . . and could You grant . . ."

But prayer is not about vain repetition, and prayer is not about getting
what we want.

Prayer is about worship. We must be careful to worship God and
not ourselves.

DAY 220

Matthew 6:9

Pray, then, in this way: Our Father who is in heaven,
Hallowed be Your name.

The Lord was gracious to give us a model for prayer, but it wasn't His design that we be so consumed with the mechanics that we miss the motivation.

Our Father is the reason we pray.

We pray because of what He has done and because of what He is doing. We pray because of the perfect obedience of Jesus Christ. We meet with God—commune with Him—when we call on His name.

Hallowed be His name should be the prayer of our hearts.

We pray because Isaiah 45:7 says: "I form light and create darkness, I make well-being and create calamity, I am the LORD, who does all these things" (ESV).

We pray because it would be ridiculous for us to run to anyone or anything else in the hope of fixing our problems or solving our dilemmas. *Our Father* is the architect behind every event in our lives and He uses each incident to make us more like His Son.

Why would we rather talk to anyone else? In 1889, B.P. Hall wrote:

> It is not the arithmetic of our prayers, how many. It is not the
> rhetoric of our prayers, how eloquent. It is not the geometry of our
> prayers, how long. It is not the music of our prayers, how sweet. It is
> not the logic of our prayers, how argumentative. It is not the method
> of our prayers, how orderly. But, how fervent and how believing are
> our prayers?

DAY 221

Matthew 12:21

*AND IN HIS NAME THE GENTILES WILL **HOPE**.*

Hope is never the product of an internal search.

No amount of examining personal motives or purifying private thoughts will generate what only God is able to give to us.

All man-made hope is therefore artificial.

From the beginning of time, God has been the sole source of His people's hope.

Isaiah 9:2 speaks of a difficult period for the people of God in which they lived in "a land of deep darkness." And then with a promise that would forever alter the course of history, a light shone that caused them to rejoice exceedingly.

This light was hope, recorded four verses later: "For to us a child is born, to us a son is given; and the government shall be upon his shoulder, and his name shall be called, Wonderful Counselor, Mighty God, Everlasting Father, Prince of Peace" (Isaiah 9:6 ESV).

Into dark moments, God delights to provide His hope.

God has only ever been the true hope for His people.

In Matthew 12, when the Pharisees were conspiring how they might destroy Christ, He was still interested in bringing hope to those who would receive it.

In our own moments of darkness—knowing we cannot generate the hope that we need—we must trust the One who has promised to be hope for us all along.

DAY 222

Matthew 14:23

*After He had sent the crowds away, He went up on the mountain by Himself to **pray**; and when it was evening, He was there alone.*

When waiting is most difficult, we never go wrong by praying.

It could be argued that if anyone who walked on this earth was strong enough to do it without prayer, it was Christ. He was perfect after all, and totally equipped for His earthly ministry (2 Corinthians 5:21).

Yet He spent time alone in prayer.

Sending everyone else away so He could spend time communing with His Heavenly Father, Jesus prepared Himself for the trials yet to come. And even in His darkest hour—while enduring tremendous pain on the cross for our sins—He continued praying to God.

Christ's final words were in prayer: "Then Jesus, calling out with a loud voice, said, 'Father, into your hands I commit my spirit!' And having said this he breathed his last" (Luke 23:46 ESV).

We, too, must fortify ourselves with prayer.

We must pray before we encounter a difficulty, when in the midst of the difficulty, and after the difficulty subsides.

We must recognize that when we don't pray, we are, in essence, casting doubt on its ability to make any difference in our lives.

Prayer—communion with God—fortified Jesus Christ, and will do the same for us.

DAY 223

Matthew 21:22

*"And all things you ask in **prayer**, believing, you
will receive."*

You will never receive an answer to a prayer you never offer.

In the margin of our Bible, alongside James 5, we wrote those words.
And time and again we were reminded of them when unpetitioned
requests went unanswered.

It's easy to throw our hands in the air and accuse God of not answering
our prayer when—if the truth were told—we really aren't praying the
type of prayer that deserves to be answered.

Why should the God of heaven respond to the grunts of men?

Throughout the Book of Matthew, believers are exhorted to petition
the Lord. Matthew 7:7 is perhaps the most well-known of the verses:
"Ask, and it will be given to you; seek, and you will find; knock, and it
will be opened to you" (ESV). We would do well to read the thoughts
in reverse.

*Don't ask and you won't receive. Don't seek and you've won't find.
Don't knock and the door will not be opened.*

If the verse were written that way, how would it change our perspective
of prayer?

We must be serious about our prayer life. God would not repeatedly
tell us to do something that was of little value to Him. That He
repeatedly prompts us to approach His throne with our requests
should persuade us that prayer is a powerful tool.

In the process of waiting on God, we would be wise to pray.

DAY 224

Matthew 26:36

*Then Jesus came with them to a place called Gethsemane,
and said to His disciples, "Sit here while I go over there
and **pray**."*

Christ never alleviated His suffering by abandoning obedience to God.

At the worst times—in the most difficult moments—He did what the Father desired.

On the lower slopes of the Mount of Olives, in a grove of weathered olive trees, there exists a garden whose most worthy purpose may have been to provide a place of prayer for the Son of God on the night He would be betrayed.

That Jesus turned to prayer—when His human, physical strength was threatened by the distress of His situation—should illustrate to us the imperative nature of obedience to God's commands.

Instead of viewing obedience as something to do in spite of our troubled times, we must view our obedience to God as something to do to make our suffering better.

God doesn't give us commands, after all, to make our struggle worse.

If we love God, we will obey Him (John 14:15).

There were times during our wait when shortcuts out of obedience to God looked very appealing. Because our paperwork necessitated that we not make any major changes in our lives—including address, employment, income, and a host of other details—we were forced to make difficult decisions to maintain accurate paperwork. Honesty or ease was often the choice. But here is what the Bible says: "For this is the love of God, that we keep his commandments. And his commandments are not burdensome" (1 John 5:3 ESV).

DAY 225

Matthew 26:39

*And He went a little beyond them, and fell on His face and
prayed, saying, "My Father, if it is possible, let this cup
pass from Me; yet not as I will, but as You will."*

We should be grateful that the same God who gives to us according
to His will does not give to us according to ours. Sometimes the most
gracious response to our request is "No."

No example of this is clearer than Jesus' request in the Garden, shortly
before His crucifixion. Christ, the perfect man, petitioned God to
spare His life. Never since then has a more perfect, more pure, or
more rightly-related child requested anything of God the Father.

And yet God said, "No."

The Father's "no" wasn't in response to the Son's failed performance,
lack of faith, or hidden sin. His "no" was the best response in that
moment so that an entire host of people might be saved.

And because of that, we have the opportunity to commune with
Christ for all eternity.

If God said, "No" to His only begotten, how could we question that a
"No" to us is anything less than the absolute best response?

> *We should be grateful that
> the same God who gives to us
> according to His will does not give to us
> according to ours.*

DAY 226

Matthew 26:41

*"Keep watching and **praying** that you may not enter into temptation; the spirit is willing, but the flesh is weak."*

Christ understands temptation.

Had Matthew 26:41 been spoken by someone who never witnessed the attraction of sin or never felt the pull of Satan's sway, we might smile or nod and go our way upon hearing it. But that Matthew 26:41 was spoken by Christ in the midst of an already challenging circumstance—when temptation seems most likely to rear its ugly head—we can be confident that our Savior understands the necessary tools to combat wrongdoing.

"For we do not have a high priest who is unable to sympathize with our weaknesses, but one who in every respect has been tempted as we are, yet without sin" (Hebrews 4:15 ESV).

Christ's response to fighting temptation was to watch and pray.

"Watch" carries the idea of being on guard. We might say that "watching" is waiting expectantly. And while waiting expectantly, we are instructed to pray.

Temptation abounds in seasons of waiting. That we are prone to wander is evident in situations where longevity and endurance are the necessity. We are tempted to question the wisdom of God, for instance, or to charge Him with the accusation that His goodness doesn't look good to us at all.

Christ understands temptation. But He never exonerates us from violating God's laws.

We must watch and pray.

DAY 227

Matthew 26:42

*He went away again a second time and **prayed**, saying, "My Father, if this cannot pass away unless I drink it, Your will be done."*

The Bible never demands that we be apathetic about our circumstances.

Recognition that God allows only what is ultimately good into our lives does not mean we cannot ask God to remove the source of our anguish.

Indeed, honest prayer means we *should* ask God to act on our behalf.

But it also means we must be content with His response.

In addition to the example of Paul (in 2 Corinthians 12) in which he asked the Lord three times to remove the "thorn," we have also been given the most powerful illustration of all in the Garden of Gethsemane. Hours before Christ would be crucified, He is seen kneeling in prayer—asking God to remove the source of His pain.

But in both cases—with Paul and Jesus—we see the response that the Bible warrants of us: "Father, if you are willing, remove this cup from me. Nevertheless, not my will, but yours be done" (Luke 22:42 ESV).

We should say with the Puritan writer, Richard Baxter, "Lord, whatever you want, wherever you want it, and whenever you want it, that's what I want."

Recognition that God allows only what is ultimately good into our lives does not mean we cannot ask God to remove the source of our anguish.

Matthew 26:44

*And He left them again, and went away and **prayed** a third time, saying the same thing once more.*

Prayer is hard work.

Consistent, persistent, enduring prayer is hard work, particularly when our requests do not appear to be answered.

Yet the Bible instructs that our prayer be a proactive, intentional, deliberate activity, not governed by whether or not what we want is always what we get.

That Christ "went away and prayed a third time" in Matthew 26:44, indicates that prayer should be a consistent, persistent, calculated practice in our lives—especially when the request isn't granted—as was the case in the life of our Savior.

No doubt, at times, the weariness from months of disappointing answers catches up with us, and we struggle to pray the way we should. At least, for us, the temptation existed to neglect prayer. Why pray when God will obviously do what He intends anyway?

Because it is commanded.

Because it is helpful.

"Therefore, confess your sins to one another and pray for one another, that you may be healed. The prayer of a righteous person has great power as it is working" (James 5:16 ESV).

Never in Scripture is the pattern to pray once and walk away. Nor is the pattern that if we pray God is obliged to answer in the way we see fit. Acceptance of God's ordained desires for us does not mean we do not pray. It means we pray as Christ did: "Nevertheless, not my will, but yours, be done" (Luke 22:42 ESV).

DAY 229

Mark 1:35

*In the early morning, while it was still dark, Jesus got up, left the house, and went away to a secluded place, and was **praying** there.*

Fellowship with the Father is sweeter the more we endure with Him.

Many times in His ministry, Christ separated Himself from others for the purpose of prayer. Though He would often spend an entire evening working on behalf of others—serving them—He still resolved to rise early for the purpose of communing with His Father.

So it is for us, as we wait for news of our son, that our sweetest times of fellowship with God are often in the morning, dedicating our day to Him and asking for Him to be glorified through whatever transpires.

Many mornings, we find ourselves begging God for good news. No doubt, heaven will be sweeter because of the painful disappointments we have experienced with His grace.

We choose not to forget that God is capable of doing incredible things on our behalf.

Martin Luther said of God: "He is like an eternal, unfailing fountain. The more it pours forth and overflows, the more it continues to give. God desires nothing more seriously from us than that we ask Him for much and great things."

So since we believe that God cannot give us a bad gift (Matthew 7:11), then we must subsequently believe that this wait is, for us right now, a good gift. And we must seek to persevere appropriately by praying persistently, knowing that heaven will be perfect because our faithful Father is there.

Mark 6:46

*After bidding them farewell, He left for the mountain
to **pray**.*

We must believe God.

We were not oblivious to the fact that there were some who believed
our adoption attempt was futile. As the number of obstacles continued
to climb, so did the number of those who quietly—not unkindly—
dropped their heads, withheld their eye contact, suspended their
verbal encouragement that we should "hang in there."

We heard through the grapevine of those who thought we
should quit.

We did not disparage those who were not given the necessary grace
for our situation. But we chose to believe God. We chose to believe
that He wanted us to pursue the adoption of this little boy we had
grown to love. We knew that if ever He wanted to thwart the adoption,
which He could do in His wisdom at any time, then He would do it
and make it clear to us.

We wanted the kind of belief that A. W. Tozer spoke about when
he said:

> Unbelief says: Some other time, but not now; some other place, but
> not here; some other people, but not us. Faith says: Anything He
> did anywhere else He will do here; anything He did any other time
> He is willing to do now; anything He ever did for other people He is
> willing to do for us! With our feet on the ground, and our head cool,
> but with our heart ablaze with the love of God, we walk out in this
> fullness of the Spirit, if we will yield and obey.

We chose to believe God.

And in doing so, we chose to believe that prayer makes a difference. At
times, this meant we bid our cynics a good day and went to a private
place to get alone with God.

DAY 231

Mark 11:24

Therefore I say to you, all things for which you pray and ask, believe that you have received them, and they will be granted you.

God will always meet us in our present need.

Since God has graciously invited us to be part of His means and methods of accomplishing His plans for us through prayer, it is our responsibility to pray.

Sometimes it is the temptation of God's children to spend more time attempting to figure out what God has planned—or how He could possibly accomplish what He has promised—as opposed to meeting God in prayer and asking for wisdom to handle whatever comes next.

Since we cannot possibly know what specific events God has ordained for our future, we must simply be obedient to pray.

God has made it clear that prayer is what He wants for us right now.

During our time of waiting, we often came across promises in the Bible, such as Mark 11:24, that simply seemed too good to be true. Where we failed to understand or fathom how God could accomplish His good purposes in us, we said with the father whose child was healed of the evil spirit in Mark 9:24 (ESV): "I believe; help my unbelief!"

For though our faith needed strengthening during our time of waiting, we knew this much: God's promises are never too good to be true.

> *Since we cannot possibly know what specific events God has ordained for our future, we must simply be obedient to pray.*

DAY 232

Mark 11:25

*Whenever you stand **praying**, forgive, if you have*
anything against anyone, so that your Father who is in
heaven will also forgive you your transgressions.

When we fail to forgive, we fail to recall what God has done for us.

At its essence, forgiveness is what gives us the right to stand before God. As God's children, we are trophies of God's grace and demonstrations of God's forgiveness.

So it is no surprise that God is uninterested in the prayers of His unforgiving children.

The process of adoption lends itself to frustration.

We spent hours on the phone, on e-mail, in offices, and in interviews. Very quickly, we learned who the people were who would do everything they could to help us and who really didn't seem to care outside of the check we wrote for them on our way out the door.

More than at any other time of our lives, it was tempting to want to give people a piece of our mind, slam a door on the way out of the office, or throw the phone.

Though we have been forgiven much, it is part of our sinful nature to forgive little.

As a family member reminded us more than once, "No one has offended me as much as I have offended God." This truth, coupled with God's forgiveness to us, enabled us to forgive.

Forgiveness is a key aspect of prayer. We cannot seek from God what we are unwilling to give to others.

> *When we fail to forgive, we fail to recall what God has done for us.*

DAY 233

Mark 14:35

*And He went a little beyond them, and fell to the ground and began to **pray** that if it were possible, the hour might pass Him by.*

We must battle the cynicism that threatens the prayer life of waiting children.

The later our wait became, the more our prayer became about faith.

In the beginning, our prayer was enthusiastic, eager, and wholehearted. As our wait persisted, our prayer became desperate, pleading, and earnest. When the "worst case scenario" came and went, our prayer became this: "Ah, Lord GOD! It is you who have made the heavens and the earth by your great power and by your outstretched arm! Nothing is too hard for you" (Jeremiah 32:17 ESV).

We understood that prayer is the fruit of faith. And if our prayer was going to survive the disparagement that threatened to destroy it as our wait progressed, we needed God to strengthen our faith. Luke 18 begins with an interesting, Divinely-inspired choice of words: "And he told them a parable to the effect that they ought always to pray and not lose heart" (Luke 18:1 ESV).

Losing heart is the enemy of prayer.

Faith that God's plans are perfect is the friend of prayer. Stephen Merritt was quoted in *Streams in the Desert*:

> Cease meddling with God's plans and will. You touch anything of
> His, and you mar the work. You may move the hands of a clock
> to suit you, but you do not change the time; so you may hurry the
> unfolding of God's will, but you harm, and do not help, the work. You
> may open the petals of a rosebud, but you spoil the flower. Leave all
> to Him. "Hands down. Thy will, not mine."

Mark 14:38

*Keep watching and **praying** that you may not come into temptation; the spirit is willing, but the flesh is weak.*

The flesh is weak.

When we believe this truth about ourselves and accept that we can do nothing apart from God, we will pray. And our prayer will be less motivated by *discipline* and more motivated by *deprivation*. Though it is a Scriptural command to pray, it is our Father's desire that we *want* and *need* to commune with Him.

It is self-sufficiency that drives us to neglect the gift of prayer.

It is not the pious of heart who pray persistently but the poor of spirit.

In Mark 14:38, "watching" yields the idea of vigilance. Christ was telling Peter, James, and John to pay attention. Yes, there would be temptations and attacks in their lives, just as there are in ours, but they were instructed to avoid spiritual overconfidence and be on guard by praying faithfully.

We are instructed to do the same.

"Rejoice in hope, be patient in tribulation, be constant in prayer" (Romans 12:12 ESV).

We are weak. We learned this with confidence as we waited on God. We faced wave after wave of disappointment, which translated into temptations of many kinds.

Doubt. Despair. Discouragement.

We learned that when the flesh is weakest, prayer is wisest.

DAY 235

Mark 14:39

*Again He went away and **prayed**, saying the same words.*

We must love our lives less than we love our God.

That Jesus asked His Father to spare His life—yet ultimately went to the cross and suffered on our behalf—is evidence that He loved God more than He loved life.

That Jesus went to the cross and died for us is evidence that He loved us more than He desired His own freedom to live.

With finite understanding, these are hard truths to comprehend.

Here is what we can understand: Christ's suffering for us on the day He died did not begin on the cross. Before ever feeling the weight of the beams on His back, Jesus carried the weight of our sin. He grieved in prayer, as Mark 14:39 alludes.

A girl in the youth group where we were serving while we waited for our son reminded us of these words from C.J. Mahaney's book, *Living the Cross Centered Life*:

> When you're tempted to doubt God's love for you, stand before the cross and look at the wounded, dying, disfigured Savior, and realize why He is there. I believe His Father would whisper to us, "Isn't that sufficient? I haven't spared My own Son; I deformed and disfigured and crushed Him for you. What more could I do to persuade you that I love you?"

Though it is eternally weak by comparison, we too must love God more than we love our life.

We must love God more than we love the object of our waiting.

"We love because he first loved us" (1 John 4:19 ESV).

DAY 236

Luke 1:10

*And the whole multitude of the people were in **prayer**
outside at the hour of the incense offering.*

The prayer that pleases God is incense to Him.

Prayer that doesn't please Him is ritualistic and academic—the opposite of worship.

Biblically speaking, incense was used as a picture of prayer ascending to heaven. In the Old Testament, people made a practice of offering incense each morning and evening on the golden altar before the veil of the sanctuary, as a means to honor and reverence the Lord.

Prayer is our spiritual sacrifice. A sacrifice we should offer often.

In the scene displayed in Luke 1:10, prayers were being offered outside the Temple while inside, a prayer was being answered. Zechariah had long sought God's goodness in the gift of a son. This had been his prayer for many years, offered as incense to His Father.

In time, God gave Zechariah a son who would be called *John the Baptist.*

God delights to answer prayer that is offered as incense to Him.

So it is we should say with the psalmist: "Let my prayer be counted as incense before you, and the lifting up of my hands as the evening sacrifice!" (Psalm 141:2 ESV).

> *Prayer is our spiritual sacrifice. A
> sacrifice we should offer often.*

DAY 237

Luke 5:16

*But Jesus Himself would often slip away to the wilderness
and* ***pray.***

There are advantages to getting away.

Milestone birthdays are challenging enough as adults, but when
you reach them without accomplishing the correlating goals or
expectations set for yourself, they can be amplified in their irritation.
Such was the case for us. So on the advent of one of our milestone
birthdays, we slipped away for a weekend.

Brilliant plan. We went to an out-of-state zoo and saw more three-
year-old children in one concentrated location than we had seen
throughout the course of our entire adoption process. And a few of
them even looked similar to the photo of our three-year-old son that
we carried in our pockets. Who were we kidding? We couldn't put the
adoption out of our minds if we tried.

We were reminded of Luke 5:16 and the reality that there really is
only one place to slip away in time of testing. Christ demonstrated the
right kind of escape when He went into the wilderness to pray. He got
alone with His Father and poured out His heart.

No doubt, Christ's wilderness prayer fortified Him for the difficulties
He was called to endure. He was wise to believe that prayer was of
more value than leisure.

Consistent communication with God is vital to the task of waiting.
Too often we seek His face only when all other options are exhausted.
For Christ, talking to God wasn't His first option—talking to God was
His only option—and His best.

"Seek the Lord and his strength; seek his presence continually!"
(1 Chronicles 16:11 ESV).

DAY 238

Luke 6:12

It was at this time that He went off to the mountain to
pray*, and He spent the whole night in* ***prayer*** *to God.*

All of our decisions should be marked by prayer.

We didn't enter into the adoption process lightly. Prayer motivated us to begin the proceedings and motivated us to continue when things got tricky. At the first sign of something disappointing in our case, we endeavored to pray. At the first sign of God's provision, we endeavored to pray.

From the largest activities of our lives to the smallest, God has instructed us to pray.

That Christ spent whole nights in prayer, as evidenced in Luke 6:12, is indicative that our commitment to sessions of personal private prayer must be taken seriously.

We need only think about the implications of having access to the ear of God to understand what an incredible opportunity and privilege we have to pray to Him.

Jonathan Edwards said in a sermon:

> The Most High is a God that hears prayer. Though he is infinitely above all and stands in no need of creatures, yet he is graciously pleased to take a merciful notice of poor worms of the dust. He manifests and presents himself as the object of prayer, appears as sitting on a mercy-seat, that men may come to him by prayer. When they stand in need of anything, he allows them to come, and ask it of him, and he is wont to hear their prayers. God in his Word hath given many promises that he will hear their prayers. The Scripture is full of such examples, and in his dispensations towards his church, manifests himself to be a God that hears prayer.

DAY 239

Luke 6:28

*Bless those who curse you, **pray** for those who
mistreat you.*

Bitterness is pointless.

There was an individual involved in our adoption who made life difficult. Determined, it seemed, to stand in our way, he failed to meet deadlines, failed to respond to e-mail or phone calls, failed to fulfill his obligation to us and our case.

But he cashed our checks before the ink dried.

When we knew it was time to reach out to him for something, a part of us would rather have taken a flying leap off the Empire State Building than call for his assistance.

Though it was his paid job to help us, he didn't make life easier.

Christ would not have grown bitter.

We knew that.

The adoption scene is ripe with opportunity to grow bitter. Here is a list of things for which we could have nourished toxic hearts: childlessness, disappointment, unsympathetic people, carelessness, bribery—the list could go on.

Praying for those who hurt us goes against all human nature, but was exemplified by Jesus (Luke 23:34). Christ could pray as Luke 6:28 commands because of His trust in His Father's plan.

Bitterness is futile. Grace is accessible.

***Praying for those who hurt us goes against all human
nature, but was exemplified by Jesus (Luke 23:34).***

DAY 240

Luke 9:29

*And while He was **praying**, the appearance of His face became different, and His clothing became white and gleaming.*

Talking with God changes things.

Luke 9:29 refers to the transfiguration of Christ in which His disciples were encouraged to wait and work for Him. As Christ prayed, His face and clothes changed.

A second remarkable example of the powerful presence of communing with God was recorded in Exodus 34:29: "When Moses came down from Mount Sinai, with the two tablets of the testimony in his hand as he came down from the mountain, Moses did not know that the skin of his face shone because he had been talking with God" (ESV).

The presence of God should change how we live.

Though our own experience in this life will not resemble the luminous Moses or radiant Christ, people should see a difference in us after we spend time with God.

People should observe a change in the way we handle waiting when we've communed with God about it.

Prayer may not change our appearance, but it should absolutely change who we are.

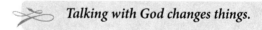 *Talking with God changes things.*

DAY 241

Luke 11:1

*It happened that while Jesus was **praying** in a certain place, after He had finished, one of His disciples said to Him, "Lord, teach us to **pray** just as John also taught his disciples."*

Jesus was a man of prayer.

Christ did incredible things on earth. He walked on water, He calmed the storms, He withstood temptation, and He brought dead people to life. Yet the only recorded request of His disciples in which they asked Him to give them an education, was this: "Lord, teach us to *pray*."

It is common for students to notice the nuances of their teachers.

It was obvious to the disciples that Jesus had a special relationship with God. Jesus rose early to pray, prayed often, and prayed with great fervency. He prayed before performing miracles, and He prayed before enduring a difficult death on the cross.

The disciples apparently took note of the Savior's habit—paid attention to its accomplishment. No doubt, they drew the obvious link between Christ's strength to do what the Father wanted Him to do and Christ's persistence in prayer.

The disciples wanted Christ's prayer life and so they asked Him to teach them to pray.

So should we.

How much more do we need prayer than He who was sinless?

DAY 242

Luke 11:2

*And He said to them, "When you **pray**, say: Father, hallowed be Your name. Your kingdom come."*

The way we view God determines how we address Him.

Why is it that amid all of our fears, we fear arriving at the place in our lives where our one remaining option is depending on God?

At various points in our wait for our son, we had zero options outside of God's intervention. The workers on our case were often at a loss. Our hands were tied from doing anything that would help our situation. And more than once, when our response to someone's request for how we were doing was, "It is in God's hands," we received apologies.

We understood these apologies, certainly we did.

As human beings, we don't comprehend that God's power far surpasses anything we can do or see or touch. But we didn't crave the apologies.

We desired to be at the place in our lives where God was best suited to work on our behalf. When we most needed God, we best communed with Him.

In prayer, we have an amazing ability as Christians to go directly to the God of the universe and make requests of Him. And the great truth is that we do not go as one who needs to fear Him; we go to Him as His child. Thus, we address Him as *Father*.

We understood throughout our wait that we were not without options.

God is more than sufficient and we are in the best spot when we rely on Him.

DAY 243

Luke 12:36

*Be like men who are **waiting** for their master when he returns from the wedding feast, so that they may immediately open the door to him when he comes and knocks.*

We must willingly wait for God.

We are not privy to the timetable of God. We are simply expected to wait for Him.

It is a simple instruction with difficult implications: *Wait on God.*

Like the servants who waited for their master in Luke 12:36, so we should eagerly wait for the activity of the Lord. They didn't know when their master would return or what he would request of them or how he would reward them, but they waited.

That was their instruction as it is ours.

We wait for God with little insight into what He will do.

It is easy to believe that waiting on God is punishment for some wrong committed. "We don't have what we want because we've done something that displeases God."

Yet, that is not God's way. Though there is a sowing and reaping principle (Galatians 6:7), sometimes we are expected to wait to demonstrate our faithfulness to God and our trust in Him. Likewise, we wait so that He can demonstrate His faithfulness to us and His strength manifested in us.

"Let us not grow weary of doing good, for in due season we will reap, if we do not give up" (Galatians 6:9 ESV).

DAY 244

Luke 18:1

*Now He was telling them a parable to show that at all times they ought to **pray** and not to lose heart.*

It is the natural response of the child of God to faint instead of pray.

If this were not the case, men like Paul would have spent much less time in the epistles exhorting believers to do just that: pray instead of faint.

We must pray and not lose heart no matter how difficult the day may get.

When a walk through the valley grows into a short-term residence—where we set up a tent and submit a forwarding address from life as we knew it—it is challenging to "maintain heart." We can handle what we think is short-term waiting, but long-term?—different story.

Seeing God's work, and acknowledging that it is His, is critical.

We must believe that God can and will continue to work in the situation in which we find ourselves. Late into our short-term residence in the land of difficulty, we discovered these words in a letter by Samuel Rutherford:

> I believe that when Christ draweth blood, He hath skill to cut the right vein; and that He hath taken the whole ordering and disposing of my sufferings. Let Him tutor me, and tutor my crosses, as He thinketh good. There is no danger nor hazard in following such a guide, howbeit He should lead me through hell if I could put faith foremost, and fill the field with a quiet on-waiting, and believing to see the salvation of God.

We took heart in these words: our Great Physician always cuts the right vein.

DAY 245

Luke 18:10

*Two men went up into the temple to **pray**, one a Pharisee and the other a tax collector.*

Depending on God is always the expectation.

The parable of the Pharisee and the tax collector, recorded in Luke 18:10, draws attention to the gross sin of depending on self to the neglect of depending on God.

The Pharisaical prayer, "God, I thank you that I am not like other men" (Luke 18:11–12 ESV), is the prayer of one who, though outwardly praying to God, is inwardly depending on himself for all that he has.

And it's utterly unattractive.

Though we would not be foolish enough to say certain things in prayer as blatantly as the Pharisee, we, at times, demonstrate their same Pharisaical attitude about life.

I deserve this. God owes me that. Here is what I have done to deserve what I want.

Otherwise, we would not struggle so hard when things do not go our way.

Looking to what we have done to justify confusion about what we do not have is unwise at best and Pharisaical at worst.

Though we would not be foolish enough to say certain things in prayer as blatantly as the Pharisee, we, at times, demonstrate their same Pharisaical attitude about life.

Luke 18:11

*The Pharisee stood and was **praying** this to himself: "God,
I thank You that I am not like other people: swindlers,
unjust, adulterers, or even like this tax collector."*

We must be deeply thankful for Christ.

Luke 18:11 records a prayer that stands in direct opposition to every
righteous prayer recorded in the Bible. The very act of prayer, after
all, is a humble acknowledgement of our lack of ability and God's all-
sufficiency.

We cannot be thankful for *who we are* or *who we are not* without an
accurate picture of *who He is* and *what He has done* for us.

We discovered this prayer, known as "God, the Source of All Good"
in *The Valley of Vision*, and we prayed it together.

I thank thee for thy riches to me in Jesus,

for the unclouded revelation of him in thy Word,

where I behold his Person, character, grace, glory,

humiliation, sufferings, death, and resurrection;

Give me to feel a need of his continual saviourhood,

and cry with Job, "I am vile,"

with Peter, "I perish",

with the publican, "Be merciful to me, a sinner."

And in praying this prayer, we were deeply thankful for Christ.

DAY 247

Luke 21:36

*But keep on the alert at all times, **praying** that you may have strength to escape all these things that are about to take place, and to stand before the Son of Man.*

Easy, comfortable, fun Christianity does not prepare people for suffering.

We will bail on Christ in the moment of trial if we only perceive God to be the author of peace or ease. There are many in this world who cannot tolerate the idea that God would choose cancer, cause catastrophe, or create calamity.

Yet He does (Isaiah 45:7).

Coupled with God's wisdom is His all-surpassing love.

Who would we rather be in control? Would we prefer that God have no control over evil? Would we rather serve a God who can be shaken by circumstance?

God is the author of all that is good.

If something difficult enters our lives, it is for our good. We must therefore take care not to shake our fists at heaven in exchange for His good gifts (James 1).

Though it is a temptation in times of waiting, we must not command God in prayer—dictate to Him what His decisions for us will be—but rather, we must pray, submit, and wait.

And we must believe that whatever He decides is, for us, the best decision.

Coupled with God's wisdom is His all-surpassing love.

Matthew Henry wrote of Luke 21:36, "Pray always: those shall be accounted worthy to live a life of praise in the other world, who live a life of prayer in this world. May we begin, employ, and conclude each day attending to Christ's word, obeying his precepts, and following his example, that whenever he comes we may be found watching."

DAY 248

Luke 22:32

*But I have **prayed** for you, that your faith may not fail;*
and you, when once you have turned again, strengthen
your brothers.

Praying for something that we think is impossible is not a prayer of faith.

We prayed that we would hear something by Christmas. To some people in our lives, the prayer seemed impossible after months of hearing nothing. Some people made it clear that there was a greater chance that God would once again raise the dead to life or cause the blind to see.

But to us, God could do whatever He wanted.

And so we prayed that we would hear something by Christmas.

If we doubted that God could do it, we would not be praying a prayer of faith.

During our time of waiting, we came to love and respect a man named Dr. Michael Barrett who wisely said: "The power of faith is not in its exercise but in its object—it is not just the exercise of faith that makes it something worthwhile. But it is rather its object—it is what we believe and what we are putting our confidence in and our trust in—that makes faith a worthwhile exercise at all."

We had faith that God was capable of giving us news by Christmas. And we prayed that He would. James 1:6 says unequivocally: "But let him ask in faith, with no doubting, for the one who doubts is like a wave of the sea that is driven and tossed by the wind" (ESV).

The answer to insecurity is faith in God.

DAY 249

Luke 22:40

*When He arrived at the place, He said to them, "**Pray** that you may not enter into temptation."*

We need help to wrestle against our weakness.

We may know that the Lord is our strength (Exodus 15:2; Psalm 28:7), yet so often we rely on ourselves to make things happen. We still attempt to do things in our own power.

We were dreading the twenty-first month of waiting, in part because it brought with it the holiday season, and in part because we were just getting tired. The back-and-forth between caseworkers and government officials combined with pending expirations on our paperwork combined with questions we had no answers to was, at times, exhausting.

Our weakness always loomed in every challenge to remind us of what we could not do.

And then we received a card in the mail from someone who had been an incredible source of kindness and encouragement through our wait. The card read in its entirety: "Be strong and take heart, all you who hope in the LORD, (Psalm 31:24 NIV). Hang on to hope. God is faithful."

God *is* faithful to show us our weakness and to compensate it with His grace.

We must pray that we would not surrender to the wrong source.

> *God is faithful to show us our weakness and to compensate it with His grace.*

DAY 250

Luke 22:41

*And He withdrew from them about a stone's throw, and
He knelt down and began to **pray**.*

In a single, unforgettable scene in Scripture, we see Jesus in the
Garden of Gethsemane hours before He would be crucified. And
in what must have been an excruciating wait for the will of God to
be performed in His life—by His death on the cross—Jesus did the
absolute best thing.

He prayed.

In words that offer us tremendous insight into the character of the
Son of God, He said, "Father, if you are willing, remove this cup from
me. Nevertheless, not my will, but yours, be done" (Luke 22:42 ESV).

And in those words, spoken in a moment of supreme submission to
His Almighty Father, Christ gave us the perfect example of what we
should do when we are called to wait, even in our darkest hours.

We must pray.

*In words that offer us tremendous insight
into the character of the Son of God, He said,
"Father, if you are willing ..."*

DAY 251

Luke 22:44

*And being in agony He was **praying** very fervently; and His sweat became like drops of blood, falling down upon the ground.*

Receiving a *no* to a request or petition is not the same as unanswered prayer.

Funny—isn't it?—the way people talk about "unanswered prayer" when really they mean to discuss the prayer which wasn't answered in the way they wanted it to be done.

God always answers our prayers.

In His own words He says, "Call to me and I will answer you" (Jeremiah 33:3). And while, perhaps, the verse would be more appealing if it read, "Call to me and I will give you what you want," we cannot mistake God to be unresponsive simply because we don't always like what He says.

We received *no* as an answer hundreds of times during our adoption journey.

No doubt we received hundreds of *waits* as well, but there were many times we prayed for decisions to be made by certain dates or invitations to be extended by certain deadlines. And time and again, we received the dreaded answer, *no.*

God was still answering every prayer.

It was His kindness that dispensed the *no* when we very much wanted to receive the *yes.* It is the kindness of God that doesn't yield to our nagging when what we need isn't what we want.

Christ prayed in Gethsemane that—if possible—God would withhold the cross.

It was the kindness of God—to us as sinners—that God said, *no* on that night.

DAY 252

Luke 22:45

*When He rose from **prayer**, He came to the disciples and found them sleeping from sorrow.*

Prayer during difficulty is paramount to victory.

Slacking during difficulty is paramount to disaster.

It could be argued that the disciples' powerlessness over sin after their time in the garden originated with their inability to remain active in prayer as Christ instructed.

It has always been the temptation of those who experience hardship to depend on their own power to persevere.

On the day Christ died, we see examples of victory and disaster.

Christ commanded the disciples to pray and yet they fell asleep on multiple occasions. This slacking led to all sorts of miserable consequences on the evening they most needed the strength of God.

On the other hand, Christ prayed to God throughout His painful betrayal and crucifixion—right up until the moment of His death. This prayer led to God's abundant grace and mercy demonstrated visibly on the cross.

Christ endured more difficulty than did the disciples.

And He did so with greater strength and more resolve.

We must pray for steadfastness.

Prayer during difficulty is paramount to victory.

DAY 253

Luke 22:46

And said to them, "Why are you sleeping? Get up and
pray *that you may not enter into temptation."*

Prayer is always our command, but especially our need when we are struggling.

Interesting that prayer is established in Luke 22 as the way to avoid temptation.

Yet too often, like the disciples at the time of Christ's betrayal, we find ourselves overcome with our own weakness when we should be privy to prayer.

For us, as for the disciples, failure is a part of life.

The failure to pray is not only a sin against God, but it is the most unwise response to our disappointments. God has provided a way for us to suffer better and yet we choose to make it worse.

We know so much of God and His promises. We know of His faithfulness. Yet somehow we still fail to trust Him. There is a prayer in the *Valley of Vision* aptly titled, "Yet I Sin":

Work in me more profound and abiding repentance;
Give me the fullness of a godly grief
that trembles and fears,
yet ever trusts and loves,
which is ever powerful, and ever confident;

Grant that through the tears of repentance
I may see more clearly the brightness
and glories of the saving cross.

DAY 254

Acts 1:14

*These all with one mind were continually devoting themselves to **prayer**, along with the women, and Mary the mother of Jesus, and with His brothers.*

God has given us a refuge in prayer.

Acts 1:14 was written when the disciples of Christ were experiencing great difficulty. They had witnessed the death, and now the departure, of their Savior. They were confused about many things, yet they understood that prayer was God's answer to human anxiety.

And so banding together with those who were like-minded, they prayed.

So it is for us that the best posture to maintain during trials is the posture of prayer.

For us, prayer was a major component in our decision-making.

Before we made the decision to adopt, we spent much time in prayer. We prayed throughout our adoption process that God would be glorified. We banded with other like-minded people who would pray for God's will to be done.

We, like the disciples of Acts 1:14, found prayer to be the perfect refuge.

"Praying at all times in the Spirit, with all prayer and supplication. To that end keep alert with all perseverance, making supplication for all the saints" (Ephesians 6:18 ESV).

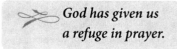

God has given us a refuge in prayer.

DAY 255

Acts 1:24

*And they **prayed** and said, "You, Lord, who know the hearts of all men, show which one of these two You have chosen."*

We must make it a priority to search out the will of God for everything we face.

Acts 1 sets the scene of the disciples trying to make a difficult decision. They were seeking to replace Judas and were at a loss to choose between two men—Joseph called Barsabbas (also known as Justus) and Matthias.

No doubt the decision was made more difficult since Jesus was not present to guide them as He had been previously.

Sometimes loss compounds our confusion.

The disciples prayed, as recorded in Acts 1:24, and they were led to select Matthias. They made their decision the way God intends all of His children to make decisions: *with His help.*

The same God that orchestrates everything in our lives knows our hearts. The disciples understood this, which is why they asked the Lord to direct their decision.

We, too, must depend on God to direct us, guide us, lead us, and sustain us.

"And he who searches hearts knows what is the mind of the Spirit, because the Spirit intercedes for the saints according to the will of God" (Romans 8:27 ESV).

DAY 256

Acts 2:26

*THEREFORE MY HEART WAS GLAD AND MY
TONGUE EXULTED; MOREOVER MY FLESH ALSO
WILL LIVE IN* **HOPE.**

We need no less grace to live our daily lives than we needed to be saved.

How do you deal with it? How can you keep going? How have you not given up?

We heard these questions from friends when one of our caseworkers made a mistake in our process that could have cost us thousands of dollars and (more importantly) caused added months of delay.

Our answer to those who graciously showed concern for us was that we had to choose to trust God and not man. And though the default reactions in life are not to trust, hope, and pray, they are the essentials to surviving the difficulties.

Every day we live on this earth, we are sustained by God's amazing grace.

In Acts 2:25, Peter quotes Psalm 16 where David says his strength comes from knowing that God is by his side. And that is also our strength. We are not self-sustaining, strength-producing machines. We are sheep in need of a loving Shepherd.

God alone gives us joy in our hearts. We know that it is because of Christ that we find the strength to endure. Walking with God is the product of sustaining grace.

"Now may our Lord Jesus Christ himself, and God our Father, who loved us and gave us eternal comfort and good hope through grace, comfort your hearts and establish them in every good work and word" (2 Thessalonians 2:16–17 ESV).

DAY 257

Acts 2:42

They were continually devoting themselves to the apostles'
teaching and to fellowship, to the breaking of bread and
*to **prayer**.*

We are only absent from God physically.

It is His desire that, while we are here on earth, we would grow in Him.

In Acts 2:42, the groundwork for the Christians' growth in Christ was a devotion to teaching, fellowship, and prayer. This dedication to God's instruction would sustain them in the plethora of difficulties yet to come.

Looking to anything in this world to satisfy or comfort us while we are traveling heavenward is the trigger of discontentment. We must grow in Christ by devoting ourselves to the same teaching, fellowship, and prayer that sustained the infant New Testament church.

That they were steadfast should encourage us to do the same.

As Samuel Stone penned:

'Mid toil and tribulation,

And tumult of her war,

She waits the consummation

Of peace forevermore;

Till, with the vision glorious,

Her longing eyes are blest,

And the great Church victorious

Shall be the Church at rest.

Acts 4:31

*And when they had **prayed**, the place where they had gathered together was shaken, and they were all filled with the Holy Spirit and began to speak the word of God with boldness.*

God writes the story.

It is God's delight to draw all things to a conclusion that glorifies Him.

God does not always answer prayer in the same way. From a fireball falling from the sky to consume Elijah's sacrifice to the earthquake that freed Paul and Silas, we always seem to desire the amazing answer to prayer.

No doubt, God delights to do the impossible.

But this is not the customary means by which God provides for His children. The word *miracle* would not exist if "miracles" were the normal means in which God chose to work.

They are "miracles" because they are rare.

No, it is often the little things God uses to encourage us. It was, for us, the unexpected strength or the grace for the day that sustained us in the worst of times. It was the lack of a major car problem or the surprise lowering of our monthly mortgage that enabled us to cover the expenses that thrilled us.

No matter the means, God writes the perfect scenes that will best display His splendor.

From Old Testament times, God delighted to do remarkable things: "To grant to those who mourn in Zion—to give them a beautiful headdress instead of ashes, the oil of gladness instead of mourning, the garment of praise instead of a faint spirit; that they may be called oaks of righteousness, the planting of the LORD, that he may be glorified" (Isaiah 61:3 ESV).

DAY 259

Acts 6:4

*But we will devote ourselves to **prayer** and to the ministry of the word.*

God, alone, is sufficient.

In the moment of personal crisis, our typical, human support systems are not adequate enough to meet our needs. Other people—friends perhaps—are battling difficulties of their own.

How could we expect them to be for us what we cannot be for them?

The thrills of this life are short-lived and shallow. No hobby or distraction can take the place of God for us.

But God is ever present.

Always rich in grace, He is available to meet us with mercy and to help us in the moment of disappointment with wisdom to guide us in the proper way.

He has given us access to His throne by prayer and access to His wisdom via the Bible.

So many times in our disappointment we cried out to God, feeling like we were in the dark about what to do next. But His support—He Himself—was adequate to meet our needs.

"Your word is a lamp to my feet and a light to my path" (Psalm 119:105 ESV).

And so we commit with Paul in Acts 6:4 to devote ourselves to prayer and to the Word.

His task was ministry.
Ours is waiting.

> *He has given us access to His throne by prayer and access to His wisdom via the Bible.*

Acts 8:22

*Therefore repent of this wickedness of yours, and **pray** the Lord that, if possible, the intention of your heart may be forgiven you.*

Prayer over sin is not merely to escape the consequences.

When we sin against God, we should not pray primarily because we want forgiveness or because we hope that God will bless our contrite heart. Rather, our prayer should be because we have wronged our Heavenly Father.

There is nothing in this world we should detest more than our own sin.

In the language of Acts 8:22, we pray "that, if possible" we will be forgiven—meaning we should pray to God and confess our wrongdoing whether or not He would grant us forgiveness.

But we know that our good God has promised to forgive.

Says Psalm 103:12: "As far as the east is from the west, so far does he remove our transgressions from us" (ESV).

How many times, during our difficult wait, did we call upon God and reflect upon these verses. And God was good to grant us forgiveness, grace, and peace to continue on this journey with renewed faith and confidence in Him!

"As far as the east is from the west, so far does he remove our transgressions from us"

DAY 261

Acts 9:11

*And the Lord said to him, "Get up and go to the street called Straight, and inquire at the house of Judas for a man from Tarsus named Saul, for he is **praying**."*

Moments of weakness drive us to our knees.

Paul had just had a supernatural encounter with Christ on the road to Damascus that left him unable to see, so he had to depend on others to lead him to the city. In cases where we are obviously not in control, it is easy to pray. It is natural.

Blinded by sadness or concern or fear, we depend on God to lead us.

When our eyes are opened to what little strength we have to accomplish what we need, our love for God grows in proportion to our need of Him.

God alone accompanied us on our wait. He alone strengthened us for the disappointments. He alone equipped us with the ability to persevere. While we were not always faithful to Him, He was perfectly faithful to us.

For these truths, we thank Him now and for eternity.

Here are the verses we claimed:

But whatever gain I had, I counted as loss for the sake of Christ. Indeed, I count everything as loss because of the surpassing worth of knowing Christ Jesus my Lord. For his sake I have suffered the loss of all things and count them as rubbish, in order that I may gain Christ and be found in him, not having a righteousness of my own that comes from the law, but that which comes through faith in Christ, the righteousness from God that depends on faith—that I may know him and the power of his resurrection, and may share his sufferings, becoming like him in his death. (Philippians 3:7–10 ESV)

Acts 10:2

*A devout man and one who feared God with all his household, and gave many alms to the Jewish people and **prayed** to God continually.*

It is not easy to always remain in a spirit of prayer.

Though we are commanded to pray (1 Thessalonians 5:17), it is something we must learn to do, improve upon, develop.

We must pray to the Lord that He would do for us what we are insufficient to do for ourselves.

Like the disciples, we must ask God to teach us to pray.

Prayer betrays in us our attitude of self-sufficiency, as we think we will handle the little things while God can take care of the big. God handles all or handles nothing.

God cultivates in us the character He desires when we come to His throne and dump out our ridiculous knapsack of needs and desires. He shows us what it is we really need—Him.

We learn, through prayer, that God is good when He gives and He is good when He withholds. Believing anything less about God is not understanding who He is or how He operates in the world.

Acts 10:2 is speaking of a man named Cornelius, a centurion who prayed to God continually. What a wonderful commendation to be called one "who prays continually."

From his actions, he demonstrated his dependence.

And so should we.

DAY 263

Acts 10:4

And fixing his gaze on him and being much alarmed,
he said, "What is it, Lord?" And he said to him,
*"Your **prayers** and alms have ascended as a memorial*
before God."

God blesses His children for their sincerity of life and worship.

Acts 10:4 refers to the prayer of Cornelius—the centurion who, the Bible says, ". . . was a devout, God-fearing man, as was everyone in his household. He gave generously to the poor and prayed regularly to God."

We do not know much about Cornelius, but we know he pleased the Lord when he prayed.

Of Acts 10:4, the Geneva Study Bible notes: "This is a borrowed kind of speech which the Hebrews used very much, taken from sacrifices and applied to prayers: for it is said of whole burnt sacrifices that the smoke and smell of them goes up into God's nostrils, and so do our prayers, as a sweet smelling sacrifice which the Lord takes great pleasure in."

We please the Lord when we pray. But herein is the irony: we would be foolish to seek out anyone else.

So if He is pleased and we are blessed, why would we *not* pray?

> *So if He is pleased and we are*
> *blessed, why would we not pray?*

DAY 264

Acts 12:5

*So Peter was kept in the prison, but **prayer** for him was being made fervently by the church to God.*

Life is full of complexities.

Why does a car accident take the life of one and not another? Why does an illness destroy one person and let another live? Why does the faithful brother suffer wrongly while the unfaithful man is free to live as he pleases?

In Acts 12, Herod gave James a death sentence and sent Peter to prison. Both were guilty of the same crime—preaching and teaching Christ—yet one died and one lived.

We cannot know the mind of God in full, but we can change our perspective of difficulty.

In talking about thinking of suffering from a new point of view, Martyn Lloyd Jones wrote in his book, *Spiritual Depression*:

> I must admit also that I am weak, that I lack the necessary powers and propensities. But instead of stopping there I must go on to say: "Yes, I know it all, but—" And the moment I use that word "but" I am doing what the Apostle wants me to do. I say: "But—but the Spirit of God is in me; God has given me his Holy Spirit." The moment I say that the whole outlook changes. In other words, we have to learn to say, that what matters in any of these positions is not what is true of us but what is true of Him.

Life is full of complexities, but this much is uncomplicated:

God is sovereign.

DAY 265

Acts 16:25

*But about midnight Paul and Silas were **praying** and singing hymns of praise to God, and the prisoners were listening to them.*

Songs that honor God are gifts to us in our pain.

When words fail us in moments of hurt and frustration, we are permitted to borrow the words of songwriters who have faithfully recorded what it is we wish to say.

Music, after all, honors God.

God not only permits us to employ music in our worship, He requires it (Colossians 3:16). And often in our distress, God uses the music—intended to exalt Him—to minister to us in our need.

One of the songs that we grew to love almost as tangibly as a human friend was *Jesus, I My Cross Have Taken*, written by Henry Lyte in the early nineteenth century. The third verse reads:

Go, then, earthly fame and treasure!
Come, disaster, scorn and pain!

In Thy service, pain is pleasure;
with Thy favor, loss is gain.

I have called Thee, "Abba, Father";
I have set my heart on Thee:

Storms may howl, and clouds may gather,
all must work for good to me.

DAY 266

Acts 26:6

*And now I am standing trial for the **hope** of the promise
made by God to our fathers.*

To claim the promises of God when we need them, we must first
know them.

Paul had a hope worth dying for, as illustrated in the courts of a
ruthless Roman judge. But he didn't develop this hope on the day he
stood trial. Long before his day of reckoning came, Paul claimed the
promises of God, as made to his fathers.

Which meant Paul sought to make the promises his priority.

Paul's hope was eternal—lodged in the reality that Christ died for
Him and would someday come again—and was therefore untouchable
by man. This hope had far-reaching consequences, including Paul's
uncompromising confidence in the face of castigation and death.

Paul was so concerned about eternity that, by comparison, his life
on this earth meant little to him. He was less worried that he would
die and more concerned that those around him would die without
Christ.

In the words of Jesus, "And do not fear those who kill the body but
cannot kill the soul. Rather fear him who can destroy both soul and
body in Hell" (Matthew 10:28 ESV).

To his death, Paul maintained his hope in God.

Consider this: we, as children of God, can share the same hope that
belonged to Paul. That though everything seems to crumble around
us—our freedom, our security, our health, our life—we can have hope
worth dying for.

DAY 267

Acts 27:20

Since neither sun nor stars appeared for many days, and
*no small storm was assailing us, from then on all **hope** of*
our being saved was gradually abandoned.

We will abandon hope if we think God's love is translated as our success in this life.

Getting what we want in this life is no more an indication of God's love than not getting what we want is an indication of His lack of love.

God never promised that life on this earth would be free of the consequences of sin and evil. In fact, the Bible is clear that we will experience heartache and disappointment until we are united with Christ for eternity.

"Beloved, do not be surprised at the fiery trial when it comes upon you to test you, as though something strange were happening to you" (1 Peter 4:12 ESV).

It is not God's fault if we do not have hope in Him.

In the poem, "The Eternal Goodness," John Greenleaf Whittier wrote these words,

> *Yet, in the maddening maze of things,*
> *And tossed by storm and flood,*
> *To one fixed trust my spirit clings;*
> *I know that God is good!*

As we were reminded by a friend during our time of waiting, we must think true thoughts about God through the pain. We must cling to the truth that God is good.

Then we will maintain hope in Him.

DAY 268

Romans 1:10

*Always in my **prayers** making request, if perhaps now at last by the will of God I may succeed in coming to you.*

We must readily relate God's working in our lives to those around us.

Comforting those who need it is necessary—even required by God (Romans 12:15)—but human consolation is not enough. "Weeping with those who weep" is kind, but giving people God's truth, which translates into enduring hope, is kinder still.

We found, during our testing, that those who offered us encouragement from the Bible or promised to pray for us or sent us little notes of exhortation were some of God's greatest gifts to us. Christian relationships which edify the body are glorifying to God.

Our journals filled up quickly with truths we immediately began sharing with others.

Receiving a note of encouragement is one of the kindest gestures from a friend. We received such a note, which began: "I came across these verses in Isaiah this morning, and I thought they might be an encouragement."

When, along the path of affliction, we have the opportunity to share God's goodness with others—by explaining His perfect orchestration of the events of our lives—we must take the opportunity to do so. God delights in the praise of His children.

And here are the verses we received in the note from that dear friend: "Fear not, for I have redeemed you; I have called you by name, you are mine. When you pass through the waters, I will be with you; and through the rivers, they shall not overwhelm you; when you walk through fire you shall not be burned, and the flame shall not consume you" (Isaiah 43:1–2 ESV).

DAY 269

Romans 4:18

*In **hope** against **hope** he believed, so that he might become
a father of many nations according to that which had been
spoken, "SO SHALL YOUR DESCENDANTS BE."*

Short-term opportunities to wait on our Heavenly Father do not
provide a picture of the long-term character of God.

God is good when the bills get paid. He is good when traffic clears
or the lines at the bank are short. He is good to us when the weather
brightens in time for the outdoor event or the headache dissipates
before the test. And we should certainly thank Him for His provision
to us in those circumstances. Every gift to us from God is worthy of
our praise.

But short-term events portray only one side of our Savior—that He
is able and willing to meet our immediate needs—and therefore do
not give the best proof of the long-term sufficiency we find in Christ
during times of waiting.

God's goodness is sufficient when receiving the diagnosis is four
months away. His goodness is sufficient when the pregnancy is
complicated or the economy takes a nosedive. His goodness is
sufficient when the house is placed on the market or the ministry
situation is bleak.

Every gift to us from God is worthy of our praise—the gift of learning
to trust God long-term included.

We may not fully understand the *why* or *how* of our struggle, but we
must put our trust in God. Abraham was ninety-nine years old when
he was promised a nation of descendents (Genesis 17:1–6). From
a human perspective, this promise was bleak. Abraham was an old
man! (Romans 4:18). But the God of the universe is the God of the
impossible and what He promises, He fulfills

We must have faith in the long-term goodness and sustainability
of God.

DAY 270

Romans 5:2

Through whom also we have obtained our introduction by faith into this grace in which we stand; and we exult in **hope** *of the glory of God.*

Everything exists to glorify God.

As children, visiting Christian camps for the summer, we were often encouraged to recite 1 Corinthians 10:31, "So whether you eat or drink, or whatever you do, do all to the glory of God" (ESV). It became a sort of "mealtime verse," which we said before prayer.

But, though the verse applies to our meals, 1 Corinthians 10:31 is so much more than a verse about food.

Everything exists to glorify God. Our eating, our drinking, our talking, our praying, our sharing—all of these things are the canvass on which God can glorify Himself through us.

Which means even our waiting must glorify Him.

A good parallel verse to 1 Corinthians 10:31 is Colossians 3:17: "And whatever you do, in word or deed, do everything in the name of the Lord Jesus, giving thanks to God the Father through him" (ESV).

Because we know that God's glory will be accomplished, with or without our consent, we can exult in the hope of this glory. God's work will be done in our lives regardless of how much we understand right now.

Because He is perfect we can count on that!

DAY 271

Romans 5:4

*And perseverance, proven character; and proven character, **hope**.*

The discomfort we experience during testing is growing pain.

Romans 5:3–5 explains: "More than that, we rejoice in our sufferings, knowing that suffering produces endurance, and endurance produces character, and character produces hope, and hope does not put us to shame, because God's love has been poured into our hearts through the Holy Spirit who has been given to us" (ESV).

The imagery of Romans 5:4 is that of testing or "proving" metal to see its consistency and validate its purity. For the believer, this "testing" comes in the form of trials and troubles.

But because it is the goal of God to produce in us greater conformity to Jesus Christ, this testing does more than just "verify" or "validate" the extent of our purity or impurity. It further produces in us the quality that Christ wants in our lives.

If we experience the domino effect of Romans 5:3–4—in which suffering produces perseverance and perseverance produces character and character produces hope—we know that God is graciously working and we are correctly responding.

Feeling the discomfort of trials, while simultaneously holding on to our heavenly hope, is a work of God in us.

 "...God's love has been poured into our hearts through the Holy Spirit who has been given to us."

DAY 272

Romans 5:5

*And **hope** does not disappoint, because the love of God has been poured out within our hearts through the Holy Spirit who was given to us.*

That God loves us no matter what should cause us to rejoice. No matter what.

We do not have the capacity necessary to comprehend the love of God which is found in Christ. And though His love is part of our conversation and part of our Sunday worship on a regular basis, we still struggle to *get it.*

When we think we have all we need to exist in this life without God, He has a way of leaving us to our own devices. But when we realize that He is what we need and want, we call on Him and He pours out on us the fullness of His resources.

His hope never disappoints.
His goodness never deceives.
His kindness never dissolves.
His strength never dissipates.

> But when the goodness and loving kindness of God our Savior
> appeared, he saved us, not because of works done by us in
> righteousness, but according to his own mercy, by the washing of
> regeneration and renewal of the *Holy* Spirit, whom he poured out on
> us richly through Jesus Christ our Savior, so that being justified by
> his grace we might become heirs according to the hope of eternal life.
> (Titus 3:4–7 ESV)

That is the love of God which is found in Christ.

DAY 273

Romans 8:19

*For the anxious longing of the creation **waits** eagerly for the revealing of the sons of God.*

Trials produce in us a greater homesickness for heaven.

Likewise, a greater hunger for heaven creates for us a set of lenses through which we view the world and our experiences in it very differently. Yes, life hurts right now, but heaven is coming, and being with Christ forever will make everything we've experienced here worth the pain of waiting.

Passages such as 2 Corinthians 4:17–18, which speak of our current trials as "light afflictions," are not so much minimizing our current pain as they are comparing that pain to the enormity of the good that is awaiting us in glory.

If the cancer hurts or the miscarriage disappoints or the death devastates—and they will!—imagine what heaven must be like for God to have inspired words like "light" and "momentary" to describe what He knows is destructive.

God is neither unfamiliar with our pain, nor is He unfamiliar with what is coming! He has the vantage point of both and encourages us to hunger for heaven.

Christ Himself endured suffering on the cross because of the joy set before Him, viewed through the lens of someone anxiously longing for the future (Hebrews 12:2).

> *God is neither unfamiliar with our pain, nor is He unfamiliar with what is coming!*

DAY 274

Romans 8:20

For the creation was subjected to futility, not willingly, but because of Him who subjected it, in **hope.**

When the pressures of life press into us, we must make a point to press into the Lord.

Matthew Henry's commentary says of Romans 8:18:

> The sufferings of the saints strike no deeper than the things of time, last no longer than the present time, are light afflictions, and but for a moment. How vastly different are the sentence of the word and the sentiment of the world, concerning the sufferings of this present time! Indeed the whole creation seems to wait with earnest expectation for the period when the children of God shall be manifested in the glory prepared for them.

Throughout our difficult wait, we were often reminded that, despite the hardships and pain that we were experiencing while waiting to meet our son, it would fade into memory when we finally received that letter—held in our hands the invitation to travel—and were able to go pick him up. The twenty-four-hour journey to meet him would be worth every minute.

So, too, for our final hope that rests in Christ. It will be worth it all when God invites us to come home to be with Him. The disappointments of this life will fade to oblivion when we see Him.

"Behold, you have made my days a few handbreadths, and my lifetime is as nothing before you. Surely all mankind stands as a mere breath! Selah" (Psalm 39:5 ESV).

Until then, we press into Him.

DAY 275

Romans 8:23

*And not only this, but also we ourselves, having the
first fruits of the Spirit, even we ourselves groan within
ourselves, **waiting** eagerly for our adoption as sons, the
redemption of our body.*

We eagerly await our adoption as children of God.

As time marched on, we grieved a lot of things for the adoption of our child. We mourned the absence of our son at the table, his presence with our family at celebrations, and the relationship we were not building with the boy we loved.

Grief, we learned, is not just expended on people.

We grieved the loss of dreams—the hopes that did not make it to fruition. There were so many plans we had for our child; and yet for years, we sat in a quiet house and mourned the lack of footsteps and laughter and childish chatter. And we clung to Psalm 34:18: "The LORD is near to the brokenhearted and saves the crushed in spirit" (ESV).

God is near, even as we groan within ourselves.

For us, it was easy to forget that we were not the only ones waiting for this adoption.

True, grandparents waited. Aunts and uncles waited. Cousins waited. Future friends waited.

But we cannot forget that our son also waited.

The way we wait to be reconciled to God, he waited to be reconciled to family.

"For in this tent we groan, longing to put on our heavenly dwelling" (2 Corinthians 5:2 ESV).

Romans 8:24

*For in **hope** we have been saved, but **hope** that is seen is not **hope**; for who **hopes** for what he already sees?*

Hope in God makes all the difference.

The worst things we endure in this life are still just that—things. They cannot follow us into eternity or rob us of the life which God has promised. God's guarantees are locked tightly in His fist, which is exactly where we are if we are His (John 10:28).

Compared to our unsaved counterparts, our future is bright, regardless of how dark today may be. We have the hope of all future fellowship with Christ. And that cannot be reversed.

We were saved with hope and we *are saved* with hope.

We must encourage the hope that God has given us for a world yet to come.

This is a hope that cannot be shaken, cannot be robbed, cannot be overturned.

Late into our wait, a well-meaning, unbelieving colleague inquired about our adoption. After hearing that we were nearing year two without our son, she held up a hand and said, "I will keep my fingers crossed for you," and went on her way.

Though her words were nothing short of sincere affirmation for us, we were grateful in that moment that we have so much more hope than the promise of superstition or good luck.

We have the hope of God in our hearts. We can say with C. H. Spurgeon: "My hope lives not because I am not a sinner but because I am a sinner for whom Christ died. My trust is not that I am holy, but that being unholy, He is my righteousness. My faith rests not upon what I am, or shall be, or feel or know but in what Christ is, in what He has done and is now doing for me."

DAY 277

Romans 8:25

*But if we **hope** for what we do not see, with perseverance
we **wait** eagerly for it.*

Waiting is God's instrument for our good.

The psalmist said in Psalm119:71: "It is good for me that I was
afflicted, that I might learn your statutes" (ESV).

So might we have said at various times during our testing, "It is good
for us that we have been required to wait on God, that we might learn
and love Him more."

We know that hope for the important things of this life rarely sees
fruition quickly. We are not promised quick answers or results in
Scripture, but we are given multiple commands to persevere (James
1:12).

By learning to wait, we learn to trust.

As we entered yet another month—several in a row since the previous
positive sign of movement—we were reminded by these words,
written in a letter by Henry Venn, when he had lost his wife:

Did I not know the Lord to be mine, were I not certain his heart

feels even more love for me than I am able to conceive, were not this

evident to me, not by deduction and argument but by consciousness,

by his own light shining in my soul as the sun doth upon my bodily

eyes, into what deplorable situation should I have been now cast.

Our hearts ached with understanding. *Did we not know the Lord to
be ours . . .*

Yet even in our disappointment, we acknowledged that waiting is a
tool for our growth.

Romans 8:26

In the same way the Spirit also helps our weakness;
*for we do not know how to **pray** as we should, but the*
Spirit Himself intercedes for us with groanings too deep
for words.

The whole Trinity is involved in prayer.

We have an intercessor, the Holy Spirit, who mediates between us and God through the work and in the name of Jesus. No other Christian discipline demands the full attention of the entire Godhead. That, along with scores of verses that prove the point, should give us tremendous confidence that prayer is a sacred privilege.

If we misunderstand prayer to be a task and not a benefit, it will never be for us what God intended it to be.

Paul never advocates the power of positive thinking as the answer to our weakness. He never suggests we find our strength in other people. He always admonishes that we pray. And even when it seems our words are not sufficient to communicate what is in our hearts, Paul reminds us that we have a gracious Intercessor who makes as His mission the task of bearing our burdens for us so we can endure as Christ commands.

There is no good reason to faint in the day of affliction (Proverbs 24:10). God has given us the tools that we need to thrive in the face of adversity.

We have His undivided attention.

Horatius Bonar wrote:

'Tis what I know of Thee, my Lord and God,

That fills my soul with peace, my lips with song:

Thou art my health, my joy, my staff, and rod;

Leaning on Thee, in weakness I am strong.

DAY 279

Romans 10:1

*Brethren, my heart's desire and my **prayer** to God for them is for their salvation.*

More than the immediate desires of our hearts, there are things we should want.

As hard as it might be to imagine, there was something we prayed for more earnestly than the invitation to meet our child.

We prayed for the salvation of our son before we ever knew him.

One of the main questions we were asked was why we selected the country we did to adopt our child. From our perspective, it was not a difficult decision.

For a handful of reasons, God made it clear we should proceed.

For one, we met the qualifications to adopt from the country—always a bonus when beginning the process. For another, we were drawn by the knowledge that 95 percent of the country where our child was born worshiped a god who was not God.

From early in our marriage, we prayed for any children that God might give us. We prayed for their salvation, for their service in whatever area God called them to, and for their ultimate conformity to the image of Christ.

We believed that to adopt a child and teach him about the goodness and holiness of God would be the greatest privilege we could have as parents.

The day we began the adoption process, we claimed Micah 6:8 as our parenting verse: "He has told you, O man, what is good; and what does the LORD require of you but to do justice, and to love kindness, and to walk humbly with your God?" (ESV).

More than what we want, we must ultimately want what God wants.

DAY 280

Romans 12:12

*Rejoicing in **hope**, persevering in tribulation, devoted to prayer.*

It will be worth it.

Anything that causes us to rejoice, persevere, and pray to God is good.

Though we must not confuse *good* with *pain-free*—because some of life's hardest events actually hurt us to the deepest parts of our souls—we can trust that God allows "the hard stuff" to purify and not punish us.

Though the sowing and reaping principle applies at times, God does not allow tribulation into our lives for the sole purpose of bringing us pain. God's goal in testing is never limited to retribution; it always involves purification.

God wants us to be like Christ.

Anything that causes us to be more like Christ, therefore, is good.

We should agree with Dr. Sam Horn who said, "There is nothing in our life—there is nothing in our Christian experience—that will test our metal or that will try the strength of our walk with God more effectively than suffering."

When we can arrive at that conclusion, even with tears streaming down our face, we can begin to give testimony to the faithfulness of God.

"So that the tested genuineness of your faith—more precious than gold that perishes though it is tested by fire—may be found to result in praise and glory and honor at the revelation of Jesus Christ" (1 Peter 1:7 ESV).

DAY 281

Romans 15:4

*For whatever was written in earlier times was written
for our instruction, so that through perseverance and the
encouragement of the Scriptures we might have* **hope.**

Persistent, exultant, triumphant endurance—that is the purpose of God for our lives.

Romans 15:4 is clear. Our anchor in the storms of life is as strong as our trust in the Word of God. It is through reading the Bible that our perseverance and encouragement is strengthened. Practically speaking, that means we should comb the Scriptures, locating the promises of God. And then we should place them where we can readily reflect on them in moments of hesitation or uncertainty.

As Joshua was commanded to encourage and fortify his heart through the reading of God's promises, so we should do the same, heeding the words of Joshua 1:8: "This Book of the Law shall not depart from your mouth, but you shall meditate on it day and night, so that you may be careful to do according to all that is written in it. For then you will make your way prosperous, and then you will have good success" (ESV).

At various times in our adoption ordeal, our home looked like a museum of biblical affirmations. A quick tour of our house would find verses posted on the walls, the doors, the desk, the counters, and the mirrors.

We placed the promises of God where they would be seen when we would be likely to struggle with some new bit of discouraging news or troublesome hearsay. Our diligence to post the index cards, greeting cards, or church bulletins on which the verses had been written served us well.

Whether or not we felt like meditating on Scripture in a particular moment of despondency was no matter—we had to whether or not we felt like it—the verses were everywhere we could go in our house. And they gave us hope.

Romans 15:12

*Again Isaiah says, "THERE SHALL COME THE ROOT OF JESSE, AND HE WHO ARISES TO RULE OVER THE GENTILES, IN HIM SHALL THE GENTILES **HOPE**."*

Following Christ is less about convention and more about conviction.

Christianity isn't primarily about rules; it is about faith in God.

The Pharisees of the New Testament made the mistake of trusting in a set of rules and standards to demonstrate their righteousness before God.

Thankfully, as Isaiah prophesied, our true hope is found in Christ.

God is our sole source of hope.

People on occasion asked us how it was possible for us to maintain our hope during various difficult moments in our adoption. We were also asked this when we were waiting for terrifying health diagnoses and when we were mourning the loss of loved ones.

The darker it got, the more people questioned our hope.

Our answer: why *wouldn't* we hope?

In our moments of exhaustion, it is then that we most need to hope in God. In moments when we are tempted to doubt or quit or fail, it is then that we most need to hope in God. In the hardest times, hope in God most surely makes obedience to Him easier.

When we trust God, we most naturally obey Him.

"Be strong, and let your heart take courage, all you who wait for the LORD!" (Psalm 31:24 ESV).

DAY 283

Romans 15:13

*Now may the God of **hope** fill you with all joy and peace in believing, so that you will abound in **hope** by the power of the Holy Spirit.*

Take it all away and we still have all we need.

Materialistic-driven happiness is elusive and deceptive. A lust for things is not easily satisfied. Most often, this form of happiness manifests itself as a colorfully-wrapped package just out of reach. And then, like a cruel mirage on the desert sand, it disappears when we reach its location—only to appear again a few more feet away.

Which is why our happiness must be found and maintained in Christ alone.

C.S. Lewis said, "God cannot give us happiness apart from Himself, because there is no such thing."

So what does true happiness look like for the waiting child of God?—a subdued, quiet confidence and anticipation that God is working everything together for our good and His glory.

This assurance enables us to rejoice with others as they experience good news in their lives. We need not pity ourselves when others receive what we do not have—pity would indicate selfish pride, the thing God hates. Instead, we must rejoice with others, recognizing that the same God who gives good things to them is carefully awaiting the appropriate time to bless us in the very best way.

The command in Romans 12:15 to "Rejoice with those who rejoice, weep with those who weep" (ESV) is as much about being glad for others as it is about weeping with them.

Christ gives us the grace to do both.

DAY 284

Romans 15:30

*Now I urge you, brethren, by our Lord Jesus Christ and
by the love of the Spirit, to strive together with me in your
prayers to God for me.*

Difficulties grow our awareness for our need of a Savior.

When we realize how truly inadequate we are, we will pray most effectively.

Our awareness of our capabilities must be adjusted to God's revelation: "I am the vine; you are the branches. Whoever abides in me and I in him, he it is that bears much fruit, for apart from me you can do nothing" (John 15:5 ESV).

Nothing is a tough word. *Nothing* means *zero, zilch, zip, zippo.*

At few other times are we as aware of our inadequacy as when we are staring in the face of something we cannot accomplish on our own. For us, it was the magnitude of getting to our child who lived on the other side of the planet—and aligning all of the people and paperwork necessary to make it happen. For others, it is an illness that is incapacitating or a financial situation that looks impossible.

We must recognize that we have all of the ability of a fistful of branches stuck in the ground and told to bear fruit, unless, of course, we abide in our Heavenly Father.

Boldness, like that which the apostles possessed, is often born out of desperation to see God act in a situation completely out of our control. In Romans 15:30, Paul was begging his brothers and sisters in Christ to pray for him.

Though we are incapable of doing many things for those we love, we are able and invited to pray. And, likewise, we are encouraged to ask others to pray on our behalf.

DAY 285

1 Corinthians 4:5

*Therefore do not go on passing judgment before the time, but **wait** until the Lord comes who will both bring to light the things hidden in the darkness and disclose the motives of men's hearts; and then each man's praise will come to him from God.*

We honor God when our obedience costs us something.

It is easy to obey when the command is simple. Being kind to those who are kind to us, for instance, does not take a lot of effort on our part. Singing when our heart is light is not a difficult challenge for the musically-inclined. Confidence about something for which there is no risk is not a threat.

But trusting when God is silent, hoping when the day is dark, and praying when the heart is heavy—that is the kind of obedience that honors God. Obedience that costs us something is obedience that indicates selflessness.

Over time, we came to understand that our chief goal could not be meeting our son. Our chief goal could only and always be obedience to God.

"The end of the matter; all has been heard. Fear God and keep his commandments, for this is the whole duty of man" (Ecclesiastes 12:13 ESV).

As 1 Corinthians 4:5 indicates, God is concerned with our motives. He is not just interested in *what* we do. Though righteousness of action is paramount to holiness of living, He wants us to please Him for the right reasons.

God will reward those in due time who obey Him because they love Him and not because they want something.

We must wait correctly.

1 Corinthians 9:10

*Or is He speaking altogether for our sake? Yes, for our sake
it was written, because the plowman ought to plow in* **hope**,
and the thresher to thresh in **hope** *of sharing the crops.*

Contentment is so much better than happiness.

On day 603 of our adoption wait, we struck the words "by now" from
our vocabulary.

Though we had long before retired our timelines, guesstimates, or
speculations, there was still the nagging voice that reminded us, "He
should have been here by now."

Trips to visit friends, dinners to commemorate accomplishments, or
holidays to celebrate family reminded us that he hadn't arrived when we
had anticipated him. We had saved up vacation days at work to spend
with him, but the year was expiring and the days were untouched.

We were sad. He obviously *was not* meant to be with us yet. That much
was clear.

And so we chose contentment.

True hope is trusting even when the outcome is unknown. As farmers
plant in the spring with the hope of a good harvest, so the new
treatment is started in hopes of stopping the cancer or the room is
prepared in hopes of bringing the child home.

And then we wait.

"But we have this treasure in jars of clay, to show that the surpassing
power belongs to God and not to us. We are afflicted in every way, but
not crushed; perplexed, but not driven to despair; persecuted, but not
forsaken; struck down, but not destroyed" (2 Corinthians 4:7–9 ESV).

Amid all of our questions, we knew this much: Christ, alone, can fulfill
our desires.

DAY 287

1 Corinthians 13:7

*Bears all things, believes all things, **hopes** all things, endures all things.*

God graciously provides every tool we need to endure the way He requires.

The greatest gift God gives us in moments of uncertainty is His unfailing presence. When our wait reached twenty months, we began listening to the Psalms whenever we had an opportunity. There was rarely a moment of quiet in our home that wasn't filled with the comfort of these sustaining words. And always—regardless of where we began our meditation—we were careful to include Psalm 23.

One day, we were stopped in our tracks by the truth of Psalm 23:3: "He restores my soul. He leads me in paths of righteousness for his name's sake" (ESV).

For His name's sake.

God has obligated Himself to lead us through whatever difficulty He has ordained us to travel. And if that is not enough, God commands us to talk to Him and to ask for the things we need. It is for His name's sake that He does all good things on our behalf.

What else could we possibly require in order to believe, hope, and endure all things?

Isaiah 41:13 says, "For I, the LORD your God, hold your right hand; it is I who say to you, 'Fear not, I am the one who helps you,' " (ESV).

This reference to God holding our "right hand" is a demonstration that He is always and ever present. We do not suffer outside the watchful care of our Heavenly Father.

He is with us now and forever. His name is on the line.

DAY 288

1 Corinthians 14:15

*What is the outcome then? I will **pray** with the spirit and I will **pray** with the mind also; I will sing with the spirit and I will sing with the mind also.*

Praying with the mind means we must align our thoughts with God's truth.

Specifically when our hearts are heavy, we should be careful to avoid the pitfalls of erroneous thinking which leads naturally to incorrect praying and faulty living.

"Finally, brothers, whatever is true, whatever is honorable, whatever is just, whatever is pure, whatever is lovely, whatever is commendable, if there is any excellence, if there is anything worthy of praise, think about these things" (Philippians 4:8 ESV).

Though Paul is speaking, specifically, of tongues in 1 Corinthians 14, he makes the point that correct praying involves correct thinking.

At few other times is thinking correctly as paramount as when we are battling unbelief.

In times of testing, we must fixate on God's truth.

When we understand how great God is, the details of our waiting will be secondary to the details of His glory. We will be more consumed with pleasing Him than getting what we desire. We will want what He wants more than what we want.

We will pray and sing in a language that is understood.

Praying with the mind means we must align our thoughts with God's truth.

DAY 289

1 Corinthians 15:19

*If we have **hoped** in Christ in this life only, we are of all men most to be pitied.*

The object of our hope in this life will be the object of our hope in the next life.

If there were no hope to be had outside of this life in this world, we would be smart to live it up. In the words of Ecclesiastes 8, we would be foolish not to eat, drink, and be merry. What more would there be but death and the grave?

But there is hope to be had.

The hope is Christ.

We endure in this life because we are confident of the life to come.

In the words of Matthew Henry, "Let all that suffer for Christ and with Christ comfort themselves with this, that yet a little while and they also shall say, 'It is finished.'"

It is finished!

We longed to say those words about our exhausting wait for our son. We could taste the words at times, longed to shout them from the rooftop. But so much more, we longed to say those words about our strenuous wait to see Christ.

We must be eager to maintain a perspective during periods of hard waiting that readily reflects on what Christ has accomplished and will accomplish in our lives.

Our moment to say "It is finished!" will come soon enough.

DAY 290

2 Corinthians 1:7

And our **hope** *for you is firmly grounded, knowing that as you are sharers of our sufferings, so also you are sharers of our comfort.*

The true and lasting comfort in this life is found in belonging to God.

It is through the weakness of man that God delights to demonstrate His power (2 Corinthians 12:9). In 2 Corinthians 1:7, Paul explains in his letter to the Corinthian believers that, because they shared in Christ's suffering, they too could share of Christ's comfort.

The benefit of Christ's comfort—the provision of His presence—belongs to believers.

At no other time is this comfort more viable than in the valley.

There is no greater theme in the life of the Christian than that of the great love of God.

The later our adoption progressed, the quicker we were to recognize the grace of God in our lives. A wave would hit—in the form of delays or fee increases or silence—and we would wait for the subsequent wave of grace. *That*, we were confident, is God's comforting love.

Dying of tuberculosis, Henry Lyte was inspired to write the hymn, *Abide with Me*. As the story goes, he finished the words on the Sunday he gave his last sermon in the church where he had long been faithful. Three weeks later, he was with the Lord. His words—particularly the seventh verse—were of great comfort to us as we waited for our son:

I fear no foe, with Thee at hand to bless;

Ills have no weight, and tears no bitterness.

Where is death's sting? Where, grave, thy victory?

I triumph still, if Thou abide with me.

DAY 291

2 Corinthians 1:9

*Indeed, we had the sentence of death within ourselves so that we would not **trust** in ourselves, but in God who raises the dead.*

God uses broken people.

One of the wonderful insights we glean from the Bible is the number of people that God chose to humble before He chose to employ. Many great men and women of God were first tested by trial and strengthened by tribulation before—or in order that—God could use them.

Though we do not always have insight as to why certain circumstances occur, we can rightly conclude that trials that humble us prepare us for greater usefulness by God.

God allowed Paul to reach the edges of his own abilities so that he was forced to rely on God and not himself. Paul gave testimony to this fact in 2 Corinthians 1:9.

"So that we would not trust ourselves" is a sufficient reason to experience difficulty.

But God does not desire to leave us broken or bewildered, bitter or bereft. Though at times we may serve Him best by experiencing pain or suffering, He has given us a proven stronghold in which to take comfort: Himself.

No one else and nothing else comes close to measuring up to God's stability.

It is this stability—in Christ alone—that enabled Paul to say, without any sign of fear or dread, that he had the sentence of death within himself. No doubt he understood, as C. H. Spurgeon would later understand, that: "Saints will not die prematurely; they will be immortal until their work is done."

And how much better that work will be if the saint is broken for service!

DAY 292

2 Corinthians 1:10

Who delivered us from so great a peril of death, and will deliver us, He on whom we have set our **hope.** *And He will yet deliver us.*

God never experiences the panic that threatens the human heart.

What, to us, looks perilous, to Him looks planned. God knows how He is going to work things out. He is not struck with the same horror when He looks at our situation as we are when we examine it.

What may look hopeless to us is not hopeless at all.

He who designed it sees it best from any angle, knows how He will work it for our good.

In the case of 2 Corinthians 1:10, it is always the purpose of God to deliver His people, either in this life or the next. What is terrifying to us is not terrifying to Him.

He is in control. He promises to deliver us.

At a very opportune time, a friend reminded us of these words from the hymn, *Jesus Lives and So Shall I*:

Jesus lives, and reigns supreme,

And, his kingdom still remaining,

I shall also be with him,

Ever living, ever reigning.

God has promised: be it must:

Jesus is my Hope and Trust.

DAY 293

2 Corinthians 3:12

*Therefore having such a **hope**, we use great boldness in our speech.*

Gospel certainty produces indestructible hope.

We did not shy away from discussing why we were able to maintain hope during our difficult adoption process. There were days when, by all means, we should have put our hands up and walked away.

Yet, because of what Christ did for us through the gospel, we had strength to continue.

It is not always popular, in a culture that values self-sufficiency, to admit that we cannot handle something on our own or in our own strength.

But it is true.

Without the hope of God, we are hopeless indeed.

With the hope of God, we have all the hope we need.

Many times when we would get discouraging news about some aspect of our process, we had to remind ourselves that God was in control. We watched to see if certain things would happen in our case even after we were told they wouldn't.

When they did, we found more boldness to tell others of our hope in Christ.

According to 2 Corinthians 3:12, Paul was able to preach the gospel with conviction because he believed with certainty the promises of God.

The same God who strengthened Christ to endure, strengthens us to endure.

"I can do all things through him who strengthens me" (Philippians 4:13 ESV).

2 Corinthians 9:14

*While they also, by **prayer** on your behalf, yearn for you because of the surpassing grace of God in you.*

Every day, God supplies us with the grace we need.

We know that we were saved by grace (Ephesians 2:8), but if we think of grace as only pertaining to salvation—and not profitable and available to us daily for everything that we need—we will live confused and frustrated lives.

New testing will always be supplied with new grace.

The day we found out a worker on our case was not being helpful, God provided the grace we needed to respond correctly to the difficult individual and the grace to fill out the hundreds of forms. Had God required we give up on adopting our son instead of dealing with the frustrations, He would have provided the grace for that.

But we always had enough grace to do what we were expected to do that day. *Always.*

On the inside of our Bible is affixed a slip of paper with these words, written by John Piper:

What is sustaining grace?

Not grace to bar what is not bliss,

Nor flight from all distress, but this:

The grace that orders our trouble and pain,

And then, in the darkness, is there to sustain.

DAY 295

2 Corinthians 13:9

*For we rejoice when we ourselves are weak but you are strong; this we also **pray** for, that you be made complete.*

Joy, for Christ, made His suffering worthwhile.

Suffering is often the origin of joy.

Joy is not just a possibility during suffering. Joy is actually a product of suffering.

When the Bible speaks of suffering, there is usually a blessing involved. In the Scriptures, suffering and blessing are linked; it is difficult to find verses where one is mentioned to the exclusivity of the other.

And most often, joy *is* the blessing.

At least eighteen times in the New Testament Scriptures, joy and suffering are mentioned together. It is the purpose of God for our lives that we find joy in Him while suffering, regardless of where on the spectrum of pain we endure.

But to find and experience joy in hardship, we must desire it.

"Therefore, since we are surrounded by so great a cloud of witnesses, let us also lay aside every weight, and sin which clings so closely, and let us run with endurance the race that is set before us, looking to Jesus, the founder and perfecter of our faith, who for the joy that was set before him endured the cross, despising the shame, and is seated at the right hand of the throne of God" (Hebrews 12:1–2 ESV).

Likewise, joy, for us, will make our pain worthwhile!

DAY 296

Galatians 5:5

For we through the Spirit, by faith, are waiting for the
hope *of righteousness.*

Our waiting—for whatever it is—is only meant to be for a season.

The greatest object of our waiting is the hope of Christ's return. We know with the certainty of the Word that seeing Christ will only be a matter of time.

Though, as children of God, we have already received Christ's righteousness, imputed to us at salvation, we are still "waiting for our blessed hope, the appearing of the glory of our great God and Savior Jesus Christ" (Titus 2:13 ESV).

Though Galatians 5 speaks of works versus faith for salvation, the truth carries through to the rest of our lives. Faith in God is the most important element of our walk with Him.

The reality is this. God doesn't always end our stories on earth the way we hope He will. He does not owe us the picture perfect conclusion or the made-for-television finale. But we should watch with a keen eye for His work in the details. For He is the God of redemptive ends. He will redeem us. He will cause all things to work for our good and His glory.

If not in this life, we will have our perfect ending in the life to come— in which there will be no ending at all.

As the Spirit equips us with the faith necessary for salvation, so the Spirit equips us with the hope necessary to believe these things and to endure the way we have been instructed.

Alexander Maclaren rightly said that "Hope is faith directed to the future."

DAY 297

Ephesians 1:12

*To the end that we who were the first to **hope** in Christ would be to the praise of His glory.*

God is often most glorified—not in delivering us from hard things—but in giving us the grace to endure them.

No greater example exists than the supreme purpose of God in man's redemption.

In all of human history, God was most glorified the day Christ suffered on the cross as the perfect atonement for sin, making possible the salvation of those in whom God delights. Christ's death on the cross was glory's climatic moment in the purposes of God.

God could have rescued Christ from Calvary, certainly He could have done so with a look or a word or a nod, but He was most glorified to ordain the death of His beloved Son.

Did God allow Christ's death or design it?

Undoubtedly, He designed it. The sovereign plan was revealed in Genesis 3.

That God doesn't always deliver us from pain and suffering in this life isn't an indication that He cannot do it or does not love us. If God doesn't deliver us from hardship, it is because He is most glorified for us to endure.

And God can never be less than right about His plans for us.

That God doesn't always deliver us from pain and suffering in this life isn't an indication that He cannot do it or does not love us.

DAY 298

Ephesians 1:18

*I **pray** that the eyes of your heart may be enlightened, so that you will know what is the **hope** of His calling, what are the riches of the glory of His inheritance in the saints.*

When the day is dark, it is easier to miss the blessings all around us.

Orphan Sunday and daylight savings coincided on the same day in November while we were waiting for news of our son. To say the day was darker for us is to be literal as well as figurative.

Our hearts broke for the millions of children worldwide without families. Of course, our hearts were heavy for our own son who was growing up in an orphanage 8,500 miles from our front door. We longed to bring him home.

On days when it is darkest, it is wise to meditate on the goodness of God.

There is a song, written in 1897, that encourages believers to count their blessings one by one. This is a practice we found to be of particular encouragement. On the roller coaster of life, the lows can multiply quickly and feel longer in duration than the highs. It is at these moments when discouragement can take root in our hearts which makes it all the more important to acknowledge the blessings that we do have from God, no matter how minor the kindness may be.

As Ephesians 1:18 explains, a spiritually enlightened heart is the key to understanding the blessing of hope and the inheritance of God. God has truly given us much to be thankful for!

"For God, who said, 'Let light shine out of darkness,' has shone in our hearts to give the light of the knowledge of the glory of God in the face of Jesus Christ" (2 Corinthians 4:6 ESV).

DAY 299

Ephesians 2:12

*Remember that you were at that time separate from
Christ, excluded from the commonwealth of Israel, and
strangers to the covenants of promise, having no **hope** and
without God in the world.*

For the child of God, there is always hope to be found.

There is nothing more hopeless than being estranged from God. Ephesians 2:12 paints the picture of an unregenerate individual, without access to the precious promises of God.

The image is bleak and off-putting.

Nothing should pump fear into the human heart like the inability to be known by God.

On the other hand, there is nothing more hopeful than fellowship with the Father.

We have done nothing—could do nothing—that would bring us closer to the hope that is found in Him. The only thing that makes God's perfect hope attainable is the blood of Christ and His work on the cross.

"But now in Christ Jesus you who once were far off have been brought near by the blood of Christ" (Ephesians 2:13 ESV).

Throughout our wait, we have heard the statement many times, "I don't know how you have managed to endure through all of this."

The truth is, on our own, we can't. But through the strength and hope found in God as His children, we can. Because of Christ's suffering, our suffering on this earth is less severe.

DAY 300

Ephesians 4:4

*There is one body and one Spirit, just as also you were called in one **hope** of your calling.*

God did not equip us to be self-sustaining during suffering.

In addition to having the Holy Spirit for guidance and comfort (John 14:16), we were given the gift of companionship within the body of Christ. As one body, we don't suffer separately: "If one member suffers, all suffer together; if one member is honored, all rejoice together" (1 Corinthians 12:26 ESV).

Available today are an amazing number of help networks and support groups for every conceivable illness, hardship, or addiction. A quick search on the Internet will turn up thousands of links for nearly every one of life's complexities.

Going through our cancer scare and then adoption journey, we were inundated with opportunities to meet with others who were experiencing the same things.

The professional community has acknowledged that people deal with the issues in their lives better when they can communicate their troubles to others. When facing a devastating illness or loss, one of the first things physicians will do is point a person in the direction of a group or counselor.

But community support groups are really only weaker versions of what God intends for the body of Christ. God has ordained flesh and blood to care for His children in their moments of need, whether physical or spiritual. But unlike a neighborhood support group, the body of Christ can pray and offer truth when it needs to be vocalized.

"Bear one another's burdens, and so fulfill the law of Christ" (Galatians 6:2 ESV).

DAY 301

Ephesians 6:18

*With all **prayer** and petition **pray** at all times in the Spirit, and with this in view, be on the alert with all perseverance and petition for all the saints.*

We glorify God when we endure.

If there were no other reason for us to endure than God's glory, we would have sufficient reason to do so. We honor God when we endure the way He commands.

What could be better than that?

Since the purpose of man is to glorify God, it would make sense that we understand what motivates endurance so we can do it correctly. Like the other disciplines of the Christian life, perseverance is not intended to be an act of human resolve.

Perseverance is a work of God within us.

God desires that we endure persistently by praying continually.

Ephesians 6:18 defines the Christian's prayer life in the way that pleases God.

With prayer . . . persevere.

John Wesley explains Ephesians 6:18 this way: "Praying always—at all times, and on every occasion, in the midst of all employments, inwardly praying without ceasing."

We must persevere, believing that the only prayer life worth having is the kind that endures storms.

Ephesians 6:19

*And **pray** on my behalf, that utterance may be given to me in the opening of my mouth, to make known with boldness the mystery of the gospel.*

Our prayer during periods of waiting should not be for escape but for growth.

It is a good possibility that, according to God's providential design, Paul encountered his greatest ministry opportunities in prison, while praying for his fellow Christians and writing letters that would be read by believers for centuries.

One reason his ministry was effective was because of the requests he made while sitting in that cell. He didn't petition primarily for personal comfort, assistance, or release—though, who would blame him for doing so?

Paul wanted spiritual growth in the form of boldness to witness to non-believers, including the men who were imprisoning him.

No doubt Paul understood that a utopian society on this earth was not to be found. And so, instead of placing comfort and freedom above growth and godliness, he prayed for opportunities to be used by God.

In essence, Paul's perspective graduated from temporal to eternal when he prayed for boldness to preach the gospel.

Lord, grant that our trials would expose our superficial cravings.

> *... instead of placing comfort and freedom above growth and godliness, he prayed for opportunities to be used by God.*

DAY 303

Philippians 1:4

*Always offering **prayer** with joy in my every **prayer** for you all.*

When we are discontent, we tell the world that God is not enough.

Being freed from the bondage of disappointment, childlessness, illness, or pain would be a wonderful thing. And certainly, we are invited to offer our prayer to God for all of those things. As Paul did, it is essential that we exhibit joyfulness in the midst of our waiting.

When Paul wrote Philippians 1:4, he was sitting in a Roman prison, and not the type of jail cells our society maintains today with prepared meals and warm showers and outdoor recreation. Paul was writing in a cell that lacked any sort of nod to any prisoner's rights.

Yet when he prayed for those he loved, he did so joyfully. He expressed without reservation that he was pleased to pray for those to whom he ministered.

By his attitude, Paul confirmed that God was enough for him.

So it is, in the midst of our waiting for God to deliver us—now or in the life to come—that we have the opportunity to demonstrate for others that we have all we need in Christ.

Prayer takes us out of the prison of our anxiety and places us in the throne room of grace.

Isaac Newton explained it well: "I can take my telescope and look millions and millions of miles into space, but I can lay it aside and go into my room, shut the door, get down on my knees in earnest prayer and see more of Heaven and get closer to God than I can assisted by all the telescopes and material agencies on earth."

DAY 304

Philippians 1:9

*And this I **pray**, that your love may abound still more and more in real knowledge and all discernment.*

Discouragement breeds bad theology.

Five minutes in the furnace will yield the well-meaning counsel of those who have a weak understanding of God's desire for suffering. In fact, it takes no time at all in the valley for us to realize how fragile our own theology at times can be.

"I don't deserve this!" and "Nobody cares!" are illustrations of weak and unbiblical thinking. Though it is not a popular memo to receive during difficulty, we must be reminded that, fundamentally, we deserve much worse than what we're experiencing.

Are our circumstances painful? Absolutely.

Are we being spared from worse? Absolutely.

We must understand that our present, discouraging circumstances are not necessarily the direct result of our choices—cancer or loss, for instance, isn't the product of a poor prayer life—but these difficulties should encourage us that God is good. And God does care.

That we are only experiencing cancer or loss and not hell and eternal separation from Christ is the benevolence of our good God.

When we are tempted to believe that God doesn't care, we must return to truth.

> *Discouragement breeds bad theology.*

DAY 305

Philippians 1:14

*And that most of the brethren, **trusting** in the Lord
because of my imprisonment, have far more courage to
speak the word of God without fear.*

We must never doubt that God is able to do His greatest work in us
when we are waiting.

Paul's willingness to endure his waiting the way Christ intends made
those who watched him grow in their boldness to witness for Christ.
How many people heard about the Savior because of one man's
humble submission to the mission of God for his life?

Though Paul trusted God throughout his ministry, while in and out
of prison, there is no doubt that God worked mightily through him
while he waited.

And waited. And waited.

Paul suffered much as a result of his calling (2 Corinthians 11:24–29).
Yet, throughout all of this, he did not lose faith. Instead, the opposite
occurred and his courage/trust increased because of God's faithfulness
to him in trials.

We are no less usable to God when we submit as He desires.

A.W. Tozer, in his book, *Root of the Righteous*, said: "The devil,
things, and people being what they are, it is necessary for God to use
the hammer, the file, and the furnace in His holy work of preparing a
saint for true sainthood. It is doubtful whether God can bless a man
greatly until He has hurt him deeply."

So the pain being what it is, let us pray for God to render us most
useful to Him!

DAY 306

Philippians 1:19

For I know that this will turn out for my deliverance through your **prayers** *and the provision of the Spirit of Jesus Christ.*

Paul's confidence that things would turn out for his deliverance resulted from faith that was motivated by correct thinking about God. His assurance was not located in himself. It was rooted in Christ.

Our faith, too, must be strengthened by Scripturally-informed thinking.

The reality is that we can't change how we feel about something. We can't alter the circumstances that have been providentially ordained. But we can modify the way we think—and therefore—the way we view God. And sometimes our feelings are changed when our thinking is corrected.

Like trust, hope, and prayer, faith is not a feeling at all. It's a choice. Whom we trust in difficulty makes all the difference.

We can experience Paul's confidence when we have faith in someone greater than ourselves. In the words of Charles Wesley:

Other refuge have I none,

Hangs my helpless soul on Thee;

Leave, ah! Leave me not alone,

Still support and comfort me!

All my trust on Thee is stayed.

All my help from Thee I bring;

Cover my defenseless head

With the shadow of Thy wing.

DAY 307

Philippians 1:20

*According to my earnest expectation and **hope**, that I
will not be put to shame in anything, but that with all
boldness, Christ will even now, as always, be exalted in my
body, whether by life or by death.*

Why?

This is the quiet, nagging question for the child of God who
experiences disappointment.

Why does terminal illness exist? Why do car accidents happen?
Why do children suffer? Why, in a single day, are thousands killed in
natural disasters or terrorist attacks? Why?

And while there is no easy response to offer the parent, the spouse,
or the wounded, there is a straightforward answer: The universe—
everything God made—exists to display God's glory. By His omniscient
design He has crafted for our lives the events and circumstances that
will best glorify Himself. Everything happens according to the eternal
purpose of God.

Confirmed throughout the Bible is the reality that suffering is
necessary for Christ to demonstrate His grace. Consider the Garden of
Eden. In Genesis 3, man, by his willful decision to sin, was introduced
to the suffering of a sin-cursed world. God's gracious response to
this complicated circumstance was to send His Son to die on the
cross in the greatest display of His grace that man would ever know.
Additionally, in another demonstration of suffering and grace, Christ's
anguish on the cross made possible God's grace in eternal salvation.

Without suffering there is neither the need nor the arena for God's
grace to be displayed.

Philippians 1:20 is, in part, Paul's personal mission statement—that
in everything, whether that be in life or death—he would magnify
Christ. If the point of everything in the world is to make God's grace
observable, then Paul's response is the only and proper way we can
react to disappointment. The answer to every "why?" question is the
unambiguous reply, "to display God's glory!"

DAY 308

Philippians 3:20

*For our citizenship is in heaven, from which also we
eagerly **wait** for a Savior, the Lord Jesus Christ.*

Contentment is not included in conversion.

In addition to our own experience with discontentment, we have
Paul's words in Philippians 4:11: "Not that I am speaking of being
in need, for I have learned in whatever situation I am to be content"
(ESV).

That Paul had to learn to be content indicates it is not innate.

So how can we learn to be content, and even experience joy, during
difficulty?

For the Christian to be able to "count it all joy"—as the Bible
commands (James 1:2 ESV)—it is imperative that the child of God
bear in mind the Father's sovereignty in every situation.

Joy—or the eager waiting mentioned in Philippians 3:20—is not
manufactured from feelings. Contentment, resulting in real and
lasting joy, grows out of the belief that God is sufficient.

At the heart of contentment is Christ.

Of these truths, Dr. Michael Barrett said, "I think we understand well
that spiritual happiness is a contentment and a satisfaction of the soul
that is absolutely independent of and unaffected by the stuff of life.
There is an indestructibility in Christian joy because it is founded in
the Lord and not in circumstance."

DAY 309

Philippians 4:6

*Be anxious for nothing, but in everything by **prayer** and supplication with thanksgiving let your requests be made known to God.*

God forbids worry.

As children, we were taught to avoid using words like "nothing" and "everything," because they most often made the sentence impossible or untrue.

Philippians 4:6 uses them both—and in so doing—becomes one of the most unsuspecting, yet difficult verses in the Bible to obey. Worry about *nothing*. Pray about *everything*.

Of Philippians 4:6, Hudson Taylor said, "Do we fail to be anxious for nothing, and to bring everything by prayer and supplication with thanksgiving before God? We may bring nine difficulties out of ten to Him, and try to manage the tenth ourselves, and the one little difficulty, like a small leak that runs the vessel dry, is fatal to the whole."

God is aware of how little it takes to upset us or distract us from the course. Though we would like to believe it is only the larger problems that disorient us, we are often more distressed by rumors or perceived slights than we are the diagnosis or the loss of something dear.

Perhaps this is why we are reminded to take *every* concern to Him and leave it there.

The God-ordained response to worry is prayer.

DAY 310

Colossians 1:3

*We give thanks to God, the Father of our Lord Jesus Christ, **praying** always for you.*

"God has a plan for me in this."

These are the words we became accustomed to repeating on the long days when we waited for test results or updates about our child.

God is governing all things. The future is His.

What an amazing thought that God knows everything there is to know about us. He is acquainted with our choices; he is attentive to our path; and He is infinitely aware of our needs, even more aware of our needs than we are.

Better still, according to Philippians 4:19, He has promised to supply.

Men and women throughout the ages have rested in the realization that God had a plan for their lives—though at times the path traveled through deep waters or low valleys—and it always arrived at a destination better than their choosing.

Words spoken to Joshua would do well to be heard by us: "Have I not commanded you? Be strong and courageous. Do not be frightened, and do not be dismayed, for the Lord your God is with you wherever you go" (Joshua 1:9 ESV).

Contentment with God produces rest.

> *What an amazing thought that God knows everything there is to know about us.*

DAY 311

Colossians 1:5

*Because of the **hope** laid up for you in heaven, of which*
you previously heard in the word of truth, the gospel.

The way to endure difficulty is to remember God's goodness in salvation.

We learned during our time of waiting that there is comfort and strength to be found in the gospel, not just for those who have never heard, but for those who know and love the Lord.

We are mistaken if we do not believe that the gospel provides strength for us daily.

When we arrive at the place where we know that God owes us nothing, then we will stop believing life is unfair because of our trials. And when we arrive at the place where we know everything in our lives is a gift from Him, then we begin believing that life is unfair because of our blessings.

"When I consider your heavens, the work of your fingers, the moon and the stars, which you have set in place, what is man that you are mindful of him, the son of man that you care for him?" (Psalm 8:3–4 ESV).

Yet, God cares for us more than anyone else ever could. We will never outlive His love.

When it comes to the gospel:

The same faith that saves, sustains.

The same Word that convicts, comforts.

The same God that grants, guides.

DAY 312

Colossians 1:9

*For this reason also, since the day we heard of it, we have not ceased to **pray** for you and to ask that you may be filled with the knowledge of His will in all spiritual wisdom and understanding.*

The card arrived in the mail the same day we received difficult news from the adoption agency. It was a simple card from our friend, which said: "This is just a note to say that I am praying for you today!"

We could have received a letter from the President of the United States, and it wouldn't have meant as much. We affixed it to the bedroom door of our waiting child to remind us each time we passed it that God was hearing the prayers of others on our behalf.

We were likewise prompted to pray for others.

 Because we need prayer does not exempt us from praying for others.

We prayed for the lady whose son lived with ours—only her son had H.I.V. and needed to be adopted so that he could begin medication. We prayed for our sister in Christ who battled breast cancer. We prayed for members of our church heading to the mission field.

It is easy to forget praying for others when our own lists are long, but doing so is unacceptable. Paul, the author of Colossians, was in jail when he prayed for the recipients of his letter.

Because we need prayer does not exempt us from praying for others.

DAY 313

Colossians 1:23

*If indeed you continue in the faith firmly established and steadfast, and not moved away from the **hope** of the gospel that you have heard, which was proclaimed in all creation under heaven, and of which I, Paul, was made a minister.*

Waiting tests the strength of our faith.

When the skies are blue and the bills are paid, when the family is healthy and our relationships are strong, it is easy to have faith in the Almighty. When everything is going well, our God *apparently* has everything under control.

But trusting God on sunny afternoons is like doing chin ups with our feet planted firmly on the ground. Our strength isn't tested until our limits are challenged.

And waiting challenges our limits like very little else.

Grace abounds for those who wait in silence, trusting God and relying wholly on His promises. And what has He promised?—that He is the same yesterday, today, and forever (Hebrews 13:8). Meaning God is the God of the good days and of the bad. He is worthy of our worship in the storm and in the sunshine. He is good all the time.

God always has everything under control.

One way that He demonstrates His goodness is that He allows our faith to be tested so that we can know, as He already knows, how much or little we truly rely on Him.

DAY 314

Colossians 1:27

*To whom God willed to make known what is the riches
of the glory of this mystery among the Gentiles, which is
Christ in you, the **hope** of glory.*

Hope is always at our disposal.

In light of God's incredible gift of the gospel, we can rejoice in Him
during our darkest hours.

Even when filled with illness, loss, or loneliness, our lives are far
better than the lives of those who are lost in sin though happy in
circumstance. For though we encounter very real trials and pain, at
the end of it all, we have the enormous wealth of the gospel in our
possession.

And because losing the gospel is impossible for the believer, we always
have a reason to hope.

Knowing that the riches and the hope of glory await us if we are a child
of God, we ought to find contentment in whatever circumstances we
face. But we will not find contentment in life until we are satisfied
with Christ.

When we realize Christ is more than enough, life is as it should be.

God is always and only good. We have every reason to hope in Him.

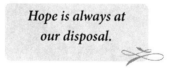

*Hope is always at
our disposal.*

DAY 315

Colossians 4:2

*Devote yourselves to **prayer**, keeping alert in it with an attitude of thanksgiving.*

Glorifying God is not primarily something we do with our lips.

Undoubtedly, during times of waiting, there are opportunities at our disposal to glorify God in verbal testimony. And we should be quick to praise Him. But people who know we are experiencing difficulty are waiting to see what we do and not just hear what we say.

It is one thing to say that God is good and another thing entirely to live as if we believe it.

Trials are often opportunities to preach the gospel with our lives. We should never miss an opportunity to trust God publicly for the sake of those who do not know Him. Neither should we neglect trusting God publicly for the sake of those who will someday encounter trials of their own.

Colossians 4:2 provides us with an essential instruction for enduring well. Without prayer, we cannot accomplish our appointed tasks—including glorifying God with our lives. Certainly we cannot sustain an attitude of thanksgiving without the grace God promises to supply us through prayer.

We participated in an adoption forum, we "bumped into people" in places like the grocery store or the bank who were trying to adopt, we talked to people at church. Each opportunity existed for us to demonstrate God's goodness or to complain about a process that was exhausting.

Remember that rejoicing is a choice.

Colossians 4:3

Praying *at the same time for us as well, that God will open up to us a door for the word, so that we may speak forth the mystery of Christ, for which I have also been imprisoned.*

We must never underestimate the opportunities that exist in affliction.

It is entirely possible that Paul's greatest earthly ministry transpired while he was in prison. Among his greatest duties, he wrote letters and prayed for the body of Christ. Both of these activities had spiritual, historical significance—not only for his direct recipients, but for us as well.

If Paul ever believed that his ministry could be greater served outside of prison, he would have grossly underestimated what God planned to do with his pain.

Likewise, we have no idea what God intends to do with ours.

In Colossians 4:3, the term *door* denotes "opportunity." Opportunities abound when we endure hardships. For one, we have occasion to talk to other people who are experiencing the same struggles—to offer to them what has been encouraging to us. For another, we can communicate with those who stop to ask us how we're doing, whether or not they understand.

We were blessed to have an incredible church family who reached out to ask us about our adoption weekly.

Each time we talked to someone, we knew we had the chance to express the goodness of God in our lives. Those connections with people may have been God's purpose for us in waiting. We may never know. But whenever He opened up a door for His Word to be shared, we took it.

Opportunities are plentiful in the lowlands.

DAY 317

1 Thessalonians 1:3 ESV

*Remembering before our God and Father your work of faith and labor of love and steadfastness of **hope** in our Lord Jesus Christ.*

God is faithful.

The waiting may feel like it's going to kill us, but it won't. Throughout our experience, people were quick to remind us that when we finally had our son in our home, it would feel like the waiting was short.

Though we were not confident that the wait would feel anything other than long, we did agree that holding our son in our arms would be worth the wait.

No doubt about that.

And until then—and even thereafter—God would be faithful to us.

In allowing the difficulties into our lives that ultimately cause us to wait for and depend upon God, God is actually keeping His promise to give us exactly what we need.

"And my God will supply every need of yours according to his riches in glory in Christ Jesus" (Philippians 4:19 ESV).

The truth is we need God above everything else. And in seasons of testing, it seems we have more of Him than we do at any other time.

He is faithful to us. We must be faithful to Him.

 The truth is we need God above everything else.

DAY 318

1 Thessalonians 2:19

*For who is our **hope** or joy or crown of exultation? Is it not*
even you, in the presence of our Lord Jesus at His coming?

That Christ would be on display in our lives.

Our goal is that when people look at us, they don't see us for who
we are, but rather they see Christ for who He is: matchlessly holy,
perfectly good, and unfathomably wise.

We must be willing to embrace anything that makes us more like
Christ—that reflects Him in an otherwise troubling time.

Anything.

These words, taken from a portion of a prayer from Bennet's *Valley*
of Vision are written on a piece of paper, torn from a steno pad, and
taped on a door in our home where we can see it daily.

> *Thou hast done for me all things well, hast remembered,*
>
> *distinguished, indulged me. All my desires have not been gratified,*
>
> *but thy love denied them to me when fulfillment of my wishes*
>
> *would have proved my ruin or injury. My trials have been fewer*
>
> *than my sins, and when I have kissed the rod it has fallen from thy*
>
> *hands. Thou hast often wiped away my tears, restored peace to my*
>
> *mourning heart, chastened me for my profit. All thy work for me is*
>
> *perfect, and I praise thee.*

Yes, that Christ would be on display in our lives.

It's the least we can do for all He has done!

DAY 319

1 Thessalonians 3:10

*As we night and day keep **praying** most earnestly that we may see your face, and may complete what is lacking in your faith.*

God is sovereign over all our deficiencies.

Where we lack knowledge, God provides wisdom. Where we lack ease, God provides grace. Where we lack confidence, God provides assurance.

And so we must have faith that His way is best.

Waiting strengthens our faith. And we know that the stronger our faith is, the more useful we can be in accomplishing God's purpose for our lives.

"In this you rejoice, though now for a little while, if necessary, you have been grieved by various trials, so that the tested genuineness of your faith—more precious than gold that perishes though it is tested by fire—may be found to result in praise and glory and honor at the revelation of Jesus Christ" (1 Peter 1:6–7 ESV).

In 1 Thessalonians 3:10, Paul writes in a letter that he is praying for his brothers and sisters in Christ that what is lacking in their faith would be strengthened.

We received similar kindness from friends and family who prayed earnestly for us. One family member wrote, "I think of you often and pray that God would give you the desires of your hearts. That he would give you wisdom while you wait and that He would be near to you both."

That's exactly what we need. We need God to complete what is deficient in us.

For we know that He is sovereign over our lacking.

1 Thessalonians 4:13

*But we do not want you to be uninformed, brethren, about those who are asleep, so that you will not grieve as do the rest who have no **hope**.*

Because of who God is, we have confidence in sorrow.

It is important to understand that there is nothing inherently wrong with grieving. At least twice in the Bible we see Christ weeping, once for Lazarus and once for Calvary. And none among us could make a good case that proved Christ was wrong for His tears.

In one sense, Christ's weeping proves His humanity and affirms His compassion.

Grieving is a natural, human response to difficult things. "We should not grieve like those who have no hope" is infinitely different than "we should not grieve."

But, though grief is not pleasant, there is something good about grieving, especially when the tears are spilled in prayer to God for help or comfort or healing.

Grief is honest.

But it is essential to understand that Christ's grieving wasn't hopeless. And God desires that ours won't be without hope either. God gave us verses like 1 Thessalonians 4:13 so that our hope wouldn't be threatened even in our pain.

Even in the face of tremendous loss, it is not surprising that our hope returns to the gospel. 1 Thessalonians 4:14 reads, "For since we believe that Jesus died and rose again, even so, through Jesus, God will bring with him those who have fallen asleep" (ESV).

How kind that God gives us insight into difficult things.

DAY 321

1 Thessalonians 5:8

*But since we are of the day, let us be sober, having put on
the breastplate of faith and love, and as a helmet, the **hope**
of salvation.*

Hope isn't just something for the future.

Like faith and love, hope is essential for the Christian life *right now*.
Hope in God protects us from despair and from the temptation to
believe that God's plan isn't best.

On the first day of November, we awoke with the recognition that
October was gone and we wouldn't be meeting our son in the month
we had been told to anticipate. October, for us, had been the month to
"count down to" for the nineteen previous months.

And then it was gone. And we did not have our son.

So on the first of November, we were forced to admit that what we
had hoped for had not happened. By all accounts, we should have
experienced despair. Nineteen months is a long time to wait.

Yet, we awoke with hope that was fueled by the recognition that God
had sustained us in the journey thus far and would continue to do so.
Yes, hope in the future salvation of our souls from hell is essential. But
so is a hope in the salvation of our souls here on earth.

God is entirely committed to doing good for His people (Jeremiah
32:40–41). If that doesn't cause us to hope, nothing on earth ever will.
On the first day of November, we said with the psalmist, "You are
good and do good; teach me your statutes" (Psalm 119:68 ESV).

> *Like faith and love, hope is essential for
> the Christian life right now.*

DAY 322

1 Thessalonians 5:17

Pray *without ceasing.*

If Bible reading is our daily bread, then prayer is our oxygen.

One of the reasons that difficulty is a blessing is because it prompts us to pray without ceasing, as the Bible commands.

The idea of ceaseless prayer is not repetitious prayer in the way that some might count out prayer beads or chant a collection of lines into ecstasy. Praying as God designs is praying persistently, eagerly, frequently.

In the way that some are hasty to judge or worry, we must be hasty to pray. Imagine being accused of running to God too quickly!

It is no surprise that the instruction to pray without ceasing comes on the heels of the charge to rejoice always. For neither could exist without the other.

Late into our experience of waiting, we came to appreciate Ecclesiastes 7 in a new and profound way. Truly wisdom for the waiting, verse 2 reads: "It is better to go to the house of mourning than to go to the house of feasting, for this is the end of all mankind, and the living will lay it to heart" (ESV).

It is a gift to experience trouble if it motivates us to separate out the true needs from the trite, the meaningful experiences from the menial. Anything—*anything*—that incites us to pray without ceasing is a good and gracious thing.

We must pray as automatically as we breathe—continually!

DAY 323

1 Thessalonians 5:25

*Brethren, **pray** for us.*

Distress in this life does not indicate a failure in God's perfect plan.

Our adoption paperwork was on the verge of expiring, which meant we had to begin the process of going back to doctors and re-visiting records offices and writing checks. One afternoon we spent several hours sitting in an empty exam room waiting to see a doctor for one signature. When we finally left his office, in the midst of a heavy storm, our car wouldn't start.

If ever in our adoption process we were tempted to wonder if setbacks existed in the sovereign plan of God, it would have been that day. The half-hour we sat in the rainy parking lot trying to get our vehicle to work was the longest, quietest half-hour of our marriage.

Tears didn't come because we had already spent so many of them.

During the next several days, whenever anyone asked how we were doing, our response was simple. "Pray for us." Sometimes the wisest thing we can do is seek out people who know and love God's Word and ask them to pray. Details aren't necessary. Complaints aren't helpful. But the prayer of God's people is always beneficial. (James 5:16).

Andrew Fuller said, "It is not under the sharpest, but the longest trials, that we are most in danger of fainting. In the former case, the soul collects all its strength, and feels in earnest to call in help from above; but, in the latter, the mind relaxes and sinks into despondency."

Prayer is always the best response to sorrow.

2 Thessalonians 1:11

*To this end also we **pray** for you always, that our God will*
count you worthy of your calling, and fulfill every desire
for goodness and the work of faith with power.

God's approval is of more value than all the good in this world combined.

If the goal of our lives is to be worthy of our calling, then God's approval is of far more importance than our ease or comfort in this life. The glory of God is the achievement we should want above everything and anything else.

Easy to say. Difficult to desire.

The Thessalonian Christians understood that suffering was evidence that Christ was working to perfect their character (2 Corinthians 12:10). Though they encountered various difficulties at the hands of the unjust, they persevered, knowing what God's will for their lives was: "Rejoice always, pray without ceasing, give thanks in all circumstances; for this is the will of God in Christ Jesus for you" (1 Thessalonians 5:16–18 ESV).

God's will for our lives consists of the same directives: rejoice, pray, be thankful *for everything*.

Though it is not always easy to follow the instructions, it is what God wants. And what God wants is infinitely more important than what we want.

Herein is the truth that makes the task worthwhile: Nothing about Christ's suffering for us was easy. He did the hardest things for us. What we do for Him is minor by comparison. So no matter how difficult our task at times may be, God's approval is of more value than all the good in this world combined.

DAY 325

2 Thessalonians 2:16

*Now may our Lord Jesus Christ Himself and God our Father, who has loved us and given us eternal comfort and good **hope** by grace.*

God may not answer our prayer the way we want Him to, but He will never dissatisfy.

Success in this life is never guaranteed in Scripture.

In his book *A Passion for Faithfulness*, J. I. Packer wrote, "The world's idea that everyone, from childhood up, should be able to succeed at all times in measurable ways, and that it is a great disgrace not to, hangs over the Christian community like a pall of acrid smoke."

In a world that teaches us that success is the result of working harder, talking louder, and being tougher, it is incomprehensible to imagine not getting what we want in this lifetime.

In our faulty thinking, family members remain unsaved because we haven't explained salvation well enough, or people are sick because we haven't prayed the right way, or our prayer request hasn't been granted because we must have failed to account for something in our plea for forgiveness of a wrongdoing.

But God doesn't operate the way our world does. He isn't moved to act because someone talks louder or tougher. He has made no promises to give us what we want—only what is best.

In 2 Thessalonians 2:16, Paul cites God's love and comfort to be sufficient for our hope in this world.

The best answer is not always in the affirmative.

DAY 326

2 Thessalonians 3:1

*Finally, brethren, **pray** for us that the word of the Lord will spread rapidly and be glorified, just as it did also with you.*

The conclusion is certain: Christ will be glorified in everything.

He neither needs our submission nor our endorsement to accomplish His will in this world. But we would be foolish not to yield to Him. We know the ending! We know He will be glorified!

Like a child, unwilling to jump in the pool for fear that his parent—whose arms are outstretched—will not catch him, so we—as God's children—often stand at the sidelines of our lives with naive and ignorant fears.

Will God take care of me? Will He forget me? What have I done to deserve what I'm facing? Does He really care?

God has proven Himself. He sent His Son (John 3:16). He gave us His Word (2 Timothy 3:16). He has always met our needs. (Philippians 4:19).

So why do we doubt Him for any detail, large or small, in our lives?—like this will be the first time He fails to catch His child.

Let us pray with the words of C. H. Spurgeon:

> *Oh, for grace to let my trials bless me! Why should I wish to stay*
> *their gracious operation? Lord, I ask thee to remove my affliction,*
> *but I beseech thee ten times more to remove my impatience.*
> *Precious Lord Jesus, with thy cross engrave the image of thy*
> *patience on my heart.*

DAY 327

I Timothy 1:1

Paul, an apostle of Christ Jesus according to the commandment of God our Savior, and of Christ Jesus, who is our **hope.**

Like Paul, we have hope because of Christ.

Christ died for our sins, sustains us in our present pain, and will come again to receive us unto Himself. Christ does not just provide us with hope. He is our hope (Colossians 1:27).

If we have any doubt about God's love or role in the details of our present testing, we need only go to the cross and look up. There, amid the scene of horrid suffering and human betrayal, we reflect on these words: "For Christ also suffered once for sins, the righteous for the unrighteous, that he might bring us to God" (1 Peter 3:18 ESV).

And we know that God designed that horrible occurrence in history for our good—as He does the painful particulars of our present situation. In essence, Christ experienced the agony of abandonment so that we would never be alone in our moments of truest need.

That is reason to hope. Christ is always with us.

He decrees the means and the ends of our pain. And no matter how baffling our circumstances at times may be, this is a reality: All suffering makes sense to God.

> **Christ does not just provide us with hope. He is our hope.**

I Timothy 2:1

*First of all, then, I urge that entreaties and **prayers**,*
petitions and thanksgivings, be made on behalf of all men.

Trials naturally lead to self-absorption.

We can be so focused on what we are going through that we can become blinded to the needs of others—specifically those whose needs are greater than our own.

The lost need God more than we need our child, for instance.

The longer our trial persisted, we found encouragement ourselves in the opportunity we had to support others in ways we had been encouraged (2 Corinthians 1:4).

Where we once were intimidated by our lack of experience with certain afflictions faced by other people, we found grace to comfort them because of the comfort we received from God.

We were certainly more motivated to share God with those who did not yet know Him.

And in being able to better love other people, we accepted our trial as even more precious and more beneficial in our lives. Praying for other people takes our eyes off ourselves and focuses our attention on encouraging people who need God's grace as much as we do.

John Newton often used his difficulties to encourage others, writing in a letter to someone who needed encouragement, "Our all-sufficient God can give seasons of refreshment in the darkest hours, and break through the thickest clouds of outward affliction or distress."

He knew this first-hand and so do we.

We must encourage others with the truths we have learned from God!

DAY 329

I Timothy 2:8

*Therefore I want the men in every place to **pray**, lifting up holy hands, without wrath and dissension.*

The foundation for a pure prayer is a pure life.

That Paul wrote in 1 Timothy 2:8 about "lifting up holy hands, without wrath and dissention" was less about his concern with the physical stance of a person's posture in prayer and more about the spiritual position of the person's heart.

We cannot presume upon the throne of grace that God should listen to us when we are harboring sin in our lives. Certainly we can't come to Him swinging our fists over what He has not given us or what we perceive that He will not do.

"We have served You for seven years in ministry. Why won't you give us our son?"—could have been our prayer. Certainly the thought crossed our mind on occasion. It was no small sacrifice of time or money to enter the ministry—valuable commodities from our point of view.

But these thoughts would no more start their slow decline when the truth would resound, "God gave His Son for you. The least you can do is live for Him."

In moments of temptation to sin against God, we would do well to remember the words of the psalmist, "If I had cherished iniquity in my heart, the Lord would not have listened" (Psalm 66:18 ESV).

The lack of communing with God is a high price to pay for muddied hands.

"Draw near to God, and he will draw near to you. Cleanse your hands, you sinners, and purify your hearts, you double-minded" (James 4:8 ESV).

DAY 330

1 Timothy 4:5

*For it is sanctified by means of the word of God
and prayer.*

It is not difficult to endure correctly without Bible reading and prayer—it is impossible.

On the morning we learned that a large portion of our paperwork had been "lost," we knew instinctively that there was nothing we could do to fortify ourselves outside of prayer and Bible-reading.

At times, our adoption felt like an illustration of Murphy's Law.

Anything that can go wrong, will go wrong.

But in finding solace in God, we found the strength that we needed to face the difficulty.

Sanctification, as it was used in the Bible, was a term meant to signal the setting aside of something for the use or purpose of the Almighty. In 1 Timothy 4:5, the issue in question was the Mosaic dietary restrictions that had long governed the eating habits of God's people. God sanctified food and marriage, recorded in 1 Timothy 4, as good gifts for His people.

On our journey toward heaven, God has given us many good gifts— among them the opportunity to read His Word and talk to Him in prayer. To not avail ourselves of these good gifts is to make our pilgrimage more complicated.

How can we charge God with not being the perfect Giver when there are unwrapped packages at our feet?

"Now may the God of peace himself sanctify you completely, and may your whole spirit and soul and body be kept blameless at the coming of our Lord Jesus Christ" (1 Thessalonians 5:23 ESV).

DAY 331

1 Timothy 4:10

*For it is for this we labor and strive, because we have fixed our **hope** on the living God, who is the Savior of all men, especially of believers.*

Sometimes God's choicest work for His children involves waiting.

The same hope in Christ that saves us from eternal damnation is the hope that sustains us in the difficulties of this life. Fixing our hope on the living God, as 1 Timothy 4:10 says, is the assignment of those who *would* believe and those who already *do*.

The same hope that sustains us in this life will satisfy us in the next.

Whatever we face on this earth—as being directly from the hand of God—is made considerably better because we hope and trust in Him.

As we neared the finish line of the second year of our wait with no earthly reason to believe our adoption would be completed soon, we did so with the awareness that God gave us everything we needed to endure correctly. We trusted that our little boy was being taken care of in the best possible way, and that if the eye of God is on the sparrow, it most certainly was on our son (Matthew 10:31).

What better provision for our child could there be?

We had no doubt that the longer our wait became, the greater our hope in God grew.

As we were reminded late in our wait, "Everything is okay in the end. If it's not okay, then it's not the end."

For the child of God, we hope in Him now and we hope in Him later.

I Timothy 5:5

*Now she who is a widow indeed and who has been
left alone, has fixed her **hope** on God and continues in
entreaties and **prayers** night and day.*

The carving process never feels good.

Molding and chiseling are not without discomfort. But when we
have been whittled down—the impurities of weakness and rot peeled
away—we can more accurately fix our hope on God. And there is no
better feeling or freedom in the world.

That God is committed to making us Christlike means there will be
discomfort. The Master Designer is seeking to make a diamond out
of dirt! But it also means the end product will be incomparably better
and more useful than the original material.

Why is this painful process necessary? Because in the language of
pottery, the fewer impurities there are in the clay of faith, the greater
the usefulness of the creation to the Potter. And isn't that the goal—to
be used by God?

"But now, O LORD, you are our Father; we are the clay, and you are
our potter; we are all the work of your hand" (Isaiah 64:8 ESV).

So let us pray, then, not that the transformative process will end,
but that we will desire the final product like nothing else we've
ever wanted.

> *So let us pray, then, not that the transformative process will
> end, but that we will desire the final product like nothing else
> we've ever wanted.*

DAY 333

I Timothy 6:17

*Instruct those who are rich in this present world not to be
conceited or to fix their **hope** on the uncertainty of riches,
but on God, who richly supplies us with all things to enjoy.*

This life is not all there is—not even close.

The Thanksgiving holiday rolled around for the second time during
our wait. The previous year we had busily been compiling our son's
baby book, fully anticipating that the pages would be filled with
photos within the year.

But for Thanksgiving season number two, the book was collecting
dust in a closet that was rarely opened. Our son was once again
missing from the family celebration.

As we listened to people talk about the things for which they were
grateful, at the top of the list was an improving economy.

When the economy took its downward spiral the year before, sending
investors and bankers into panic mode, it seemed all people wanted
to talk about was "security"—secure investments, secure loans, secure
mortgages.

And if riches were the only contributing factor to security, we would
have panicked too.

But for the child of God, we have so much more to hope in than the
"uncertainty of riches." What a wonderful, reliable truth that God
provides for us so much more security than life on earth can ever
offer! (Matthew 6:19–21).

Here is what we were thankful for on Thanksgiving number two: the
best is yet to be!

DAY 334

Titus 1:2

*In the **hope** of eternal life, which God, who cannot lie, promised long ages ago.*

That God cannot lie is a truth our souls should cling to.

We live in a world where people say things they don't mean and mean things they don't say. But God was gracious to give us His Word—full of exactly what He meant for us to know.

And all of it is true.

If we are tempted to doubt God's goodness to us, it is not because He has not already given us everything we need to hope in Him.

God is the fundamental need of our hearts. And we have been given all we need to trust Him fully. He is worthy of that trust.

The storms of life will toss us up and down—we've been told to expect that much (John 16:33)—but we are also given the encouragement to believe that everything God says is true.

He cannot lie. He cannot fail. He cannot love us any more than He does right now.

So how do we survive? We trust Him.

"You keep him in perfect peace whose mind is stayed on you, because he trusts in you" (Isaiah 26:3 ESV).

He cannot love us any more than He does right now.

DAY 335

Titus 2:13

*Looking for the blessed **hope** and the appearing of the
glory of our great God and Savior, Christ Jesus.*

Being loved by God is better than life.

Being loved by God is better than receiving the things for which we
pray.

In the midst of waiting for our adoption to be finalized, we continued
to pray for Christ's return. Did we want to be parents? Absolutely.
Could we fathom a life where we never enjoyed children? No.

But more than anything that we desired, we wanted Christ.

We wanted His presence, His glory, and His return.

Perspective makes the difference in times of testing. If we felt like the
most important thing in life—our son—was being withheld from us,
we couldn't function. How could we? But when we believed that the
best thing—salvation— had already been given to us and every other
gift was wonderful, yet secondary to the gift of Christ, we could bear
the struggle much better.

God is a giving God. His gift of His Son for our salvation is the
best of His gracious gifts to us. How could we question that He
was withholding something from us because of close-fistedness or
unkindness? To believe that about God would be foolish (Romans
8:32).

God longs to bless us with secondary gifts, but He wants us to
understand that He has already given us the very best thing.

Being loved by God is better than life.

DAY 336

Titus 3:7

*So that being justified by His grace we would be made heirs according to the **hope** of eternal life.*

We have been adopted to hope.

Going through the process of adoption caused us naturally to think about our own adoption into the family of God. It was no small effort for God to make us His heirs. In fact, several times in our own struggle to adopt our son, we found ourselves praising God and saying to Him, "What You did for us was amazing and we are grateful for it."

As adopted children, we have been given much (1 Peter 1:3–4).

But there is an interesting detail in connection with our adoption into God's family that became more apparent to us as we studied—a natural link between salvation and suffering.

Romans 8:15 speaks of spiritual adoption. Romans 8:16–17 read as follows: "The Spirit himself bears witness with our spirit that we are children of God, and if children, then heirs—heirs of God and fellow heirs with Christ, provided we suffer with him in order that we may also be glorified with him" (ESV).

Of these verses, commentator John McArthur says, "The suffering in this life creates reactions that reflect the genuine condition of the soul. God allows suffering to drive believers to dependence on Him—an evidence of their true salvation."

If we can endure the difficulties of this life while maintaining a genuine, Christ-centered hope, we can have confidence that we belong to God.

So, in being grateful for our salvation, we must be thankful for our suffering.

DAY 337

Philemon 1:6

*And I **pray** that the fellowship of your faith may become effective through the knowledge of every good thing which is in you for Christ's sake.*

Whatever God allows, we must accept as God's will.

We caught ourselves saying, "We don't need this" when things grew frustrating during our times of testing. One Saturday morning, desirous to get out of the house and enjoy some time as far away from our son's empty bedroom as possible, we planted ourselves in a coffee shop where we didn't anticipate seeing anyone we knew.

Moments after getting settled, someone we barely recognized approached us and informed us (loudly) that we were likely being manipulated by a fraudulent adoption agency—and hopefully we hadn't spent too much money.

"We don't need this!" ran through our minds like a news ticker at the bottom of a television screen.

But we did need that interaction. We need whatever God allows into our lives.

True trust in God necessitates our acceptance of life's events as divinely ordained. From the pesky traffic during our morning commute to the tragic car accident that claimed the life of our brother when he was twenty-four years old, God has allowed what was necessary for our growth and His glory.

We must obey 1 Thessalonians 5:18: Give thanks in all circumstances; for this is the will of God in Christ Jesus for you (ESV).

Hebrews 2:13

*And again, I WILL PUT MY **TRUST** IN HIM and again, BEHOLD, I AND THE CHILDREN WHOM GOD HAS GIVEN ME.*

We live infinitely better than what we deserve.

When we arrive at the point in our trial where we understand that God knows better than we do and gives to us better than we deserve, then we know we are putting our trust in Him.

Trust requires confidence that isn't swayed by how we feel in a given moment.

Learning to trust God this way—specifically when life doesn't make sense—is essential to the Christian life. If we cannot trust God in difficulty, we do not trust Him at all. Trust in Someone that is never put to the test is like displaying furniture that never gets used—it is all show and not useful.

And what is the value of inadequate trust?

God is infinitely trustworthy. If He went to the trouble of saving us in our hour of greatest need, why would He abandon us in our moment of lesser need?

"Oh, the depth of the riches and wisdom and knowledge of God! How unsearchable are his judgments and how inscrutable his ways! For who has known the mind of the Lord, or who has been his counselor? Or who has given a gift to him that he might be repaid? For from him and through him and to him are all things. To him be glory forever. Amen" (Romans 11:33–36 ESV).

DAY 339

Hebrews 3:6

*But Christ was faithful as a Son over His house—whose house we are, if we hold fast our confidence and the boast of our **hope** firm until the end.*

Perseverance is the litmus test of faith.

That Hebrews 3:6 speaks of holding fast our hope until the end is not specifically limited to the faith that secures our salvation; it refers to a faith that triumphs—*perseveres*—throughout life. Perseverance is the result of a faith that must outlive us.

We should understand, according to Hebrews 3:6, that endurance is an issue of gospel significance.

Our hope must take respite in the Christ who purchased us with His blood, not only for salvation, but also for all of life.

If we experience the disappointments of this life and react no differently than our unsaved counterparts by blaming Christ, losing hope, disobeying the Word, and neglecting prayer, then we give evidence that our hope isn't really in Christ after all. Our hope is in an imaginary alternative to God who only does good and comfortable things.

Christ is faithful.

The gospel is good.

Let's hold fast our confidence and hope until the very end.

Our hope must take respite in the Christ who purchased us with His blood, not only for salvation, but also for all of life.

DAY 340

Hebrews 6:11

*And we desire that each one of you show the same
diligence so as to realize the full assurance of **hope** until
the end.*

Someday we will view our present circumstances with brighter, clearer vision.

We may never receive all of the answers, but we will see the Savior and that will be sufficient.

Until then, we must trust that God alone knows how He intends to turn our trial into a triumphant display of His glory with His grace.

On the 586th day of our waiting, we discovered these words, written by William Cowper:

Ye fearful saints, fresh courage take,

The clouds ye so much dread

Are big with mercy, and shall break

In blessings on your head.

Judge not the Lord by feeble sense,

But trust Him for His grace;

Behind a frowning providence

He hides a smiling face.

And believing his words to be true, we purposed again to trust God with our waiting and hope in Him until the end.

DAY 341

Hebrews 6:15

*And so, having patiently **waited**, he obtained the promise.*

We must wait on God expectantly, knowing that the flip side of pain is joy.

We received the following words in an e-mail, written to us by someone who was adopting from the same country at the same time as we were: "The patience required to make it through this process to finally be united with our son is one that I had never imagined."

And we agreed. Though we did our homework before embarking on the journey, we still had no idea what would be involved—the tears, the sweat, the prayer, the pain—and we certainly underestimated how valuable God's promises would be to us along the way.

But God's truths sustained us.

Hebrews 6:15 refers to the story of Abraham, a man who waited a long time before God's promise to Him was fulfilled. He waited for the same thing we waited for—a son.

And God gave him the desire of his heart (Psalm 37:4).

We learned in time that wherever sadness or grief exists, joy of equal proportion or greater waits to be discovered. We trusted that at the end of our waiting, we would meet our son. And so we waited patiently.

It was John Owen who said, "Live, and pray, and hope, and wait patiently, and do not despond; the promise stands invincible, that He will never leave us nor forsake us."

DAY 342

Hebrews 6:18

*So that by two unchangeable things in which it is impossible for God to lie, we who have taken refuge would have strong encouragement to take hold of the **hope** set before us.*

The practical way we trust God in difficulty is by taking refuge in Him.

And the way we take refuge in Him is by believing the promises He has given us and resting in the reality that God has everything under control.

That Hebrews 6:18 talks about hope is not surprising since hope is one of the themes of the Book of Hebrews. The fact that Christ promises salvation—and a host of other things to His children—is, in the words of Hebrews "an anchor" for us who know Him.

And what is the purpose of an anchor?—to keep its object attached, fixed, *secure.*

The best anchor is this: God cannot lie.

So why would we doubt anything He says?

Why, at times, do we live like we have no anchor at all?

What are we saying about our Savior if we trust Him with our eternal security and not with the lesser things of this world? Or, maybe the better question is, how can we profess to be saved from eternal damnation and still have cause for concern over a health diagnosis or a good job or a relationship status?

Taking refuge in God means we trust Him to take care of it all—our salvation and everything else.

DAY 343

Hebrews 6:19

*This **hope** we have as an anchor of the soul, a **hope** both
sure and steadfast and one which enters within the veil.*

For an anchor to function properly, it must be securely attached to
something.

The strongest anchor will not make an ounce of difference if it is not
connected to the ship. Neither will the strongest anchor matter in the
moment of crisis if those in the boat act like it doesn't exist.

The purpose of God is to keep us secure in times of testing. The will of
God is that we remain steadfast.

So what, then, is the point of having Christ—who freely offers hope
for every situation we face—if we act no differently than those without
Him?

God is worthy to be trusted. We are foolish not to trust.

The hope in Hebrews 6:19 refers to a confident expectation that what
God has promised, He will perform. And God, since He cannot lie
(Titus 1:2), only makes promises that He is sure to keep and we are
welcome to trust. The promises that God makes to us are worthy to be
trusted until and even after our death.

Of Hebrews 6:19, Matthew Henry wrote, "We are in this world as a
ship at sea, tossed up and down, and in danger of being cast away. We
need an anchor to keep us sure and steady. Gospel hope is our anchor
in the storms of this world. It is sure and steadfast, or it could not
keep us so."

Christ is our anchor. We must live like we know it.

DAY 344

Hebrews 7:19

(For the Law made nothing perfect), and on the other
*hand there is a bringing in of a better **hope**, through which*
we draw near to God.

Drawing near to God is the objective of the Christian life.

Unlike the goal of those who do not know our Savior, our aim is not to live lives of happiness and ease. We exist to glorify God by being perpetually chiseled into His image.

Shortly after the one-year mark of being "matched" with our son, we crossed the nineteenth month of waiting to actually be invited to the country. The two dates converged, and we still had no idea when we would actually be united as a family.

Our adoption process was like living in a hamster's wheel—we would get great updates followed by the worst kind of news, followed by good information, followed by silence. In the space of a couple of weeks, we went from believing it was time to pack and travel to believing we might have lost him entirely. And this cycle was constant during our wait.

But as we welcomed the nineteen-month mark, we were overwhelmed with this certainty: "It is good for me that I was afflicted, that I might learn your statutes" (Psalm 119:71 ESV).

With confidence we agreed that emerging from the valley, knowing and loving God more than before, would make the trial a blessing.

Drawing near to God is the objective
of the Christian life.

DAY 345

Hebrews 10:23

*Let us hold fast the confession of our **hope** without wavering, for He who promised is faithful.*

It is bittersweet to leave the valley.

It is God's design that trials will not test His children forever. In a matter of time, permanent healing will occur. We can rightly rejoice that our pain isn't forever.

Though we want the hurting to end and our lives to resume to "normal," it is a reality: some of the sweetest fellowship with God occurs when the storms are raging.

It is when our affections are tested that we learn what and whom we really love. And it is during times of testing that we find God's promises to be utterly reliable—more dependable than on the days we give them no thought and take no care for our need of them.

It is in the valley that we most naturally affirm two facts: God always speaks the truth and God always keeps His promises. *Always.*

So with that knowledge, we must hold fast the confession of our hope. We must persevere—not because it will buy our salvation, but because it will prove that we are God's—something we know with certainty when we're passing through the tempest.

"For he will deliver you from the snare of the fowler and from the deadly pestilence. He will cover you with his pinions, and under his wings you will find refuge; his faithfulness is a shield and buckler" (Psalm 91:3–4 ESV).

DAY 346

Hebrews 11:1

*Now faith is the assurance of things **hoped** for, the conviction of things not seen.*

Our hope during times of difficulty will be in direct proportion to our view of God.

If we believe God is enough, we will be hopeful.

If we believe God is incapable, we will be anxious.

We must recognize that there is something worse than experiencing trials and difficulties, and that is experiencing trials and difficulties without hoping in God. There is also the danger of living life relatively pain-free and believing life lived without God is, therefore, not a problem.

A life of difficulty and disappointment warrants daily trust in God. Such a life is a gift.

In a sermon published in 1913, C.H. Spurgeon said:

> Believe that the deepest afflictions are neighbors always to the highest joys, and that the greatest possible privileges lie close by the darkest trials. If the bitterer your sorrow, the louder your song at the last, there is a reason for that, and that reason faith may discover and experience live upon.

Let us hope in God in magnanimous ways.

Our hope during times of difficulty will be in direct proportion to our view of God.

DAY 347

Hebrews 13:18

Pray for us, for we are sure that we have a good conscience, desiring to conduct ourselves honorably in all things.

Bystanders are always interested in how the grieving respond.

Perhaps there is meddlesome fascination involved at times, but more likely, people want to see how others respond to difficultly so that when their day of disappointment arrives, they will have confidence that endurance is possible.

George Müller was a man of prayer. The orphans in his care were constantly in need of sustenance, and Müller maintained a constant communication line with God. But no prayer is more insightful of George Müller's affection for Christ than when his wife was sick. Beside the bed of his wife, dying of the deadly rheumatic fever, he prayed:

> *Yes, my Father, the times of my darling wife are in Thy hands. Thou wilt do the very best thing for her and for me, whether life or death. If it may be, raise up yet again my precious wife—Thou art able to do it, though she is so ill; but howsoever Thou dealest with me, only help me to continue to be perfectly satisfied with Thy holy will.*

At his wife's funeral, Müller preached from Psalm 119:68: "You are good and do good; teach me your statutes" (ESV).

Perfectly satisfied with God's decreed will. *That* is honorable conduct.

James 5:7

*Therefore be patient, brethren, until the coming of the
Lord. The farmer **waits** for the precious produce of the soil,
being patient about it, until it gets the early and late rains.*

Patience is more than a virtue. It is a command.

"Rejoice in hope, be patient in tribulation, be constant in prayer,"
(Romans 12:12 ESV).

There is a temptation in difficulty to try to cut our suffering short.
And while there is nothing necessarily wrong with wanting the
pain to end, there is something very wrong with bringing about its
conclusion in the wrong way.

Suicide, divorce, abortion—the world is full of shortcuts out of pain—
and in nearly every case, the methods are made to look acceptable. So
says the world: *You shouldn't have to live without quality of life. If
the marriage is tough, get out! Who says you must carry a baby you
don't want?*

Since the Garden of Eden, alternatives to patient obedience have
been made to look attractive. Yet the Bible says as the farmer waits
for harvest, so we should wait on God, which means we must endure
patiently.

We should be encouraged by the number of people who have
successfully traveled the path we are currently taking and, in the end,
found God to be sufficient.

"And let us not grow weary of doing good, for in due season we will
reap, if we do not give up" (Galatians 6:9 ESV).

DAY 349

James 5:13

*Is anyone among you suffering? Then he must **pray**. Is anyone cheerful? He is to sing praises.*

Praise is the natural response to salvation.

Psalm 107:2 speaks of the Israelites' redemption from Egypt when it says: "Let the redeemed of the LORD say so, whom he has redeemed from trouble" (Psalm 107:2 ESV).

Yet it is an accurate portrayal of how God intends all of His children to respond to His deliverance. We must praise the Lord for His delivery—whether by the rescue of our souls or the release of our suffering—and acknowledge that all relief is from Him.

It is not hard to understand that God wants us to rejoice in His goodness.

Prayer must be the natural response to suffering.

In the words of James 5:13, if anyone is afflicted, he should pray.

God knows best how to soothe our souls, and He provides us with the resources to pray and praise Him in whatever situations we experience. It is clear that prayer and praise enhance the experiences of suffering and salvation.

Let us offer prayer and praise to our God.

Let us offer prayer and praise to our God.

James 5:14

Is anyone among you sick? Then he must call for the elders
*of the church and they are to **pray** over him, anointing*
him with oil in the name of the Lord.

Enduring difficulty should intensify our ability and desire to care for others who are hurting.

James 5:14 encourages church members who are suffering to reach out to church leadership for prayer and support. Some commentators suggest that James may have been writing about the persecuted believers and their need for medical attention. Others advocate that the "anointing" in this verse is a symbol for the comfort or encouragement that we owe members of our congregation.

Either way, Scripture is clear that when one member of the body hurts, we all hurt. And so, our own difficult walk through the wilderness should deepen our concern for those still traveling through it.

When 2 Corinthians 1:4 speaks of comforting others with the comfort that we have received, it gives every indication that—instead of simply rejoicing that our trial has concluded and moving on with life—we should look around to see who needs the comfort next. It means, at times, returning to the valley of the shadow of death, not to walk in it again for ourselves, but to walk in it with someone else.

Praying for others is an act of Christian compassion.

Our trial brings more glory to God when we look for others to encourage.

Praying for others
is an act of Christian
compassion.

DAY 351

James 5:15

*And the **prayer** offered in faith will restore the one who is sick, and the Lord will raise him up, and if he has committed sins, they will be forgiven him.*

In time, the Lord will heal.

Illness can only do so much. Death is only able to destroy certain things. Pain can only exist so long.

Health can be restored. Hearts can be mended. Lives can be made stronger than they were before. Our God is capable of more than we can imagine.

In the meantime, the worst events of this life cannot lay a hand on the Christian's gifts of trust, hope, or prayer. Safe in the bunker of God's omnipotence are the most important endowments from Him. Our heart and soul are indestructible by man (Matthew 10:28).

Early in our adoption process, we were encouraged by Katharina von Schlegel's words in *Be Still, My Soul*. Much later in the process—like bookends to our time of testing—we were once again encouraged by the hymn, specifically the fourth verse:

Be still, my soul: the hour is hastening on

When we shall be forever with the Lord.

When disappointment, grief and fear are gone,

Sorrow forgot, love's purest joys restored.

Be still, my soul: when change and tears are past

All safe and blessed we shall meet at last.

DAY 352

James 5:16

*Therefore, confess your sins to one another, and **pray**
for one another so that you may be healed. The effective
prayer of a righteous man can accomplish much.*

God has divinely appointed prayer to be a tool of His people.

According to James 5:16, "The prayer of a righteous person has great power as it is working" (ESV).

But sometimes the efficacy of prayer happens within us and not outside us.

No doubt Shadrach, Meshach, and Abednego trusted God to answer their prayer, believing in essence that their righteous prayer would accomplish their deliverance. And yet, God ordained that they would be sent to the furnace.

There was nothing more on this earth that we wanted than to bring our son home. We prayed about it. We asked others to join us in praying about it. We appealed to those working on our case to see if we could do anything else. We exhausted our creativity.

But on day 598 of our wait, with heavy hearts that wanted God's best for our family, we said with Daniel's friends: "But if not."

In one of the Bible's greatest illustrations of endurance, the young men told King Nebuchadnezzar in no uncertain terms that—even if God would not deliver them from the flames of the furnace—they would trust their God to the end (Daniel 3:18).

We, too, determined to trust God's sovereign plan for our lives. We wanted to bring our son home. We wanted to teach him about God and His goodness in our lives.

But if not, God's decision for our lives would be the very best thing.

DAY 353

James 5:17

*Elijah was a man with a nature like ours, and he **prayed** earnestly that it would not rain, and it did not rain on the earth for three years and six months.*

So that Jesus' name is glorified.

God uses men like Elijah to accomplish incredible things so that there is no question about it—the glory belongs, not to Elijah, but to Elijah's God.

Elijah, who the Bible graciously notes, had a nature like ours, provides us with an incredible illustration of the power of prayer.

Elijah knew what it meant to wait. For nearly four years, he experienced drought with those around him—drought being no small circumstance to endure in biblical times. But he endured with total confidence that God was allowing the drought for the good of His chosen people, so that their hearts would be turned away from idolatry and turned back to the Lord.

When, at the end of the three years and six months, Elijah prayed for God to end the drought, he did so with these words: "Answer me, O LORD, answer me, that this people may know that you, O LORD, are God, and that you have turned their hearts back" (1 Kings 18:37 ESV).

In the same way and with the same certainty that God ended the drought, He intends to answer our prayers—one way or another—in His timing and with His means. But how He chooses to answer and when He chooses to act will be for His glory.

We should want nothing else.

James 5:18

*Then he **prayed** again, and the sky poured rain and the earth produced its fruit.*

God's provision will be delivered right on schedule.

Twice during our adoption wait, we had financial needs that were huge and time-sensitive and met by the generosity of friends who pooled resources for a rummage sale. The first time, our driveway more closely resembled a flea market than a neighborhood garage sale.

Tables lined our driveway and every manner of household good stood sentinel.

A small band of brothers under ten years old built a lemonade stand and plastered the frame with Bible verses and words of encouragement. "Children are a heritage of the Lord!" the signs read—and what an encouragement the four little preachers were to us.

If they had faith, we absolutely could have faith as well.

Both sales—different in size and participation—met the need that we currently had. Neither brought in more money than we needed. Neither brought in less.

And, unlike the lepers in Luke 17, we made a point to return thanksgiving to God for His provision on our behalf. It is easier to remember to take requests to God instead of gratitude.

"Thanks be to God for his inexpressible gift!" (2 Corinthians 9:15 ESV).

DAY 355

1 Peter 1:3

Blessed be the God and Father of our Lord Jesus Christ, who according to His great mercy has caused us to be born again to a living **hope** *through the resurrection of Jesus Christ from the dead.*

Our future is bright because of God.

We know that we have begun to understand what hope is when we look at the difficulties in our lives and are blessed and not bitter. We know that we are beginning to trust when we realize what we thought we needed pales in comparison to what we already have. We know how to pray when our prayers begin, "Lord, thank You"–even on our darkest afternoons.

If for no other reason, our future is promising because our God is good.

If we endure the testing that God has providentially placed in our lives, we can rejoice in this truth: We won't be just survivors, champions, winners, or warriors. No, we'll be so much more than that.

"No, in all these things we are more than conquerors through him who loved us. For I am sure that neither death nor life, nor angels nor rulers, nor things present nor things to come, nor powers, nor height nor depth, nor anything else in all creation, will be able to separate us from the love of God in Christ Jesus our Lord" (Romans 8:37–39 ESV).

> *If for no other reason, our future is promising because our God is good.*

DAY 356

1 Peter 1:13

*Therefore, prepare your minds for action, keep sober in spirit, fix your **hope** completely on the grace to be brought to you at the revelation of Jesus Christ.*

Be still.

It is perhaps more difficult to be still than to be busy. It is more therapeutic to talk than to be quiet.

On the afternoon that we learned our adoption case was finally being reviewed overseas, Psalm 46:10 settled over us with certainty: "Be still, and know that I am God. I will be exalted among the nations, I will be exalted in the earth!" (ESV)

We repeated these words as we waited for news to come.

Within forty-eight hours, our anticipation turned to disappointment and we learned that, once again, we had no good news. And as if she knew, a little girl sitting in front of us in church the following Sunday turned and produced a paper she had written in her class. On it were the words that had settled our souls days before—*Be still and know that I am God.*

On the good days and the difficult, the command is the same: Fix your hope completely on grace.

On the good days and the difficult, the command is the same: Fix your hope completely on grace.

DAY 357

1 Peter 1:21

*Who through Him are believers in God, who raised Him
from the dead and gave Him glory, so that your faith and
hope are in God.*

God is not required to explain anything.

For some of us, Isaiah 55:8 is the only explanation we will receive—at least on this side of Heaven—for some of life's toughest challenges: For my thoughts are not your thoughts, neither are your ways my ways, declares the Lord (ESV).

We know that everything happens to bring glory to God, and we know that it is the glory of God to conceal things (Proverbs 25:2).

So, fortified with these truths, we must place our faith and hope in Him, regardless of whether or not we learn why we have suffered various things in this life.

Years before miscarriages, health scares, loss of loved ones, and a difficult adoption process, we chose Ephesians 3:20-21 as the Scripture to be in our wedding program. It read: "Now to him who is able to do far more abundantly than all that we ask or think, according to the power at work within us, to him be glory in the church and in Christ Jesus throughout all generations, forever and ever. Amen" (ESV).

Admittedly, we didn't know then what we know now. Nor do we know now what we will know later. But we affirm what we have believed all along: God deserves glory.

DAY 358

1 Peter 3:5

For in this way in former times the holy women also, who
hoped *in God, used to adorn themselves, being submissive*
to their own husbands.

The right thing to do during times of waiting is the next right thing.

There is no second code of conduct for someone experiencing trials. Obedience to God is always the expectation. Faithfulness to marriage, commitment to family, dedication to work, loyalty to relationships— these are things that we can do during difficulty.

Many individuals in Scripture demonstrate for us what it means to obey God even during hard times. Daniel continued to pray when told to stop. Shadrach, Meshach, and Abednego refused to worship the idol. Ruth supported her mother-in-law when both had lost their family.

All of these situations in which God blessed abundantly, began with people living in simple obedience even under duress.

Knowing that obedience to God pleases Him should give us great confidence that while we are fulfilling our responsibilities, He is working to ensure that we finish the race well. Obedience isn't just something we do to fulfill an obligation; it's something we do to honor God.

We must keep trusting and obeying Him.

"For this is the love of God, that we keep his commandments. And his commandments are not burdensome" (1 John 5:3 ESV).

Obeying God and leaving the outcome to Him is the bottom line.

DAY 359

1 Peter 3:12

FOR THE EYES OF THE LORD ARE TOWARD THE
RIGHTEOUS, AND HIS EARS ATTEND TO THEIR
PRAYER, *BUT THE FACE OF THE LORD IS AGAINST*
THOSE WHO DO EVIL.

Our testing on earth is nothing to be compared to what we will be spared.

The eyes of the Lord are toward the righteous, and Revelation 3:10 straightforwardly speaks of the future for those who endure: "Because you have kept my word about patient endurance, I will keep you from the hour of trial that is coming on the whole world, to try those who dwell on the earth" (ESV).

That Christ takes note of our endurance and promises to reward it in time with His presence is not empty, naive optimism on our parts—necessary to get through the day. Our future with Him is the guarantee of our all-wise, all-loving, all-sufficient God.

These words, by Esther Kerr Rusthoi, resonate with those who, by enduring, look forward to the day when we see Christ:

Oft times the day seems long, our trials hard to bear,

We're tempted to complain, to murmur and despair;

But Christ will soon appear to catch His Bride away,

All tears forever over in God's eternal day.

It will be worth it all when we see Jesus,

Life's trials will seem so small when we see Christ;

One glimpse of His dear face all sorrow will erase,

So bravely run the race till we see Christ.

1 Peter 3:15

*But sanctify Christ as Lord in your hearts, always being
ready to make a defense to everyone who asks you to give
an account for the **hope** that is in you, yet with gentleness
and reverence.*

God's favor doesn't fall on bitter children.

Opportunities abound in the valley to introduce people to Christ.
Call them "gawkers" or "spectators," there are many who take interest
in the tragedies or difficulties of others. People are curious to see how
those around them respond to trouble.

But no one wants to know the God of the angry. Few will take interest
in the Lord of the bitter. What good is there to be said of a God who
fails His people?

Our God makes no mistake. We must never represent Him in any
other way.

Interesting that the context of 1 Peter 3:15 is that of Christ's suffering
in addition to our own. The verse immediately preceding reads: "But
even if you should suffer for righteousness' sake, you will be blessed.
Have no fear of them, nor be troubled" (1 Peter 3:14 ESV).

We experience trials, in part, that instead of growing bitter, we may
reassure those who watch that God is good and righteous altogether.

"Blessed be the God and Father of our Lord Jesus Christ, the Father of
mercies and God of all comfort, who comforts us in all our affliction,
so that we may be able to comfort those who are in any affliction,
with the comfort with which we ourselves are comforted by God" (2
Corinthians 1:3–4 ESV).

DAY 361

1 Peter 4:7

*The end of all things is near; therefore, be of sound judgment and sober spirit for the purpose of **prayer**.*

The difficulty that God allows into our lives is not the end of the story.

Disease is temporary.

Pain is impermanent.

Disappointment is fleeting.

That Psalm 23 speaks of walking *through* the valley of the shadow of death means there's a beginning and an end to the anguish. It's not forever. For the child of God, all pain is only passing. In the blink of an eye, it will be over and we will be in Glory.

God, alone, has always been and always will be.

So let us praise Him. Let us rest in the reality that any hurt we feel today will pass. But when it is gone, God will remain. And He will be to us brighter and sweeter and better than He ever has been. Because we will know what it means to trust Him. And we will know beyond a shadow of any uncertainty that He is trustworthy. And for that reason, the difficulty we experienced will be worth it all.

"For I consider that the sufferings of this present time are not worth comparing with the glory that is to be revealed to us" (Romans 8:18 ESV).

 God, alone, has always been and always will be.

1 John 3:3

*And everyone who has this **hope** fixed on Him purifies himself, just as He is pure.*

It will be okay.

There is no fatalistic force in the universe, working to make sure everything turns out as planned. Karma won't do any of us any good. Paying it forward won't guarantee any reward.

So what is the point to all of this?

The Israelites found their answer in the words recorded in Deuteronomy 8:16: ". . . that he might humble you and test you, to do you good in the end" (ESV).

And we have the same hope recorded throughout the Scriptures. Ours, like the Israelites, is a story of redemption and not of ruin. We trust a God who does good and not guile. We know that there is more to life than this.

And because of this unwavering confidence in God, we rejoice—no matter what. He gives and He takes away. Blessed is His name (Job 1:21).

What we will experience soon enough will be worth it all.

As we began month twenty of our wait, we were reminded of these words by Andrew Murray:

> Nothing is more natural and beautiful and blessed than to be nothing, that God may be all … it is not sin that humbles but grace, and that it is the soul, led through its sinfulness to be occupied with God in His wonderful glory as God, as Creator, and Redeemer, that will truly take the lowest place before Him.

DAY 363

3 John 1:2

*Beloved, I **pray** that in all respects you may prosper and be in good health, just as your soul prospers.*

We have no guarantee that our requests will result in realization.

But we have every guarantee that God will do what is best on our behalf. Which means we can trust Him. And in so trusting Him, we can thank Him—even before we receive the final answer to our request—for the good that will surely result from His divine decision.

Here is one sentence with three truths: *Every* answer from God is perfect for us. Every answer from God *is* perfect for us. Every answer from God is perfect for *us*.

Just as John wrote in his letter in 3 John, we ask for good health and we petition for the growth of our soul in Christlikeness, and we rest in the knowledge that His will, will be done in us (Proverbs 16:9).

Over time our prayer became, "O Lord our God, grant us grace to desire You with our whole heart, that so desiring we may seek and find You, and so finding You, may love You, and loving You, may hate those sins from which You have redeemed us. Amen."

 Every answer from God is perfect for us.

DAY 364

Jude 1:20

*But you, beloved, building yourselves up on your most holy faith, **praying** in the Holy Spirit.*

What about the stories that do not have a happy ending?

Whether or not the desire is granted, the illness relieved, the loss restored—the ending for the child of God is always certain, and it is always bright. God is in control. He will allow the best thing to happen to us every time. Eventually, in the providence of God, He will bring us to Heaven where we will praise Him for eternity.

Make no mistake. Our God is faithful (Psalm 55:22).

It is our responsibility to trust, hope, and pray.

Twenty-six months after beginning the adoption process, we are still waiting to meet our child. We believe it will happen. Until then, we wait. We hope it will be soon.

But we are not naive to think we won't be waiting soon enough for something else. All of life is a series of waiting on God.

So let us cling to the promise of 2 Corinthians 4:17–18, "For momentary, light affliction is producing for us an eternal weight of glory far beyond all comparison, while we look not at the things which are seen, but at the things which are not seen; for the things which are seen are temporal, but the things which are not seen are eternal."

> *Make no mistake. Our God is faithful.*
> *It is our responsibility to trust, hope, and pray.*

DAY 365

Jude 1:21

*Keep yourselves in the love of God, **waiting** anxiously for the mercy of our Lord Jesus Christ to eternal life.*

In the midst of our waiting on God, dear friends of ours lost their husband/father in a tragic accident. We gave them these words— meant to encourage and support—but over time, they became our prayer as well.

God most high, I call for mercies new. I am weary with distress.
Having born the weight of sorrowing, I am broken—I confess.

In the furnace of affliction, And the wilderness lain bare—
You have never left me wandering—I have always found You there.

Savior, grant that I would honor You. Choose the painful path if best—
Draw me closer to Your holiness—In Your shadow, let me rest.

Mold me wholly to Your likeness, Melt the dross and purge the fray—
Shape and fashion, fortify my steps, In my weakness, lead the way.

Heavenly Father, I have found in You—Mercies new and strength to stand—Lead me where Your healing waters flow, Guide me with Your precious hand.

Since Your power knows no limits, And Your mercies never cease—
Proffer grace to rest inside the storm—Knowing this is perfect peace.

—To God be all glory.

EPILOGUE

Luke and Trisha are still waiting to meet their son.

And they still believe that God is good.

RESOURCES

Introduction: Tripp, Paul David. 2009. *Broken-Down House*. Wapwallopen: PA: Shepherd's Press.

Day 1: Cowman, L.B. 2006. *Streams in the Desert*. Grand Rapids: Zondervan.

Day 3: Cairns, Dr. Alan. 6/10/2001. *Waiting on the Lord: The Source of Unfailing Strength*. Sermon: Faith Free Presbyterian.

Day 6: Walford, William W. 1842. "Sweet Hour of Prayer."

Day 10: Bennet, Aurthur. 1975. *The Valley of Vision*. Carlisle, PA: The Banner of Truth Trust.

Day 21: von Schlegel, Katharina A. 1752. "Be Still, My Soul."

Day 28: Francis, S. Trevor. 1875. "O the Deep, Deep Love of Jesus."

Day 30: Rippon, John. 1787. "How Firm a Foundation."

Day 33: Havergal, Frances R. 1876. "Like a River Glorious."

Day 38: Augustine, Saint. 2001. *Saint Augustine's Confessions*. Mulberry, IN: Sovereign Grace Publishers.

Day 47: Elliot, Elisabeth. 2004. *Keep a Quiet Heart*. Grand Rapids: Baker.

Day 62: Barry, Henry H. 1892. "He Leadeth Me."

Day 63: Mahaney, C.J. 1996. *Suffering and Sovereignty Part 1*. Sermon: Covenant Life Church.

Day 64: Crosby, Fanny. 1875. "All the Way My Savior Leads Me."

Day 65: Minnick, Dr. Mark. 8/3/2005. *Responding to Trials.* Sermon: Mount Calvary Baptist Church.

Day 66: Newton, John. 1960. *Letters of John Newton.* Carlisle, PA: The Banner of Truth Trust.

Day 67: Spurgeon, C.H., 1885, *The Treasury of David.* Peabody, MA: Hendrickson.

Day 68: Wesley, Charles. 1740. "Jesus, Lover of My Soul."

Day 70: Wesley, John. 1754–1765. *Commentary on the whole Bible.* Public domain.

Day 75: Spurgeon, C.H., 1885, *The Treasury of David.* Peabody, MA: Hendrickson.

Day 76: DeYoung, Kevin. 2010. *The Good News We Almost Forgot.* Chicago: Moody Publishers.

Day 77: Minnick, Mark. 8/3/2005. *Responding to Trials.* Sermon: Mount Calvary Baptist Church.

Day 78: Piper, John. 10/13/1985. *All Things Work for Good: Romans 8:28–30.* http://www.desiringgod.org/resource-library/sermons/called-according-to-his-purpose.

Day 80: Müller, George. 1899. Quoted in Arthur Tappan Pierson. *George Müller of Brisol.* London: James Nisbet & Co.

Day 81: Welch, Edward T. 2007. *Running Scared: Fear, Worry, and the God of Rest.* Greensboro: New Growth Press.

Day 86: Spurgeon, C.H., 1885, *The Treasury of David.* Peabody, MA: Hendrickson.

Day 90: Murray, Andrew. 1896. *Waiting on God.* Revell: Wilder Publications, reprinted 2008.

Day 92: Maclaren, Alexander. 1893. *The Wearied Christ: and Other Sermons by Alexander Maclaren*. Alexander & Shepheard.

Day 93: Sandell-Berg, Karolina W. 1865. "Day by Day." Translated by Andrew L. Skoog.

Day 94: Lloyd-Jones, D. 1965. *Spiritual Depression: Its Causes and Cure*. Grand Rapids: Wm. B. Eerdmans Publishing Company. Horn, Dr. Sam. 9/12/2010. *Psalms: God's Refreshing Oasis*. Sermon: Brookside Baptist Church.

Day 95: Tripp, Paul David. "Psalm 27: You're Talking to Yourself" Paul Tripp Ministries, entry posted 21 January 2008, http://paultrippministries.blogspot.com/2007/01/psalm-27-youre-talking-to-yourself.html (accessed November 2010).

Day 97: Rippon, John. 1787. "How Firm a Foundation."

Day 103: Spurgeon, C.H. 1993. *Faith's Check Book*. New Kensington, PA: Whitaker House.

Day 106: Spurgeon, C.H. 8/2/1857. *Waiting Only Upon God*. Sermon: Music Hall, Royal Surrey Gardens.

Day 113: St. Augustine. As quoted in Winks, J.F. 1881. *The Christian Pioneer*. Issue 35. London: Simpkin, Marshall, and Co.

Day 116: Mote, Edward. 1836. "My Hope Is Built."

Day 117: Spurgeon, C.H. 1995. *The Practice of Praise* New Kensington, PA: Whitaker House.

Day 119: MacMillan, Hugh. Quoted in Cowman, L.B. 2006. *Streams in the Desert*. Grand Rapids: Zondervan.

Day 122: Wesley, Charles. 1742. "Jesus, My Strength, My Hope."

Day 127: Murray, Andrew. 1896. *Waiting on God*. Revell: Wilder Publications, reprinted 2008.

Day 132: Watson, Thomas. 1847. *The Christian Treasury: Rules About Contentment*. London" John Johnstone.

Day 136: Tozer, A. W. 2010. *Next Chapter After the Last*. Camp Hill, PA: WingSpread Publishers.

Day 145: Spurgeon, C.H. 1869. *Sermons of the Rev. C. H. Spurgeon*. New York: Sheldon & Company.

Day 157: Burroughs, Jeremiah. 2001. *Rare Jewel of Christian Contentment*. Mulberry, IN: Sovereign Grace Publishers.

Day 160: Wesley, John. 1754–1765. *Commentary on the whole Bible*. Public domain.

Day 161: Spafford, Horatio G. 1873. "It is Well."

Day 163: Wesley, John. 1810. *Sermons on Several Occasions*. Hudson: William E. Norman.

Day 164: Minnick, Mark. 8/10/2005. *Asking and Receiving in Trials*. Sermon: Mount Calvary Baptist Church.

Day 172: Guinness, Os. 1976. *In Two Minds: the Dilemma of Doubt and How to Resolve It*. Downers Grove, IL: InterVarsity Press.

Day 179: Piper, John. John Piper, entry posted 12/18/2009. twitter.com/JohnPiper/status/6803509843 (accessed November 2010).

Day 182: Cairns, Alan. 6/10/2001. *Waiting on the Lord: The Source of Unfailing Strength*. Sermon: Faith Free Presbyterian.

Day 191: Murray, Andrew. 1981. *Waiting on God*. New Kensington, PA: Whitaker House.

Day 194: Lewis, C. S. 1965. *The Weight of Glory, and Other Addresses.* Grand Rapids, Mich.: Eerdmans.

Day 200: Manton, Thomas. 1923. *The Complete Works of Thomas Manton, D. D., with a memoir of the author, Volume 4.* London: James Nisbet & Co.

Day 202: Byrne, Mary E. 1905. "Be Thou My Vision."

Day 205: Lewis, C. S. 2001. *The Problem of Pain.* New York: HarperOne.

Day 220: Hall, B.P. 1889. *Thirty Thousand Thoughts, section XV, Extracts Covering a Comprehensive Circle of Religious and Allied Topics.* Cambridge: MA: Harvard University Press.

Day 227: Baxter, Richard. http://twitter.com/RichardBaxter_/status/25921324178

Day 229: Luther, Martin. 2009. Quoted in *The Lutheran Study Bible.* St. Louis, MO: Concordia Publishing House.

Day 230: Tozer, A. W. 1993. *The Counselor: straight talk about the Holy Spirit from a 20th century prophet.* Camp Hill, PA: Christian Publications.

Day 233: Merritt, Stephen. Quoted in Cowman, L.B. 2006. *Streams in the Desert.* Grand Rapids: Zondervan.

Day 235: Mahaney, C.J. 2006. *Living the Cross Centered Life: Keeping the Gospel the Main Thing.* Colorado Springs, CO: Multnomah Books.

Day 238: Edwards, Jonathan.1735-6. *The Most High, A Prayer-Hearing God.* http://www.biblebb.com/files/edwards/prayer.htm.

Day 244: Rutherford, Samuel. 1891. *Letters of Samuel Rutherford: With a Sketch of His Life and Biographical Notices of His Correspondents* collected by Andrew Alexander Bonar. Edinburgh: Oliphant Anderson and Ferrier.

Day 246: Bennett, Arthur G. 1975. *The Valley of Vision: A Collection of Puritan Prayers & Devotions*. Banner of Truth.

Day 247: Henry, Matthew. 1999. *Matthew Henry's Commentary*. Zondervan; abridged edition.

Day 248: Barrett, Dr. Michael. 11/12/1995. *Not to Worry*. Sermon: Faith Free Presbyterian Church.

Day 253: Bennett, Arthur G. 1975. *The Valley of Vision: A collection of Puritan Prayers & Devotions*. Banner of Truth.

Day 257: Stone, Samuel J. 1866. *The Church's One Foundation*.

Day 264: Lloyd-Jones, D. 1965. *Spiritual Depression: Its Causes and Its Cure*. Grand Rapids, MI: Eerdmans Printing Company.

Day 267: Whittier, John Greenleaf. 1909–14. *English poetry III: from Tennyson to Whitman*. New York: P.F. Collier & Son.

Day 274: Henry, Matthew. 1999. *Matthew Henry's Commentary*. Zondervan; abridged edition.

Day 276: Spurgeon, C. S. 2003. *Morning and Evening: A New Edition of the Classic Devotional Based on the Holy Bible, English Standard Version*. Wheaton, IL: Crossway.

Day 277: Venn, Henry. 1850. *Light for the House of Mourning: a Book for the Bereaved*. London: Houlston and Stoneman.

Day 278: Bonar, Horatius. 1861. "Not What I am, O Lord."

Day 280: Horn, Sam. 7/11/2010. *Trials that Transform*. Sermon: Brookside Baptist Church.

Day 283: Lewis, C. S. 2001. *Mere Christianity*. New York: HarperCollins.

Day 289: Henry, Matthew. 1828. *Exposition of the Old and New Testament,*

Volume 3. London: Joseph Ogle Robinson.

Day 290: Lyte, Henry. 1847. *Abide with Me.*

Day 292: Gellert, Christian F. 1757. *Jesus Lives and So Shall I.*

Day 294: Piper, John. 6/16/1996. *Sustained by Sovereign Grace—Forever.* Desiring God. Website: desiringGod.org

Day 296: Maclaren, Alexander. 1907. *Exposition of the Holy Scriptures: A Commentary on the Entire Bible.* New York: A. C. Armstrong and Son.

Day 30: Wesley, John. 1754–1765. *Commentary on the Whole Bible.* Public domain.

Day 303: Newton, Isaac. 1916. Quoted in Hallimond, John Greener. *The Miracle of Answered Prayer.* New York: The Christian Herald.

Day 305: Tozer, A. W. 1986. *The Root of the Righteous.* Camp Hill, PA: WingSpread Publishers.

Day 306: Wesley, Charles. 1740. *Jesus Lover of My Soul.*

Day 308: Barrett, Michael. 7/18/2010. *How to Be Happy.* Sermon: Faith Free Presbyterian.

Day 309: Taylor, Hudson. 2010. *A Ribband of Blue.* Memphis: General Books LLC.

Day 318: Bennett, Arthur G. 1975. *The Valley of Vision: A collection of Puritan Prayers & Devotions.* Banner of Truth.

Day 323: Fuller, Andrew. 1833. *The Complete Works of the Rev. Andrew Fuller, with a Memoir of His Life, volume 2.* Boston: Lincoln, Edmands & Co.

Day 325: Packer, J.I. 1995. *A Passion for Faithfulness.* Wheaton, IL: Crossway Books.

Day 326: Spurgeon, C. H. 1993. *Faith's Check Book*. New Kensington, PA: Whitaker House.

Day 328: Newton, John. 1808. *The Works of the Reverend John Newton, volume 1*. Philadelphia: Uriah Hunt.

Day 336: MacArthur, John. 1991. *The MacArthur New Testament Commentary Romans 1–8*. Chicago: Moody Press.

Day 340: Cowper, William. 1774. *God Moves in a Mysterious Way*.

Day 341: Owen, John. 1840. Quoted in Orme, William. *The Life of the Rev. John Owen, D.d*. Philadelphia: Presbyterian Board of Publication.

Day 343: Henry, Matthew. 1999. *Matthew Henry's Commentary*. Zondervan; abridged edition.

Day 346: Spurgeon, C. H. 1883. *Fathomless*. New York: Robert Carter & bros.

Day 347: Muller, George. 2009. Quoted in Alcorn, Randy. *If God Is Good: Faith in the Midst of Suffering and Evil*. Colorado Springs: Multnomah.

Day 351: von Schlegel, Katharina A. 1752. "Be Still, My Soul."

Day 359: Kerr Rusthoi, Esther. 1941. "When We See Christ."

Day 362: Murray, Andrew. 1895. *Humility the Beauty of Holiness*. New York: Anson D. F. Randolph & Co.

Day 363: Anselm, St. 1996. *The Doubleday Prayer Collection*, compiled by Mary Batchelor. New York: Doubleday.

Day 365: White Priebe, Trisha. 2010. "God Most High."

CPSIA information can be obtained at www.ICGtesting.com
263971BV00004B/3/P